MANAGING THE LABOUR PROCESS

Managing the Labour Process

Edited by
David Knights
and
Hugh Willmott

Gower

Published by
Gower Publishing Company Limited
Gower House
Croft Road
Aldershot
Hants GU11 3HR
England

Gower Publishing Company
Old Post Road
Brookfield
Vermont 05036
USA

British Library Cataloguing in Publication Data
Managing the labour process.
1. Management — Social aspects
I. Knights, David   II. Willmott, Hugh
302.3'5   HD38

Library of Congress Cataloging-in-Publication Data
Managing the labour process.

Includes index.
1. Personnel management — Great Britain — Data processing. I. Knights, David.   II. Wilmott, Hugh.
HF5549.2.G7M36 1986   658.3   86-3110

ISBN 0 566 05000 5

Printed in Great Britain at the
University Press, Cambridge

Contents

List of Contributors

Peter Armstrong graduated in Engineering at Bristol University in 1960. After seven years in industry he took a Masters degree in Sociology at Bath University. He is co-author of *Workers Divided* (with Theo Nichols) and *Ideology and Shopfloor Industrial Relations* (with J. F. B. Goodman and J. D. Hyman) as well as a number of papers on industrial sociology. He is currently pursuing research while on secondment at the Industrial Relations Research Unit, Warwick University from his permanent post in the Department of Management Studies at Huddersfield Polytechnic.

Paul Boreham is a senior lecturer in government at the University of Queensland. His research interests are in the fields of work and organisations, political economy and social class. He is co-editor of *The Professions in Australia, Work and Inequality*, vols. 1 and 2; *The State Class and the Recession*; and co-author of *Class, Politics and the Economy*. He is currently working on a study of new middle-class occupations in the class structure of contemporary capitalism.

David Buchanan is lecturer in organisational behaviour at the University of Glasgow and Director of the Scottish Business School Doctoral Programme. His current research concerns the organisational imnplications of new computing technologies. Previous publications include, *The Development of Job Design Theories and Techniques; Organizations in the Computer Age; Technological Imperatives and Strategic Choice*, (with David Boddy), and *Organizational Behaviour: An Introductory Text*, (with Andrzej Huczynski).

Beverley H. Burris is Assistant Professor of Sociology at New Mexico University. She is the author of *No Room at the Top: Underemployment and Alienation in the Corporation* which is an attempt to go beyond technocratic analyses of the problem of over-education/underemployment. She is also the co-author (with Wolf Heydebrand) of 'The Technocratic Administration of Education' in Fischer and Sirianni (eds), *Critical Studies in Organization and Bureaucracy*. Currently, she is involved in a study of working mothers and the family/work nexus.

Teresa Capps has worked in industry (British Steel, Bass and Whitbreads) where she obtained a professional accounting qualification and in academic life (at Sheffield Polytechnic and University). She is currently completing a Ph.D. at Sheffield University on management control in the NCB.

David Cooper Ph.D. (University of Manchester) is Price Waterhouse Professor of Accounting and Finance at UMIST. He has held previous appointments at the University of Manchester, East Anglia, British Columbia and Berkeley. Recent research has combined an interest in the organisational context of management accounting with a concern with the role of accounting regulations in society. He is currently studying the relationships of the State and the accounting profession. He is associate editor of *Accounting Organisations and Society*.

Christine Cousins gained her B.Sc. from the University of Surrey, her M.A. from the

University of Nottingham and her M.Phil. from the University of London. Since 1969 she has been a lecturer, and is now senior lecturer, in sociology at Hatfield Polytechnic. From 1985 she has held a research fellowship at the Polytechnic and will be carrying out research into work organisation and management-labour relations in the health and social services.

Stewart Clegg is Professor of Sociology at the University of New England. His major research has been in the sociology of power and organisations to which he has contributed several books and numerous shorter studies. As well as his present collaboration with Paul Boreham and Geoff Dow, which has produced *The State, Class and the Recession* and *Class Politics and the Economy*. He is also the current co-editor of the Australian and New Zealand Journal of Sociology and a founder member of APROS (Australian and Pacific Researchers in Organisation Studies).

Geoff Dow is a lecturer in political economy in the School of Humanities at Griffith University. His major teaching and research interests are in political economy and the state and he is currently researching the comparative relationship between ideology and economic policy in post-war Australia, Britain and Sweden. His recent publications include the two-volume collection *Work and Inequality; The State, Class and the Recession* and *Class, Politics and the Economy*.

Trevor Hopper, currently a lecturer in Accounting and Finance at Manchester University, previously taught at Wolverhampton Polytechnic and Sheffield University. His M.A. concerned the role of accountants in industry and his recent research has focused on management control and the labour process.

David Knights is Senior Lecturer in Management Sciences, UMIST. He has conducted research into sales activities, industrial relations, equal opportunity for ethnic minorities and sex discrimination in recruitment. His (joint) publications include *Managing the Multi-Racial Workforce* and *The Theory and Practice of Management Control*.

Tony Lowe is Professor of Accounting and Financial Management at Sheffield University. He worked as a chartered accountant before entering academic life. Since graduating from LSE he has worked at Leeds and Bradford Universities and Manchester Business School, as well as having several visiting appointments in North American Universities. He has published widely in systems theory, financial management, management control and management science. He is joint editor of *New Perspectives in Management Control* and is currently studying the relationship of the State and the accounting profession.

Jan Mouritsen is currently a lecturer in Accounting at the Copenhagen School of Business Administration, where he was involved in a longitudinal study of management's use of computerised information systems. He obtained an M.A. at Sheffield University, analysing the culture of NCB collieries.

John Storey is currently a Principal Research Fellow in the Industrial Relations Research Unit at Warwick University and an Associate Fellow of the Work Organisation Research Centre at the University of Aston. He is the author of *The Challenge to Management Control* and of *Managerial Prerogative and the Question of Control*.

Ad W. M. Teulings is Professor of Sociology of Organizations at the University of Amsterdam and Director of the Sociology of Organizations Research Unit. His present research work is in the field of corporate structuring, systems of industrial democracy and union participation in government policy-making. He has published in *Sociologie du Travail, Revue Française de Sociologie, British Journal of Sociology* and *Organization Studies*. He has also written a number of books in the field of industrial sociology (in Dutch).

Hugh Willmott is Lecturer in the Management Centre, University of Aston. He has published in a number of accounting, management and sociology journals. He is currently engaged in research projects on management control and the regulation of the accounting profession.

1   Introduction

This is the third in a series of volumes in which a selection of papers presented at the annual UMIST/Aston Organisation and Control of the Labour Process Conferences has been assembled. The purpose of these conferences has been to develop a regular forum for the discussion and advancement of critical studies that explore the terrain of labour, organisation and society. The previous two collections addressed issues in job redesign (Knights, Willmott and Collinson 1985) and gender (Knights and Willmott 1986). The distinctive focus of the present volume, in contrast, is broadly that of management control. A wide range of concerns is explored. These include the role of specialist occupational groups in determining strategies of management control; the significance of culture and ideology in mediating the introduction and use of new technology; the analysis of management practice within different areas of the public sector; the political and organisational significance of developments in the work of corporate management; and the role of organised labour in macro-economic management.

The Study of Management
What is management? In orthodox treatments of the subject, management is represented as a set of technical, functionally necessary tasks, roles and processes that are present in all forms of activity (e.g. Taylor 1911; Barnard 1938; Fayol 1949; Drucker 1954; Mintzberg 1973; Kotter 1982). The basic rationale of management is seen to reside in its functional contribution to the efficient and effective achievement of objectives whose origins and legitimacy are taken for granted. In this light, competent managerial work is regarded as morally and politically neutral. That the means as well as the ends of management practice might be radically contested, displaced or resisted by anything other than 'irrational' forces is beyond the comprehension of the orthodox literature on management.

In fact, it is virtually unimaginable that management control could be deflected or resisted for reasons other than the failure of managers to effectively organise, motivate and reward their subordinates.

In opposition to conventional accounts of management, in which its practices tend to be abstracted from the power relations in which they are embedded (Willmott 1984), the papers collected here attend to management as a medium and outcome of the distinctive, historical, and often contradictory, relations of power and production. They share a deep scepticism about the adequacy and value of orthodox accounts in which consideration of the potentially problematical constitution and significance of management is either marginalised or omitted.[1] Further, in contrast to those who have focused on the internal, micro-politics of management without any sustained theoretical consideration of wider economic, political and ideological factors (e.g. Dalton 1959; Pettigrew 1973, 1985; Burns 1977, 1982; Sayles 1979; Golding 1980; Kakabadse 1983; Lawrence 1984), contributors to this volume are more attentive to the structured and contested relations of power through which management practices are articulated and reproduced.

Quite clearly, there is no one answer to the question 'What is management?' Not only is the reality of management seen to differ, historically and culturally between (and, indeed, within) contrasting structures of social and economic relations. But, just as important, the depiction of management is also clearly relative to the perspective that organises its representation. It should come as no surprise, therefore, to find the contemporary study of management in a state of flux and fragmentation – a condition that is inflamed by a growing realisation that the development of a 'scientific' study of management is 'as much an ethical, moral, ideological and political activity as it is an epistemological one' (Morgan 1983: 373; cf. Wood and Kelly 1978; Whitley 1984).

The emergence of critical accounts of management has certainly added fuel to this fire.[2] Not that elements of a critical perspective have been entirely absent from earlier studies of management and organisation. Contributions to the debate on the separation of ownership and control (e.g. Berle and Means 1932; Burnham 1941; Nichols 1969), discussions of managerial ideology (e.g. Bendix 1963; Child 1969; Fox 1966, 1974), research on bureaucracy (e.g. Gouldner 1954; Crozier 1964; Mouzelis 1967) and studies of power in organisations (Clegg 1979; Knights and Roberts 1982) have exposed the socially constructed and politically charged character of management practice. However, it was not until the publication of Braverman's *Labor and Monopoly Capital* that there emerged the foundations of a concentrated and systematic critique of the theory and practice of management in the context of the capitalist labour process.

The appearance of *Labor and Monopoly Capital* revitalised and focused critical interest in management and suggested a fresh and penetrating perspective for its study. Inspired by the neglected first volume of Marx's *Capital*, a central theme of Braverman's work is that, in the context of capitalist economies, the content and process of management is shaped, above all, by the requirements of the capitalist system. Management is seen to perform a class function: to develop and secure the organisational means of appropriating surplus value from labour. Through management's purposive subordination and deskilling of productive labour, private wealth is secured (Braverman 1974: 121). In the context of capitalism, the managerial function is seen to derive its essential features from the fact that the contract of employment secures only a potential ('labour power') for productive effort. In order for waged labour to be converted into added value, the control of labour is required. Otherwise, there can be no guarantee of the effective valorisation of productive labour. Focusing upon the distinction between labour power and productive labour, Braverman regards Taylor's principles of 'Scientific Management' as the most developed and pervasive technology of management control wherein the valorisation and the impotence of labour is secured through a purposive programme of intensification, fragmentation and deskilling of work.

Clearly, Braverman's analysis does not lead him to dismiss conventional, power-blind accounts of management, such as those of Taylor and the Human Relations writers, merely as partial or incomplete. Rather, he focuses on the strength of their impact, attributing it precisely to a managerial class-bias which, in representing management as an essentially technical, instrumentally rational, politically neutral phenomenon, has the effect of legitimising the status quo. By default, if not by design, managerialist theory's neglect or naturalisation of power and class exploitation is seen to preserve the position of those groups which derive disproportionate material or symbolic benefit from the prevailing structure of production relations. Further, its characterisation of management as a universal, functional, rational phenomenon is understood to reflect and reinforce the conventional wisdom that (advanced) capitalism is a rationally organised system in which inequalities (e.g. of class, gender and race) are a naturally occurring and/or necessary cost which are more than compensated for by the benefits of 'generalised affluence' and 'individual freedom'.

Yet, whilst recognising that management occupies a position of comparative material and symbolic advantage, Braverman also describes it as 'a labour process ... exactly analogous to the process of production', albeit that it is intentionally installed 'for the purpose of control within the corporation' on behalf of the interests of capital (ibid. 267; cf. Stone 1974; Marglin 1974; Palmer 1975; Goldman and Van Houten 1977; Clawson 1980). More specifically, management is understood to comprise the set of practices and positions that arise to secure a transfer of control over the production of goods and services from the hands of the (craft) worker into the hands of the professional manager who applies his specialist expertise in the interests of capital. Management is thus seen to effect 'the most decisive step in the division of labour taken by the capitalist mode of production' – namely, the separation of hand and brain through the establishment of 'the conceptual apparatus and trained personnel' required 'to institutionalise this separation in a systematic and formal fashion' (Braverman 1974: 126).

Critics of Braverman have been far too numerous and prolific to summarise here. It is possible to refer only to some of those whose work has the most direct bearing on the critical study of management. A central problem, identified by many commentators (e.g. Coombs 1978; Elger 1982), is the tendency within Braverman's thesis to favour a conspiratorial, one-dimensional conception of management and the means of management control. Once this is challenged, it is necessary to re-examine a number of the elements of Braverman's argument, including the unqualified contention that management has engineered a progressive deskilling and degradation of work (Wood 1982); that Taylorism has been the favoured managerial strategy for controlling the labour process (Littler 1982, 1985); and that worker resistance and class struggle play little or no part in shaping and constraining the strategies and tactics of management *vis-à-vis* the extraction and realisation of surplus value (Brighton Labour Process Group 1977; Stark 1980).

Early studies sought to correct these limitations. For example, in his longitudinal study of management strategy, Friedman (1977a, 1977b) has argued that the Tayloristic strategy of 'direct control' may be combined with, or replaced by, one of 'responsible autonomy' in which a positive value is placed upon the malleability of labour. In which case, close supervision is either displaced or moderated by 'humanistic' ideologies and methods in which 'responsible' employee initiative, flexibility and responsiveness is actively sought, encouraged and rewarded (c.t. Mayo 1933; McGregor 1966; Peters and Waterman 1982). Others, notably Edwards (1979), have suggested that the form of management control has evolved over time from an early reliance upon simple control (e.g. direct management by the owner), through reliance upon technical workflow control (e.g. the assembly line) to the current situation where management in large organisations depends heavily upon a complex, bureaucratic system in which a sophisticated battery of unobtrusive controls (e.g. job evaluation and career planning) play a central role.

Since the publication of these studies, there has been a further wave of post-Braverman literature (Littler and Salaman 1982; Storey 1983; Thompson 1983; Burawoy 1985). This has been particularly critical of the tight coupling of the relationship between the systemic demands of the capitalist mode of production for the continued generation of surplus value on the one hand, and the concrete practices of management on the other. The fundamental flaw in such a formulation, it is argued, concerns the implication that management practice is either mechanically, fatalistically determined by the functional needs of the capitalist system; or that it involves the conscious, premeditated omniscient identification and implementation of strategies that most consistently satisfy the pressures for accumulation. The shared deficiency of such conceptualisations, it is said, concerns their explanation of historical and contemporary variations in the development of management in terms of responses to the abstracted imperatives or needs of capitalism. thus, the development of strategies of control, for example, is explained exclusively in terms of their provision of a functionally appropriate solution, or panacea, for each new crisis in capitalism (Littler and Salaman 1982). Events are explained in terms of their consequences in facilitating the 'progress' of capitalism as the teleology of the system comes either to 'govern or supplant that of the actors themselves' (Giddens 1979: 112, quoted in Salaman 1982).

Those subscribing to this critique have questioned whether the position and practice of management can be fully understood simply as a product of an objective antagonism of interests between capital and labour (Burawoy 1978, 1985; Edwards 1983). In posing this question, the existence of a structural conflict of interests is not necessarily denied. However, it is found to be of limited value in studying and explaining the actual, diverse practices that comprise the design and control of capitalist labour process. For, in practice, interests are not given. Rather, they are defined, organised and interpreted through interaction and struggle. Or, as Burawoy (1985: 39) has put it, 'one cannot assume the existence of a cohesive managerial and capitalist class that automatically recognises its true interests. Rather one must examine how that class is organized and how its interests emerge historically through competition and struggle'. To repeat, the recognition of the non-automatic identification and pursuit of interests does not necessarily negate the understanding that fundamental conflicts of interest are structured into the capitalist organisation of production relations. Instead, it simply allows that a less formalistic, broader range of analytical tools must be incorporated into the study of these relations if the actors who compete and co-operate to reproduce and transform labour processes are not to be reduced to 'passive supports or cyphers for certain universal imperatives embedded in the social organisation of society' (Reed 1984: 276). So, for example, labour process analysis must penetrate the ways in which structural conflict may be obscured through management practices that have the effect of subjecting labour to the materialist and/or careerist rationale of such practices. But, at the same time, it must seek to reveal the limits and contradictory consequences of management controls – controls that may be prompted by interests of management which are not necessarily consonant with the demands of an abstractly formulated capitalist logic (Storey 1985).[3] In short, it should not be assumed that management is, or ever could become, a homogeneous, unambiguous phenomenon whose actions are programmed by any single, well-defined objective – such as that of achieving profitable growth. This may be the rhetoric. But its attainment is a constraint upon the survival of capitalist enterprise, not an adequate description of how labour processes are actually organised and controlled. For, in reality, management is routinely engaged in smoothing tensions and containing the centrapetal forces that inhere within its diverse practices (Tomlinson 1982). More generally, it is necessary to remember that the abstract logic of the economic realm is not separable from what Burawoy (1985) has termed 'the political and ideological structures' through which the social relations of production are generated and experienced.

When informed by this perspective, labour process analysis is able to reveal a number of features of management under capitalist conditions which tend to be underplayed by Braverman and others whose work falls within the tradition of Marxist functionalism (Giddens 1979: 111–12; 1982). For example, it highlights how, in practice, the co-operative and interdependent character of socialised production under capitalism and the payment of wages to 'free' labour serve to conceal the proportion of labour that is unpaid; how the existence of capital is rendered abstract, ambiguous and diffuse owing to the separation of ownership and control, the political rights of citizenship and the absorption of consumers in commodity relations;

how the exploitative relationship between capital and labour can be organised in ways that are mutually acceptable to management and workers (e.g. increases in productivity can support improvements in wages and working conditions for those in employment whilst simultaneously raising the rate of profit to capital); how the capitalist demand for profit can be extracted as much at the point of consumption as at the point of production; how the burden of capitalist exploitation can fall disproportionately on women, the unemployed and ethnic minority groups, leaving Anglo-Saxon white male workers comparatively privileged; how, despite being formally denied any participation in the social organisation of production, the provision of useful goods and services, together with the unacknowledged utilisation of a host of localised skills, rituals and 'games' can render work tolerable by providing a valued source of meaning, identity and motivation; how workers are frequently more concerned with pay comparabilities and the purchasing power of labour as a commodity than they are with the exploitative nature of the employment relationship; how unions often reflect and reproduce rather than resist such economism; and how the effect of these forces within the labour process leaves workers entrapped in a self-defeating, individualistic, instrumental relationship towards fellow workers no less than they do towards the employer, which can only heighten the vulnerability of labour to management discipline and control.

Extending the Debate

Central to recent labour process perspectives is an acknowledgement that numerous factors and forces mediate the relationship between the capitalist imperative of accumulation and the control of work and production (Cressey and MacInnes 1980). Capital is recognised to reap benefits by actively fostering, or at least allowing, space for the co-operative and committed potential of labour (Storey in this volume); and, on the other hand, labour has a stake in maintaining the existence of units of capital in which it is employed (Buchanan in this volume). Accordingly, it is appropriate to analyse management practice in terms of 'the potential terrain of compromise and consensus' as well as 'in relation to conflict and sources of conflict' (Littler and Salaman 1982: 253). In this context, managerial ideologies and informal negotiations with workers are seen to play a central, mediating role (Armstrong in this volume). Where ideologies supportive of the prerogative of management are regarded as legitimate by workers, routine subordination in processes of control is normalised. And, where informal arrangements are cultivated, moral bonds are developed that place constraints upon both strategies of management control and worker resistance.

By extending analysis beyond the point of production, it can also be seen how management in monopoly capitalist corporations is often as much, if not more, concerned with the development of favourable conditions for the realisation of surplus value in product markets as with creating the optimum conditions for the extraction of surplus value directly through the labour process (Littler and Salaman 1982; Littler 1985). Indeed, especially in the larger corporations, management controls and associated ideologies, are directed at a wide range of concerns, including the pricing and supply of raw materials, the development and penetration of product markets and the planning and siting of future capital investment (Teulings in this volume), any of which can exert greater influence than control *per se* on the organisation of labour processes at the point of production (Kelly 1985; Child 1985). Indeed, if intensification of control at the point of production results in avoidable over-production or unpredictability of output, its costs quickly outweigh any projected benefits. With this in mind, it is worth stressing that the primary imperative of capitalist production is not to reduce labour's costs or even to reduce the dependence of capital upon labour. Rather, the foremost imperative is that of accumulation. In translating this imperative into specific policies and objectives, the most technically rational approach is one that flexibly combines and integrates each of the control systems within a given organisation (Burris in this volume). However, it is also essential to appreciate how management may itself displace this objective in so far as it becomes preoccupied with maintaining control in conditions that continuously invite its subversion (Golding 1980). Finally, it is important not to forget that the organisation and control of labour processes are embedded in a wider political context; and that the State, both as a regulator of institutions and practices and as an employer (Hopper et al. and Cousins in this volume), plays a central role in shaping the relations between capital and labour (Boreham, Clegg and Dow in this volume).

However, despite the scope for a concrete co-ordination of the interests of capital and labour, tensions and contradictions in the structure of capitalist relations of production render this co-ordination uneven and uncertain. The 'comforting' appearance of consent can conceal the precarious reality of compliance – a compliance that is often dependent upon a perceived continuation or relative improvement in current working arrangements and rewards (Knights and Collinson 1985) in the face of changes in political and ideological, as well as economic, conditions that threaten their erosion. Compliant, as contrasted to consensual, forms of co-operation amongst managers as well as workers may persist indefinitely as a precarious feature of the labour process. And this is not just because the capitalist mode of production can be seen to embody a contradictory, antagonistic unity of the interests of capital and labour; nor even because it generates a social structure in which socially unnecessary suffering and inequalities are systematically reproduced. For, of no less significance is its construction and reinforcement of a dualism between individual subjects and their world, a dualism that is manifest in the socially constructed fiction of a separate skin-enveloped ego whose satisfaction continuously undermines the productive potential of consensual, communal co-operation (D'Amico 1978; Lichtman 1982; O'Connor 1984; Knights and Willmott, 1985).

From such a perspective, the preferred alternative to both conventional and orthodox Marxist accounts of the labour process, which both rely upon functionalist explanations of the reality of management, is to be sensitive to the intersubjective organisation of interests and the play of contradictory forces that support their concrete co-ordination. In this light, the practices and ideologies of management are recognised to be conditioned, but not determined, by managers' (ambiguous) position within the prevailing structure of power relations — relations that shift not only with changes in product markets, labour markets, technology and varying forms of class, gender and ethnic resistance, but also with the processes of strategic decision-making that develop in relation to such changes (Kelly 1982, 1985; Child 1972, 1985).

In the first paper, Peter Armstrong argues that specific management control strategies are best understood as outcomes of the ideologies developed by occupational groups who compete with other 'professions' to determine and occupy key positions within the global function of capital. In contrast to Braverman, Taylorism, for example, is regarded as one possible management control strategy whose appearance and application should be related to the successful efforts of engineers to convince others of its relevance and utility, and thereby reverse their profession's experience of 'an abrupt transition from independence to subordination within developing industrial hierarchies' (cf. Meiksins 1984). Armstrong's central thesis is that the content and mix of management control strategies within specific economies, sectors and organisations is shaped and mediated by processes of competiton between occupational groupings who have been more or less effective in securing recognition and influence over the organisation and control of labour processes. Through an historical examination of the professions of accountancy and personnel management, it is argued that recognition and influence depends as much upon members' ability to develop effective methods of control over the possession and transmission of specialist knowledge and techniques as it does upon the functional relevance of their distinctive skills for satisfying the needs of the capitalist system.

The following two contributions from John Storey and David Buchanan present results of research in which the relationship between technology and strategies of management control is explored. In both cases, this is done by examining the effects of the introduction of new technologies upon the organisation of the labour process. Storey presents the findings of a comparative study of three regional centres within different insurance companies. While carefully avoiding the temptation to generalise from his cases, it is noted that even in the company where the use and penetration of new technology was most developed, the potential of information technology to bifurcate, degrade and tighten surveillance over labour was by no means fully exploited. To account for this finding, Storey suggests three possible explanations. First, he considers the possibility that regional managers actively resisted change, an explanation that is rejected on the grounds that they had minimal influence on decision-making about the strategic application of new technology. Second, and of much greater explanatory value, Storey contends, is the deeply paternalistic nature of the culture in the companies studied. In this light, management's cautious, soft-pedalling approach to new technology is seen to reflect a normative desire to foster and maintain a reciprocal, co-operative orientation on the part of its employees. Third, there is a veiled suggestion that the attenuated use of technology is actually strategic in so far as it serves to maintain co-operation and goodwill in the use of new technology – an area which, arguably is expected to be of growing importance in securing a competitive advantage in attracting and repeating insurance business.

The observations of Armstrong and Storey are broadly confirmed in David Buchanan's case studies of technical change involving the application of new technology. Evidence from his cases suggests the following. First, that management does not form a homogeneous group. Rather, managers vary in their objectives and have a wide range of aspirations. For example, Buchanan observes how the practices of middle and junior managers are shaped by performance measures that encourage a parochial, low-risk orientation to technical change. Second, and relatedly, he notes that management is not preoccupied with control since commitment and effort is willingly made by the workforce. Third, he considers that decision-making in respect of the redesign and day-to-day operation of work structures is mediated by managerial preferences and ideologies which, especially at an operational level, are not rationally consistent with the imperatives of capital accumulation. Fourth, Buchanan says that the introduction of new technology frequently enhances worker autonomy and skill at the expense of middle-line management. However, in contrast to Storey, who concludes by stressing the limits to management choice and action imposed by their 'ultimate structural location' within capitalist relations of production, Buchanan emphasises managers' scope for autonomous 'rule bending', and argues that their disregard for capitalist imperatives shapes the longer-term trends in the structural organisation of these relations.

The contributions by Christine Cousins and Trevor Hopper et al. both focus upon the comparatively neglected area of the management of labour processes within the public sector. In her discussion of the recent history of the National Health Service, Cousins stresses the fundamental importance of appreciating the distinctive structural properties and contradictory rationalities that are characteristic of state agencies in advanced capitalist societies. Drawing upon neo-Marxian theories of the state (e.g. O'Connor 1973; Offe 1984), she argues that the organisation of such agencies is conditioned by political demands that are governed by non-market criteria and by the performance and requirements of an economic system that is geared to continuous capital accumulation. In this context, an expanding output of goods produced outside the market, and which know no political limits, is seen to stimulate fiscal crises as public expenditure on these goods outstrips the ability of the private sector to support their production. Efforts to solve such crises are understood to act back upon the public sector in the form of cuts, reorganisations, rationalisations, the imposition of cash limits, the re-assertion of managerial expertise and prerogatives, and the deeper penetration of capitalist rationality into the management of state labour processes. Accordingly, Cousins examines labour processes in the National Health Service as the product of conflicting objectives, shifting strategies and the absence of uncontested and consistent criteria for assessing performance. Specifically, she observes how ambiguities and inconsistencies in the structure and rationality of the NHS have been promoted and exploited by dominant professional groups (e.g. doctors) who have secured monopoly control over the priorities, content and delivery of public health provision. At the same time, a combination of state pay policies that disadvantage workers in the (labour intensive) public sector and the segmented features of internal labour markets are shown to have politicised the employment relationship, eroded the public service ethic and stimulated the growth of increasingly militant and well-organised trade unionism.

The paper by Hopper et al. is based upon an intensive case study of planning and control practices in the National Coal Board. It has three interrelated foci. The first concerns the complex and problematical methods of management in collieries where it is observed how struggles over control have been extended to the generation, availability and interpretation of information about production. The second explores the loose and sometimes decoupled relationship between HQ, Area and Colliery levels within the formal organisational structure of the NCB. This relationship is analysed as an outcome of the effort to localise and contain contradictions between, on the one hand, corporate strategy development in respect of finance and markets, and, on the other hand, operational concerns about production and engineering. In each case, the desire of professional groups to achieve or retain autonomy over their sphere of competence and power base is seen to mediate and compound this central problem of corporate control. The third focus of attention is directed to the role of the State in shaping the economic conditions in which the NCB is obliged to operate. Hopper et al.'s argument is that control over labour processes within the coal industry must be examined in the light of a consideration of the State's role in mediating the distribution of surplus value around the economy. It is observed how in recent years the State's pursuit of monetarist financial, industrial and energy policies, combined with a selective use of seemingly neutral financial measures and accounting practices, has acted as a powerful lever in redefining the politico-economic terrain of coal production. Thus, the paper reveals how the production and presentation of financial information, embodying the impersonal logic of market exchange, has underpinned and legitimised the call for the restructuring and disciplining of labour processes within the industry.

The contributions by Ad Teulings and Beverly Burris both discuss broad historical trends and contradictions in the nature of management and the means of management control over labour processes in advanced capitalism. Teulings' point of departure is Braverman's (1974: 267) characterisation of management as 'a labor process exactly analogous to the process of production' whose function is 'the operation and coordination of the corporation'. To elaborate this portrayal of management, Teulings draws upon the writings of the strategy and structure (e.g. Chandler 1962) and markets and hierarchies (e.g. Williamson 1975) debates. Specifically, he attends to the appropriation of market functions by corporate management and the development of competitive relations within the management of large, multi-national corporations. With the rise of 'organised capitalism', management is seen to become differentiated into a number of loosely coupled activities, each of which has its own, separate labour process. Developing this theme, Teulings focuses attention upon differences in the logic of action that exist within the operational, structuring, strategic and institutional activities of management. The emergence of these separate and contradictory logics, he argues, politicises relations within management whilst, at the same time, the instrumenal rationality of these logics of action inhibits effective engagement in processes of political bargaining that must occur if an optimal accommodation with other managerial labour processes is to be reached. It is for this reason, Teulings concludes, that while management in the aggregate forms an extensive machinery of power, the common experience of individual managers is one of frustration at their comparative incapacity to control their situation.

Whereas Teulings' focus is upon the internal differentiation of management activity, Burris explores what she identifies as a generalised trend towards technocratic forms of management control within modern organisations. Central to her contribution is the thesis that neither Braverman's exclusive interest in Taylorism nor the disclosure of alternative strategies of control in subsequent labour process analysis has adequately recognised and appreciated the significance of technocracy as a dialectically developing structure of domination in which elements of other (e.g. bureaucratic, professional and technical) forms of control become incorporated and integrated in a novel and potentially tyrannical combination. Concretely, the advance of technocratic control is found in the contemporary flattening of hierarchy, the extreme polarisation of experts and non-experts, the collapsing of technical and managerial functions, the growing reliance upon technological expertise as a basis of authority, and the strategic use of new technology to achieve a flexible mix of centralised power with functional decentralisation. Thus, Burris's emphasis is upon the historical process of organisational rationalisation in which the systemic features of technocracy serve to attenuate the contradictions within earlier strategies and structures of control. By bringing the insights of critical theory to bear upon the study of contemporary management practice, she points to a developing trend towards the design of the means of management control by experts who are preoccupied by the 'administration of things' in which critical reflection and democratic debate upon the substantive, human rationality of ends is effectively excluded.

In the final paper, Paul Boreham, Stewart Clegg and Geoff Dow argue that labour process analysis must engage with, and incorporate, consideration of the wider political arenas of class conflict that shape the form of management strategies and labour resistance at the point of production. Through a critique of Keynesian and monetarist economics, it is contended that private control over investment decisions lies at the heart of the recurrent crises of capitalist development. This is because, at the moment of crisis, the retention of private prerogatives is preferred to the socialisation of investment necessary to sustain non-inflationary expansion. The specific focus of the paper is upon the class politics of economic policy determination and the role of representatives of the interests of labour in corporatist relations of economic regulation. Citing the recent history of corporatist arrangements in Australia, they urge that dichotomous zero-sum assumptions about the relationship between capital and labour be replaced by an awareness and celebration of the potentially progressive contribution of corporatist control over the economy. For, it is argued, if sufficiently radical in commitment, corporatist management of the economy not only expands democratic control, and thereby advances the interests of labour, but also heightens political awareness of the presence and class nature of conflict over economic decisions. In other words, political struggle to achieve radical corporatist control over the economy is seen to provide a more fruitful and progressive instrument of change than struggle that is centred upon the point of production. However, while corporatism is regarded as a potentially progressive vehicle for achieving radical advances in the relations of production and the operation of labour markets, such change is recognised to be conditional upon effective political intervention to ensure that critical investment decisions are placed in the public arena, that the social wage is secured and that real incomes are maintained.

Overall, then, the papers collected in this volume contribute to a developing, critical perspective on the management of labour processes in advanced capitalist societies. Through the presentation of case studies and by recognising the relevance of literatures that have been neglected in labour process analysis, the papers extend and revitalise the labour process debate. By exposing the limits of Braverman's formulation of management, the papers both broaden and advance beyond earlier critiques of his seminal work. So doing, they point the way forward for analysis which, in presuming neither an unproblematic consensus nor an unmediated antagonism of interests between capital and labour, is sensitive to the heterogeneous and ambiguous character of production relations in general, and of the management of labour processes, in particular.

Notes
1. As Macintyre (1981) has argued, the very concept of effectiveness implies a manipulative mode of organisation where persons are routinely moulded or coerced into compliant patterns of behaviour (cf. Roberts, 1984).
2. Within the UK alone there has been in recent years the conference on 'Critical Perspectives on Management Studies' held at the Manchester Business School in June 1983 from which were drawn a selection of papers published in vol. 21, no. 3 of the *Journal of Management Studies*; the seminar on 'Management of the Labour Process' organised by the Department of Industrial Relations and Management Studies, University College, Cardiff in May 1984; the workshop on Management and Industrial Relations organised by the Industrial Relations Research Unit at Warwick University in July 1984; the regular meetings of the Management Control Workshop Group that has in preparation a volume of papers entitled *Critical Perspectives on Management Control*, (Macmillan). During this period a number of collections of papers have also appeared, including Clegg and Kelly 1982; Wood 1982; Gospel and Littler 1983; Thurley and Wood 1983; Knights, Willmott and Collinson 1985).
3. From this perspective, it is equally a mistake to assume that the interests of capital, for example, are unproblematical or uncontradictory. This is not only because there are differences of potential pay-off within different capitals and within their associated managements, but also because managers, the alleged guardians of the given interests of capital, can themselves become 'unreliable' and 'recalcitrant' in response to pressures and controls that bear down upon them. As numerous commentators on the class structure of late capitalist society have observed (e.g. Crompton and Gubbay 1977; Wright 1978; Carchedi 1975), many managers find themselves in an ambivalent, ambiguous position. For, whilst they are accountable through the board of directors to the owners or institutional managers of capital, they are generally dependent on the sale of their labour for the greater part of their income. And, in this latter respect, they are partly members of the proletariat, even though they exist in an exploitative relationship to labour in so far as a proportion of their wage is derived from the surplus generated by productive labour.

References
Barnard, C. (1938), *The Functions of the Executive*, Cambridge, Mass.: Harvard University Press.
Bendix, R. (1963), *Work and Authority in Industry*, New York: Harper and Row.
Berle, A. A. and Means, G. C. (1932), *The Modern Corporation and Private Property*, New York: Macmillan.
Braverman, H. (1974), *Labor and Monopoly Capital*, New York: Monthly Review Press.
Brighton Labour Process Group (1977), 'The Capitalist Labour Process', *Capital and Class*, **1**, 3–26.
Burawoy, M. (1978), 'Toward a Marxist Theory of the Labour Process: Braverman and Beyond', *Politics and Society*, **8**, 247–312.
Burawoy, M. (1985), *The Politics of Production*, London: Verso.
Burnham, J. (1941), *The Managerial Revolution*, Harmondsworth: Penguin.
Burns, T. (1977), *The BBC: Public Institution and Private World*, London: Macmillan.
Burns, T. (1982), *A Comparative Study of Administrative Structure and Organizational Processes in Selected Areas of the National Health Service*, London: Social Science Research Council.

Carchedi, G. (1975), 'On the Economic Identification of the New Middle Class', *Economy and Society*, **4** (1), 1–86.

Chandler, A. D. (1962), *Strategy and Structure*, Cambridge, Mass.: MIT Press.

Child, J. (1969), *British Management Thought*, London: Allen and Unwin.

Child, J. (1972), 'Organizational Structure and Performance: The Role of Strategic Choice', *Sociology*, **6**, 1–22.

Child, J. (1985), 'Managerial Strategies, New Technology and the Labour Process' in Knights, Willmott and Collinson, (eds), 1985.

Clawson, D. (1980), *Bureaucracy and the Labor Process*, New York: Monthly Review Press.

Clegg, S. (1975), *Power, Rule and Domination*, London: Routledge and Kegan Paul.

Clegg, S. (1979), *The Theory of Power and Organisation*, London: Routledge and Kegan Paul.

Clegg, C. W. and Kelly, J. E. (1982), *Autonomy and Control at the Workplace* London: Croom Helm.

Coombs, R. (1978), 'Labour and Monopoly Capital', *New Left Review*, **107**, 79–96.

Cressey, P. and MacInnes, J. (1980), 'Voting for Ford: Industrial Democracy and the Control of Labour', *Capital and Class*, **11**, 5–33.

Crompton, R. and Gubbay, J. (1977), *Economy and Class Structure*, London: Macmillan.

Crozier, M. (1964), *The Bureaucratic Phenomenon*, Chicago: University of Chicago Press.

Dalton, M. (1959), *Men Who Manage*, New York: John Wiley.

D'Amico, R. (1978), 'Desire and the Commodity Form', *Telos*, **35**, 88–122.

Drucker, P. (1954), *The Practice of Management*, New York: Harper and Row.

Edwards, P. K. (1983), 'Control, Compliance and Conflict: Analysing Variations in the Capitalist Labour Process', paper presented at the 1st Aston-UMIST Organisation and Control of the Labour Process Conference, Manchester.

Edwards, R. C. (1979), *Contested Terrain: The Transformation of the Workplace in the Twentieth Century*, New York: Basic Books.

Elger, T. (1982), 'Braverman. Capital Accumulation and Deskilling' in S. Wood, (ed.), *The Degradation of Work*, London: Hutchinson.

Fayol, H. (1949), *General and Industrial Management*, London: Pitman.

Fox, A. (1966), *Industrial Sociology and Industrial Relations*, Research Paper No. 3, Royal Commission on Trade Unions and Employers' Association, London: HMSO.

Fox, A. (1974), *Beyond Contract*, London: Faber.

Friedman, A. L. (1977a), *Industry and Labour : Class Struggle at Work and Monopoly Capitalism*, London: Macmillan.

Friedman, A. L. (1977b), 'Responsbile Autonomy Versus Direct Control over the Labour Process', *Capital and Class*, **1**, 43–57.

Giddens, A. (1979), *Central Problems in Social Theory*, London: Macmillan.

Giddens, A. (1982), 'Power, the Dialectic of Control and Class Structuration' in A. Giddens and G. Mackenzie, (eds.), *Social Class and the Division of Labour*, Cambridge: Cambridge University Press.

Golding, D. (1980), 'Establishing Blissful Clarity in Organizational Life: Managers', *Sociological Review*, **28** (4), 763–82.

Goldman, P. and Van Houten, D.R. (1977), 'Managerial Strategies and the Worker: A Marxist Analysis of Bureaucracy', *The Sociological Quarterly*, **18**, 108–15.

Gospel, H. F. and Littler, C. R. (1983), (eds.) *Managerial Strategies and Industrial Relations*, London: Heinemann.

Gouldner, A.W. (1954), *Patterns of Industrial Bureaucracy*, New York: Free Press.

Kakabadse, A. (1983), *The Politics of Management*, Aldershot: Gower.

Kelly, J. E. (1982), *Scientific Management, Job Redesign and Work Performance* New York: Academic Press.

Kelly, J. E. (1985), 'Management's Redesign of Work: Labour Process, Labour Markets and Product Markets' in Knights, Willmott and Collinson, (eds), 1985.
Knights, D. and Collinson, D. (1985), 'Redesigning Work on the Shopfloor: A Question of Control or Consent?' in Knights, Willmott and Collinson, (eds), 1985.
Knights, D. and Roberts, J. (1983), 'The Power of Organisation or the Organisation of Power', *Organisation Studies*, 3 (1), 47–63.
Knights, D. Willmott, H. C. and Collinson, D. (1985), (eds), *Job Redesign; Critical Perspectives on the Labour Process*, Aldershot: Gower.
Knights, D. and Willmott, H. C. (1985), 'Power and Identity in Theory and Practice', *Sociological Review*, 33 (1), 22–46.
Knights, D. and Willmott, H. C. (eds), (1986), *Gender and the Labour Process*, Aldershot: Gower.
Kotter, J. P. (1982), *The General Managers*, New York: Free Press.
Kouzmin, A. (1980), 'Control in Organizational Analysis: The Lost Politics' in D. Dunkerley and G. Salaman, (eds), *International Yearbook of Organization Studies, 1980*.
Lawrence, P. (1984), *Management in Action*, London: Routledge and Kegan Paul.
Lichtman, R. (1982), *The Production of Desire*, New York: Free Press.
Littler, C. (1982), *The Development of the Labour Process in Britain, Japan and the U.S.A.*, London: Heinemann.
Littler, C. (1985), 'Taylorism, Fordism and Job Design' in Knights, Willmott and Collinson, (eds), 1985.
Littler, C. and Salaman, G. (1982), 'Bravermania and Beyond: Recent Theories of the Labour Process', *Sociology*, 16 (2), 251–69.
Macintyre, A. E. (1981), *After Virtue; A Study in Moral Theory*, London: Duckworth.
Marglin, S. A. (1974), 'What Do the Bosses Do? The Origins of Hierarchy in Capitalist Production', *Review of Radical Political Economics*, 6, 60–112.
Mayo, E. (1933), *The Human Problems of an Industrial Civilisation*, New York: Macmillan.
Meiksins, P. F. (1984), 'Scientific Management and Class Relations; A Dissenting View', *Theory and Society*, 13 (2), 177–210.
McGregor, D. (1966), *Leadership and Motivation*, Cambridge, Mass.: MIT Press.
Mintzberg, H. (1973), *The Nature of Managerial Work*, New York: Harper and Row.
Morgan, G. (1983), (ed). *Beyond Method; Strategies for Social Research*, New York: Sage.
Mouzelis, N. P. (1967), *Organisation and Bureaucracy*, London: Routledge and Kegan Paul.
Nichols, T. (1969), *Ownership, Control and Ideology*, London: Allen and Unwin.
O'Connor, J. (1973), *The Fiscal Crisis of the State*, New York: St Martin's Press.
O'Connor, J. (1984), *Accumulation Crisis*, Oxford: Basil Blackwell.
Offe, C. (1984), *Contradictions of the Welfare State*, London: Hutchinson.
Palmer, B. (1975), 'Class, Conception and Conflict: The Thrust for Efficiency, Managerial Views of Labour, and the Working Class Rebellion, 1903–1922', *Review of Radical Political Economy*, 7 (2), 31–49.
Peters, T. J. and Waterman, R. H. (1982), *In Search of Excellence*, New York: Harper and Row.
Pettigrew, A. (1973), *The Politics of Organisational Decision-Making*, London: Tavistock.
Pettigrew, A. M. (1985), *The Awakening Giant, Continuity and Change in I.C.I.*, Oxford: Basil Blackwell.
Reed, M. I. (1984), 'Management as a Social Practice', *Journal of Management Studies*, 21 (3), 273–85.
Roberts, J. (1984), 'The Moral Character of Management Practice', *Journal of Management Studies*, 21 (3), 286–302.

Salaman, G. (1982), 'Managing the Frontier of Control' in A. Giddens and G. Mackenzie, (eds), *Social Class and the Division of Labour*; *Essays in Honour of Ilya Neustadt*, Cambridge: Cambridge University Press.

Sayles, L. R. (1979), *Leadership*, New York: McGraw-Hill.

Stark, D. (1980), 'Class Struggle and the Transformation of the Labor Process', *Theory and Society*, 9, 89–130.

Stone, K. (1974), 'The origins of job structures in the steel industry', *Review of Radical Political Economics*, 6 (2), 113–73.

Storey, J. (1983), *Managerial Prerogative and the Question of Control*, London: Routledge and Kegan Paul.

Storey, J. (1985), 'The Means of Management Control', *Sociology*, 19 (2), 193–211.

Taylor, F.W. (1911), *Principles of Scientific Management*, New York: Harper and Row.

Thompson, P. (1983), *The Nature of Work*, London: Macmillan.

Thurley, K. and Wood, S. (1983), *Industrial Relations and Management Strategy*, Cambridge: Cambridge University Press.

Tomlinson, J. (1982), *The Unequal Struggle? British Socialism and the Capitalist Enterprise*, London: Methuen.

Whitley, R. (1984), 'The Fragmented State of Management Studies': Reasons and Consequences', *Journal of Management Studies*, 21 (3), 331–48.

Williamson, O. E. (1975), *Markets and Hierarchies*, New York: Free Press.

Willmott, H. C. (1984), 'Images and Ideals of Managerial Work', *Journal of Management Studies*, 21 (3), 349–68.

Wood, S. (1982), ed., *The Degradation of Work? Skill, Deskilling and the Labour Process*, London: Hutchinson.

Wood, S. and Kelly, J. (1978), 'Towards a Critical Management Science', *Journal of Management Studies*, 15 (1), 1–24.

Wright, E. O. (1978), *Class, Crisis and the State*, London: New Left Books.

2 Management Control Strategies and Inter-Professional Competition: the Cases of Accountancy and Personnel Management

Peter Armstrong

Introduction: Management and the Labour Process

Much of the orthodox literature on management is largely neutered by its own studied ignorance of the context and purpose of management activity. Thus, reviewing the work of the 'founding fathers' (such as Fayol) and the latter day ecstatics (such as Drucker), Willmott (1984) notes a common tendency to represent management as no more than the functionally necessary — and hence politically neutral — co-ordination of differentiated labour. The writings of modern empiricists (such as Mintzberg) represent a retreat even from this modest level of interpretation, in that the activities of managers are there portrayed as quite arbitrary sets of roles with little suggestion as to why they are as they are, what purpose or circumstance gives them coherence, or how they might vary. The assumption would appear to be that management is simply *there*, unchanging in essentials, and to be taken for granted by practical men. Whilst such perspectives may serve the ideological function of reassuring the managed that their trials are in the nature of life itself, they also offer the mordant pleasure of contemplating the essential one-ness of the administration of punitive labour camps and the modern 'enlightened' corporation. From an analytical point of view, the price is that an assumption that all management is essentially similar may not be the best starting point from which to reach an understanding of the historical, cultural and corporate differences between managements which are observable even when discussion is restricted to capitalist enterprises and economies.

In order to understand this and other phenomena which are obscured by traditional approaches, Willmott (op. cit.) advocates that students of management should engage with what has come to be known as the 'labour process debate'. This is concerned, not with the production of commodities or services considered in the abstract (which is how the topic is first introduced by Marx 1976: 283–90), but with the influence upon this process of the social context within which labour is performed. In capitalist societies and enterprises, therefore, the debate starts from the recognition that the employers' wages purchase, not a set amount or type of work, but a comparatively open *potential* for labour (labour power), which is then actualised under the direction of the employer. The fundamental task of the employer, or, in later versions of capitalism, his management, is to realise this labour power so that the value added to the product or service exceeds its purchase price *and* is secured on behalf of the employer (ibid: 291–2, 300–4). The basic relationship of capitalist management to the labour process, therefore, is not that they take part in it but that they are paid to extract a surplus from it. A number of features of real-life capitalist enterprises complicate this picture, however, notably that many managers perform productive labour (for example, design work or technically necessary co-ordination) *as well* as the task of extracting surplus. In fact it could well be this sub-stratum of fact which underlies the ideological presupposition within orthodox management thought that co-ordination is the defining characteristic of management.

It is this labour process perspective which Braverman (1974) employed to account for the most important change in management control strategy (i.e. the battery of organisational designs, specialisms and techniques for extracting surplus) which has so far occurred in the progress of capitalism — the advent of scientific management. Whereas in orthodox management thought, Taylorism appears as a *more efficient* way of organising *work*, which cuts out waste effort, replaces skilled labour by cheaper unskilled labour and reduces training costs, to Braverman it is a way of reorganising the *labour process* in which the primary effect of deskilling work is to render it more transparent to management *control*, thus facilitating the extraction of surplus value. Whereas, to the main line of management thought, Taylorism generated unacceptable losses of 'work satisfaction' and was soon superseded by less psychologically naïve approaches (see, for example, Rose 1975), To Braverman (1974: 87), its control potentialities are enduring and it remains 'the bedrock of all modern management', later techniques being mere superimpositions upon Taylorism, and mostly cosmetic at that. Though Braverman's conclusion is a valuable corrective to that rose-tinted view which sees Taylorism as a kind of managerial dark age which was soon obliterated by the Hawthornian enlightenment, it does not, as it stands, much advance our understanding of the *variety* of management control strategies. As Littler and Salaman (1982) put it, 'Braverman, by positing a single control problem and deskilling as a global means of solving it, prematurely foreclosed analysis of the real means used by capital to control labour'.

However, the labour process debate, which arose in reaction to Braverman's work, has been very much concerned with re-examining these matters. Concerned in the first instance with Braverman's neglect of the role of workers' resistance in shaping management control strategies (which was quite intentional, but nevertheless ultimately misleading (Elger 1982: 24–77), later theorists have linked changes in these strategies to the type and intensity of the control problem presented by the workforce. The clearest example is Edwards (1979), for whom each management control strategy is ultimately neutralised by the characteristic form of resistance which it generates within the workforce, thus precipitating the search for alternative strategies. Rather different versions of this theme have been developed by Friedman (1977) and Gordon, Edwards and Reich (1982). These authors show that the state of the labour market and the nature of the tasks which workers are employed to perform may, in certain periods and in certain sectors, incline employers to the choice of 'responsible autonomy' strategies rather than the kind of 'direct control' exemplified by Taylorism. Gordon, Edwards and Reich (op. cit.) and Littler (1982) introduced a further dimension into the picture by considering the part played by economic crises and the consequent pressure on profits in stimulating the search for new control strategies.

These and other writers in the 'post Braverman' tradition deploy an impressive range of historical, comparative and contemporary empirical evidence. The result, taken as a whole, offers compelling insights into the variety of management strategies. However, there remains a difficulty: it is that the explanations offered for variations of management strategy within this literature are essentially functionalist in that the appearance of new strategies tends to be accounted for in terms of the problems which these solve (c.f. Salaman 1982). The problem with functionalist explanations is not so much that they are wrong but that they are incomplete. Thus it is quite reasonable to explain the *adoption* of a new strategy by citing the problems which it solves but this is insufficient to account for the *origin* of the strategy, still less for its *nature*. The object of this chapter is to offer a theoretical approach to these latter two questions supported by some evidence on the part played in developing methods of labour process control by the personnel and accounting specialisms within management hierarchies. In doing so, it is also hoped to offer a fresh illumination of the dynamics of managerial organisation, more especially within the highly differentiated and specialised personnel of the modern corporation.

In order to introduce the approach, however, I will return to the beginnings of scientific management during the first decades of this century. After reviewing the accounts of the origins of scientific management offered by a number of prominent labour process writers, I then show how these are complemented by Layton's (1969, 1971) study of the American engineering profession within which this new control strategy was generated. Generalising the pattern of origin and sponsorship of new strategies which is exhibited in this early case, I then attempt to indicate how the pattern is replicated in the trajectories of the accounting and personnel specialisms within management organisations.

Scientific Management as the Answer to a Capitalist Prayer and as a Means of Intra-Managerial Competition

In order to clarify the inadequacy of existing 'labour process' explanations of the variety of management control strategies, I will first briefly outline the 'modal' account of the advent of scientific management and allied techniques which is offered by a sample of prominent post-Braverman writers (Friedman 1977; Edwards 1979; Clawson 1980; Gordon, Edwards and Reich 1982 and Littler 1982). Stripped of historical detail and allowing for differences of terminology, their argument runs that employers' reliance on craft traditions (Friedman, Gordon et al.) or systems of internal contract (Clawson, Littler) proved inadequate as means of work intensification under the increased stress of competition brought about by slump conditions. There followed a period of experimentation with piece-rates (Friedman, Edwards, Clawson, Littler), a technique of control which began to fail, in its turn, as workers learned to regulate their efforts as a defence against rate-cutting. It was therefore the employers' need to combat effort regulation which first exposed the necessity for direct physical intervention in the process of production, and it was noticeable that Taylor explicitly directed his methods against 'systematic soldiering'. In post-Braverman writings, then, scientific management and similar techniques appear at the moment when earlier attempts at work intensification were failing for want of precisely the kind of control of production methods which the new strategies promised. If this account is read, not simply as a narrative, but as an *explanation* of the evolution of the employers' control strategies, it is, as Salaman (1982: 51) has pointed out, a functionalist one: the techniques of scientific management seem to appear *because* of the problems which they solved. Moreover, they are made to appear as the *only* solution, a position which is quite obviously untenable in the light of Littler's study of the very different development of the Japanese labour process (1982: 46).

A related difficulty occurs in the attempts of some of the accounts to periodise changes in control strategies by relating them to economic crises. The problem here is that there are *always* crises somewhere in capitalist economies; and it is highly questionable whether the search for a competitive edge is absent when and where there is no crisis. At the empirical level, the work of Littler (1982) again underlines this difficulty: whereas the experiments with scientific management occurred in the USA in boom conditions, the derivative techniques of the Bedaux system were implemented in this country during a slump.

The treatment of the techniques of scientific management within the 'labour process tradition', then, is arguably deficient in its account of the reasons for their advent, in accounting for the precise nature of the techniques, and in locating them historically. In these respects the work of Layton (1969, 1971) offers an important supplementary perspective.

For Layton, scientific management, in its criticisms of traditional supervision and in its claim that the administration of labour should be monopolised by the 'planning department', was a product of the 'ideology of engineering'. This, in turn, was an expression of the resentment of the American mechanical engineers of the day, hitherto accustomed to the ownership or substantial control of small job-bing machine shops (Calvert 1967, Ch. 1) at their subordination in growing bureaucratic organisations as industrial concentration proceeded.

There was nothing even mildly reformist about this ideology: far from expressing hostility to big business it constituted a claim that engineers were those best fitted to dominate it. Thus, at the same time as scientific management offered techniques for, and an ideological justification of, the control of labour by capital, it derived those techniques from a particular analysis of the management task – an engineering analysis – and made the claim that an application of those techniques called for the installation of a particular group – engineers — at the apex of the developing differentiation within the 'global function of capital' (a term used by Carchedi (1977) to denote that assemblage of roles which, in modern capitalism, performs the functions once carried out by the individual capitalist).

What this perspective offers is first of all a convincing periodisation of the advent of scientific management: it arose as an expression of the 'ideology of engineering' at the moment when American mechanical engineers, as a group, experienced an abrupt transition from independence to subordination within developing industrial hierarchies. More importantly, it offers an explanation of the nature of the solution which scientific management offered to the problem of controlling labour. The approach to the physical process of production grew out of the engineers' previous experience of machine design. Workers' movements were analysed and redesigned so as to achieve the most economical sequence, an approach which inherently presupposes the subordination of manual to mental labour and close directive supervision. Moreover there is an analogy between the reduction of skilled to simple labour and the earlier development by mechanical engineers of interchangeable parts as a solution to the problem of co-ordinating production (Clawson 1980: 76–9). Of course these considerations do not by themselves explain why businessmen adopted the techniques of scientific management (when they did): for that we need to return to the considerations by the labour process writers. What is being claimed is that the two perspectives are complementary and that Salaman (1982: 59) is correct in calling for a consideration of the influence of intra-organisational relationships on the development of control strategies and also of the influence of previous systems of ideas on the form they take.

Although it anticipates some later arguments, it is as well at this point to consider a major possible objection: that if scientific management was sponsored by engineers in an attempt to install themselves at the apex of the global function of capital, and if its techniques are now, as Braverman claims, the 'bedrock' of all modern management (1974: 87), how is it that engineers themselves do not now dominate the managements of all major corporations? The answer appears to lie in Larson's (1977: Ch. 4) analysis of the conditions under which a professional body of knowledge can form the basis of a 'collective mobility project'. Whilst the knowledge base needs to be sufficiently codifiable to be transmitted as a professional culture, it also needs to contain sufficient indeterminacy to debar outsiders from professional practice. In other words, however important their function, professionals can only use it as a basis for social mobility (in this case within the global function of capital), if their professional knowledge (in this case a technique for controlling labour) is sufficiently indeterminate to prevent the detachment of the function from the professionals themselves. Unfortunately for the engineers, the techniques of scientific management proved too lucid and could too easily be detached from the ambitions of the engineers, despite Taylor's protestations that scientific management could only be installed as a total system. Thus Bedaux, though a technocrat by personal inclination, was acute enough to market the techniques of scientific management to the family-dominated firms of England in a form shorn of Taylor's Messianic visions (Littler 1982: 105–8).

The Role of Inter-Professional Competition in the Generation of Control Strategies

Though the development of the techniques of scientific management occurred early in the differentiation of management hierarchies, it has features which point towards a more general model of the development of management control strategies. For brevity, in what follows I will loosely refer to specialisms within the global function of capital as 'professions'. Such a usage calls for some explanation since professionalism has traditionally been thought of as in some degree antipathetic to the values of business organisations.

This supposition was derived largely from the assumption that professions can be defined by the possession of certain traits, notably independent ethical or technical standards of performance and collegiate control of these which, virtually by definition, create the potential for conflict with capitalist priorities. Besides tending to accept at face value the professionals' own account of the reasons behind their exclusionary practices and demands for autonomy (Roth 1974), such an approach ignores the possibility that some of the techniques which certain professions attempt to monopolise have no existence outside the global function of capital and that, in the context of business organisation, demands for autonomy may express not so much a desire for independence but ambitions to be numbered amongst the controllers rather than the controlled. Thus Child et al. (1983) see professionalism amongst the staff positions in British industry not simply as a demand to be allowed to work according to the professions' own conception of proper standards but also as an imposition of these standards on managers in the production function.

It should also be pointed out that, in using the term 'professionals' to denote competing specialisms within the global function of capital, I am not intending to endorse the notion that all mental labour lies within the capital function (cf. Poulantzas 1975). It is simply that I am not directly concerned in this discussion with those elements of professional work which constitute productive labour. Finally, it is relevant to note that whereas certain segments of a profession may lie within what Abercrombie and Urry (1983) call the 'service class' (i.e. that class which discharges the functions of capital), other sections of the same profession may not – although they may nevertheless aspire to do so. Into this aspiring category fell a section of the American engineering profession at the time of the development of scientific management.

(i) At the time of the development of scientific management, American mechanical engineers had developed a relatively clear occupational ideology, one element of which was a belief that their position within the global function of capital had become unjustifiably subordinate. This suggests that, beyond a certain stage of differentiation, the global function of capital can be seen as a collection of relatively self-conscious specialisms which compete at a group level for access to the key positions of command. At stake is both the position of the profession as a whole and the promotion prospects of individuals whose careers originate within it. There is every incentive for such a competition if Wright (1979) is correct in arguing that there exists an economic return to the function of control, and (for example) the 45 per cent salary advantage enjoyed by British engineers who move into 'general' management (Berthoud and Smith 1980: 38) suggests confirmation of Wright's thesis.

(ii) As an expression of the ideology of engineers, scientific management sought to remedy their subordination by offering an engineering solution to one of the key problems within the global function of capital – that of controlling labour. Though the problem was, of course, real, the urgency of solving it was also ideologically emphasised by Taylor's criticisms of the inadequacies of traditional management. Generalising, this indicates that collective mobility for a profession within the global function of capital depends on identifying a key problem confronting capital (which need not necessarily be that of controlling labour), stressing the inadequacy of existing methods of coping with it (which may be associated with competing professions) and developing a solution based on the techniques of the profession. This process will be facilitated by the development of a professional ideology which stresses both the urgency of the problem and the irreplaceability of the profession's techniques for solving it.

(iii) As has already been pointed out, scientific management was based on an extrapolation of the principles of mechanical engineering design in that most of its key characteristics derived from an assumption that human labour could and, for optimum efficiency, should, be designed in the same way as machine movements. Thus the solutions offered by professions to crises within the global function of capital may be generated from their existing bodies of professional knowledge and their specialised techniques. Pre-professional examples of this process were the systems of internal contract and the piece-work payment methods which succeeded them. Both can be regarded as attempts to generalise the petty capitalist motives of the small entrepreneur into methods of controlling labour in relatively large organisations (Littler 1982: 81,82). However, it is also possible for professions to annex developments which occur in other fields, as (for instance) the American accounting profession later took possession of the techniques of management accountancy which were pioneered by

American industrial engineers (Chatfield 1977: 178 *et seq.*).

(iv) Professions which achieve a pre-eminence within the global function of capital on the basis of solving a problem other than that of the control of labour (for example, that of the realisation of surplus), may still influence the control strategy simply on account of their general dominance. Seeing the problem in terms of their professional expertise (or former expertise in the case of senior managers who no longer practise one), they may favour systems of control which they best understand. For example, senior managers with backgrounds in finance or accountancy may seek solutions to profitability problems by tightening up financial controls rather than by redesigning the labour process itself.

(v) For a strategy to function as a means of collective mobility for a profession, the profession needs to retain a monopoly of its practice. As already pointed out, scientific management let the engineers down badly in this respect: it was too lucid. Its techniques could be divorced from the overall dominance of the engineering profession despite Taylor's warnings of the perils of doing so. As Braverman put it, though not with quite the same meaning, the techniques of scientific management are no longer the property of a faction (1974: 87). Speaking more generally, the continued possession of a control (or other) strategy depends on the profession maintaining a certain mystique and indeterminacy about it so that the strategy can be operated only by themselves.

(vi) A feature of internal competition within the global function of capital which is not illustrated by the case of scientific management is the development of clear-cut differentiations of power, privilege and status (horizontal fissures) *within* professions, of the kind analysed in the case of accountancy by Johnson (1977a, b, 1980). However, whereas Johnson argues that horizontal fission tends to occur at the boundary between capital and worker functions, I would maintain that his analysis of accountancy demonstrates that it can also serve to isolate different levels of access to decision-making power and economic privilege *within* the global function of capital. There are at least three reasons for expecting this to occur:

(1) By consigning the routine and codifiable elements of its professional knowledge to subordinates, the élite secures for itself the elements of indeterminacy and thus reinforces its grip on the strategy on which its collective mobility project is based.
(2) By reducing the size of the élite for whom key positions are claimed, competition for these at the individual level is reduced.
(3) An internal hierarchy within the profession creates a 'managerial'

element in senior positions within it which reinforces the claim of the élite that their professional practice inherently involves managerial responsibility.

Having sketched out a model of the role of competition within the global function of capital in the development of control strategies, I will now attempt to apply it to the cases of accountancy and personnel management. Albeit with different degrees of success, both of these professions have tended to achieve their present position in management hierarchies at the expense of engineers and production managers. After a brief discussion of the place of each of these professions within the managerial and directoral élite, the discussion of each will follow the model as laid out above.

Accountants and Other Financial Specialists

As far as can be ascertained, British company directors with backgrounds in banking or accountancy substantially outnumber those with technical training (BIM 1972), membership of the Institute of Chartered Accountants being the single most common academic or professional qualification in British boardrooms (Institute of Directors Survey 1965, quoted in Tricker 1967: 20). Further, although the most common first degrees amongst the members of the British Institute of Management (BIM) are in science or engineering (Melrose-Woodman 1978: 16; Mansfield Poole, Blyton and Frost 1981: 8; Solomons 1974), the pattern of post-graduate study is such that qualifications in business, economics or accountancy predominate amongst the minority (roughly one-third) of members who are qualified to degree level. Moreover the trend over time is strongly in favour of qualification in the business and financial subjects (Melrose-Woodman 1978: 14).

Thus, understanding accountancy, not as a specific professional training but as that broader range of subjects which include its technologies as core elements, there can be little doubt of its heavy and increasing representation at the key decision-making levels within the global function of capital. Although we are here concerned with the fortunes and consequences of accountancy in this broad sense, much of what follows perforce draws on a literature which has been concerned with the profession specifically. Nevertheless this can still serve to illuminate the processes which have led to the comparative dominance of accountancy as a means of management and its consequences for the control of labour.

In this country, the accounting methods used by early manufacturers originated in the bookkeeping techniques used by estate managers, mercantile capitalists and putting-out manufacturers. Although these were quite unreliable, even as a basis for pricing, let alone internal control, these deficiencies were masked for a long time by the wide profit margins characteristic of the era. In the firms of the industrial revolution, the clerks who performed this accounting work remained few in number and comparatively poorly paid whilst their employers were more preoccupied with shortages of engineers and metalworkers (Pollard 1965: 144, 223).

Accountants owed a more substantial early position in the structures of capitalism to the audit requirements imposed by capitalists on each other, some of which were incorporated into law, both here and in the USA (Portwood and Fielding 1981: 755; Boland 1982: 116), just as later specialists in taxation were able to prosper by employing their 'impartiality and dispassionateness' (Stacey 1954: 178) to minimise the tax liabilities of the firms which employed them (Thompson 1978: 397; Boland 1982: 122).

However, at least until the mid 1920s, it was not understood by investors and entrepreneurs that 'in helping to boost company profits, the accountant has been and remains to this day, perhaps the most important management tool of private enterprise' and members of the profession 'rarely ascended to leading positions in trade, industry or commerce' (Stacey 1954: 168, 176–8, 200–2). In other words, the adaptation of audit and costing techniques to the problem of internal control within capitals as opposed to that of regularising relations between them or between capitals and the state, had not yet begun, nor had the correlative advance of accountants and former accountants to positions of command within the global function of capital.

What changed matters was the depression of the mid 1920s. If the wide profit margins of early manufacturing industry had forgiven the primitive accounting techniques of the industrial revolution, economic crisis, by a reversal of the same logic, helped to advance the cause of accountancy by stimulating a drive to locate and contain costs. It was the evolution of management accountancy in response to this pressure which completed the consolidation of accountancy as a major profession. However, despite proddings from Government during and immediately after the Second World War, the new techniques were not adopted without the vigorous advocacy of the profession itself against the resistance of 'entrepreneurs', suspicious of any 'new fangled administrative overhead' (Stacey ibid.).

Although Stacey is not very clear about the sources of resistance and not very sophisticated in his analysis of its motivation, these developments fit well with the model of an organisational profession adapting its original specialism to the problem of managerial control (in the case of audit), or annexing related techniques developed elsewhere (partly by engineers, in the case of costing [Chatfield 1977: 178 *et seq.*]) and adapting these to the same end. The profession's sponsorship of these techniques as appropriate responses to a crisis within the global function of capital served, at the same time, as a means of collective mobility in competition with other potential or actual incumbents of positions of command.

Studies of the evolution of giant corporations in the USA, carried out by Chandler and his co-workers, cast further light on the rise of accountancy, although, as Littler (1982: 50) points out, it is necessary to be careful when applying American experience to this country. In viewing giant corporations essentially as alternatives to competitive markets or cartel arrangements for carrying out the economic functions of co-ordination, monitoring and allocation, Chandler could be said to be using concepts and a frame of reference which virtually define the development of accounting controls as fundamental to the development of giant corporations (Chandler and Daems 1979: 3–4). However his historical accounts show that the rise of the accountants was accomplished not as a matter of definition but by a purposeful restructuring of large corporations in response to the economic crises of 1920–2. Until that time, the organisational structures of large American corporations were modelled on the line/staff structure first developed on the railways, in which accountants and other financial specialists were amongst the staff advisory to line managers. When applied to multi-product enterprises, the fundamental weakness of this structure was that it provided no rational way of allocating resources. Because line managers reported only to senior managers who themselves had functional responsibilities, allocation remained a matter for bargaining and in-fighting between interested parties. The consequent inability to adjust inventories to demand led to a severe crisis for American corporations in the recession of the early 1920s.

In the pioneering and prototypical restructuring of General Motors, this problem of allocation was solved by creating a multi-divisional structure, co-ordinated and controlled by a general office of financial and advisory staff who developed, from the original techniques for controlling inventories, new statistical techniques for more generally controlling, co-ordinating and evaluating the performance of operating divisions (and consequently of their managers). Senior managers were thus divorced from day-to-day operations and, what is more significant from the present point of view, they became financial rather than operational or technical decision-makers. Thus although it was an engineer – Alfred P. Sloan Jr – who played a prominent part in the restructuring of General Motors, the reorganisation was possible because the accounting and financial staffs, formerly in advisory positions, possessed the techniques of auditing and cost accounting (the latter, ironically, first developed by the early industrial engineers) from which could be developed more general methods of control which offered a solution to the crisis faced by the corporation. To put the matter very crudely, accountants displaced engineers and other operational managers from key positions within the global function of capital because decisions of allocation between dissimilar operations could only be made on a common abstract – and therefore financial – basis. However, in applying such an analysis to the United Kingdom, it is necessary to bear in mind a number of contextual differences: importantly that family capitalism persisted far longer in this country than in the USA and that here the coincidence of mass markets and mass production techniques which stimulated the development of giant multi-divisional American corporations was less common and occurred later (Chandler 1977, 1980; Chandler and Daems 1979). Whereas in the USA, the multi-divisional form became predominant amongst large corporations in the period 1945–50, in the UK, the transition was still in progress during the years 1965–70 (Steer and Cable 1978).

It is important to note that the growth of giant corporations itself is not sufficient to explain the relative ascendancy of the accounting profession. For this it was critical that accountants were already represented in the management hierarchies of British and American companies at the time of their growing pains so that they could profit by offering their characteristic remedies. As has been already pointed out, this early presence was partly a consequence of the audit requirements imposed by the securities market. In Germany and Japan, where the major sources of industrial finance were respectively the banking system (Habakkuk 1967: 167) and government (Littler 1982: 146), it is also the case that accountants are both less numerous and less senior in the management hierarchies of large companies (Hutton, Lawrence and Smith 1977: 69–87; Lawrence 1980: 67–74; Coke 1983). German management, in particular, is dominated by engineers and, instead of forming the stock-in-trade of a specialist accounting profession as in Britain and the USA, the techniques of financial control are taught to these engineering managers at undergraduate and post-graduate levels. Although German accounting controls may, in consequence, appear primitive to American eyes, this appears to be compensated by the greater emphasis on manufacture (Lawrence 1980: 89–95). Interestingly, in a German company studied by Millar (1979) the engineer-managers had devised a de-centralised system of production and a 'special' stock-control system, both of which eliminated the need for certain accounting procedures common in the UK.

The involvement of accountancy in key decision-making positions within the global function of capital has, in Johnson's view (1977a, b, 1980), created a horizontal fission within the profession whereby the activites of the élite which creates, installs and supervises control systems have the effect of routinising, fragmenting and deskilling the work of their nominal professional colleagues. For the élite, on the other hand, the delegation of routine tasks to subordinates has the effect of sustaining the 'indetermination' of its own activities, thus serving to reinforce its monopoly of them. This monopoly persists, suggests Johnson, not so much as a result of the esoteric nature of the knowledge base but only so long as it operates in the interests of capital. Testifying to the qualitative differences in different levels of accounting work are the problems of adjustment faced by accountants if and when they are promoted (McKenna 1978).

Besides these tensions internal to the profession, claims are being made for the territorial extension of the accounting domain into production management (Burchell et al. 1980) and into the 'behavioural' expertise hitherto claimed by the personnel specialists (e.g. Hopwood 1974). In reaction, resistance by operational managers to accounting controls is a routine feature of modern corporate life (Tricker 1967: 375) and, on the behavioural front, there appears to be a disputed no man's land within which 'manpower audits' are claimed for management accountancy (Benston 1977: Chs. 7.1 and 7.2) whilst 'human resource accounting' is staked out by the personnel profession (see later). Amongst the professional bodies of accountants, at least the Institute of Cost and Management Accountants is keenly aware that its members are in competition for positions of corporate power with other professions as well as with the members of other accounting institutions. At the time of writing, this institute is preparing a report identifying the sources of competition and strategies to deal with it. In particular, it is seen as necessary in the interests of the profession that it should succeed in annexing those parts of information technology which seem likely to impinge on its practice rather than suffer the consequences of the monopolisation of these by other specialists (Banyard 1983). On another front, the more recently evolved sub-specialisms of operational research and managerial economics appear to be competing for part of the traditional control function of management accountancy (Tricker 1967: 371-5) to the accompaniment of mutually denigratory occupational ideologies (cf. Esland 1980: 240).

As a system of control, management accountancy does not, in its pure form, involve physical intervention in the labour of production. However, in the larger sense, it serves to control the labour process in at least three interrelated ways. In one of its aspects it is a solution to the problem posed by the demise of the internal contract system: that of how to ensure the loyalty and motivation of salaried managers and so avoid the 'negligence and profusion' which Adam Smith believed would be the inevitable result of their relative economic security (Pollard 1965: 12; Edwards 1979: 31). Budget allocations are used to discipline and control department managers (Tricker 1967: 73–5) and the development of measures of departmental performance has been linked with practices for the evaluation and reward of their managers (Burchell et al. 1980: 16). In this aspect, management accountancy supplements the engineering transformation of the physical process of production by linking managers' careers to their success in increasing the rate of exploitation in their particular departments. Second, by rationalising decisions of allocation (see, for example, McKenna 1978: 13) it enables the concentration of capital and labour on operations which yield the greatest surplus, so indirectly acting as a disciplinary pressure on those whose livelihoods are linked with operations which yield the least. Finally, the language and presuppositions of accounting systems (Burchell et al. 1980) function as vocabularies of motive which set the terms of and limit any challenge by workers and subordinate managers to senior management decisions (Batstone 1979).

The Personnel Specialists

In the opinion of Cherns (1972, quoted in Watson 1977: 168) 'organisational leadership' in post-war Britain has successively passed from engineers, accountants and marketing specialists to personnel departments. The evidence relating to this sweeping claim is contradictory. Whereas Brookes (1979: 53) found that only 4 per cent of his surveyed companies had directors responsible solely for personnel and/or industrial relations, Brown (1981: 27) and Daniel and Millward (1983: 122) report the much higher proportions of 30 per cent and 34 per cent respectively. On the other side of the coin, between one-half (Brookes) and one-third (Brown, Daniel and Millward) of surveyed companies had no director whose reponsibilities included personnel or industrial relations. Interpretations of the figures vary as much as the evidence. Whereas Brown was impressed by the symptoms of increasing attention to personnel and industrial relations, Daniel and Millward were struck by the rarity of personnel managers and the paucity of formal qualifications amongst them. Whatever the truth of these matters, it could be argued that success is relative: the profession itself traces its origins to the 60 or so female welfare workers in British factories on the eve of the First World War (Niven 1967: 42) whereas, by 1980 membership of the Institute of Personnel Managers stood at over 20,000 (ACAS 1980: 55).

According to the literature there is a curious difference between the origins of British and American personnel management. Whereas in the USA, personnel departments were apparently created in order to administer a battery of techniques aimed at dividing and weakening the workforce (Gordon, Edward and Reich 1982: 138) and the devices of paternalistic despotism such as Henry Ford's 'Sociology Department' (Beynon 1973: 21–3), the profession in this country, as has been mentioned, claims its origins in factory welfare work. Perhaps the discrepancy arises because, in the more fragmented conditions of British industry, the less benign approaches to the control of labour were performed by employers' associations rather than by managers as such (Clegg 1979: 125). However these aspects of its origin are not emphasised in the accepted histories of the profession, though Anthony and Crichton (1969: 160) do mention the bargaining activities of employers' associations as antecedents.

History is written by the victors, and that of the personnel profession is represented as a struggle whereby 'professionalism' emerged through and was finally emancipated from, the 'welfare image' (Anthony and Crichton 1969: 149). For example, in the inter-war years, welfare workers based outside the factory were excluded from membership of the Central Association of Welfare Workers, care was taken to define welfare work as an aspect of management and even the name of the association was changed so as to emphasise its industrial concerns (Niven 1967: 51, 52, 61). In the account of Anthony and Crichton (1969: 164), the former welfare workers 'struggled to find other jobs to do for management which would entitle them to a place on the management team, in order that they could be brought in on discussions of importance such as the determination of wage rates or the deployment of staff'. In other words, it is claimed that corporate power was sought, not in the self-interest of the profession, but as a means of more effectively performing welfare work (se also Watson 1977: 52–5). Niven's account of the progress of the profession during the recession of 1925–39 is more robust: 'in the recession, welfare workers had to justify their immediate usefulness or founder ... welfare supervisors had the courage and adaptability to turn course from welfare to labour and staff management in order to meet new and pressing needs' (Niven 1967: 71). Given that the welfare needs of workers can scarcely have declined during the hungry thirties, it is likely that these 'new and pressing needs' had more to do with maintaining the welfare workers' position in industry than with anything else. Niven's passage suggests that they did so by adapting the existing means of their trade (interviewing, record-keeping and so on) so as to create a new means of labour administration. As late as the early 1970s, this aspect of the origin of the techniques of personnel management was, according to Timperley and Osbaldeston (1975: 619) still reflected in the clerical/administrative backgrounds of many practising personnel managers.

Having developed its techniques of control before the Second World War, the profession was well placed to offer them on a post-war seller's market, when full employment made the control of labour a more pressing problem. By the 1970s, the adaptation of professional values to the opportunities of the market had proceeded to the point where a concern for welfare appeared to be entirely submerged beneath a concentration on 'efficiency' (Watson, 1977: 198) and this tradition of relatively self-consciously adjusting the service provided so as to advance the profession within the global function of capital has continued (Thomason 1980: 32, 37).

However useful the personnel specialists may or may not have been, they could only have advanced their profession on the basis of that usefulness by establishing a monopoly of competence. Thus Niven (1967: 59) saw a key task of the association as that of combating the employers' tendency to assume that anyone could do the job and persuading them to employ only trained welfare workers. For Thomason (1980: 32), the essential difficulty in this is that the human relations and social skills which are part of the profession's stock-in-trade are too indeterminate to form a sufficiently exclusive and distinct basis on which to claim a monopoly (in a way, the opposite difficulty to that faced by the engineers). Like Niven, and with disarming frankness, he proposes a somewhat artificial credentialism as a solution (Thomason 1980: 32, 33), without burdening his readers with the usual claims that this is really in the clients' own interests.

Perhaps because they have not yet succeeded in gaining the autonomy which they believe possible and necessary (Thomason 1980: 35), personnel specialists are highly conscious that they face competition for positions of corporate power from engineers and financial and sales specialists, amongst others. The kind of interpersonal tactics used by individual personnel managers in such situations are most illuminatingly described by Watson (1977: 178–89) in an account which also stresses the active role played by them in defining the problems for which they purport to offer solutions.

Personnel specialists have tried to expand their sphere of influence into production planning and have competed with foremen and costing departments for the function of rate-fixing on the grounds that they possess specialist knowledge of the effects of incentives. After the Second World War, they increasingly appropriated the training of first-line supervisors and middle managers on the grounds that the hire and fire methods of control, traditional amongst these groups, were no longer appropriate in an era of full employment (Anthony and Crichton 1969: 166–70). They have become the prophets of a particular kind of behavioural science, much of which, as Rose (1975: 213) points out of the Tavistock researches, can be interpreted as an attack on the trained incapacities of production engineers. Moreover, in the industrial relations field, the general message of the kind of industrial relations policies advocated, for example by Cuthbert and Hawkins (1973), is that short-term expediency in solving industrial relations problems (characteristic of production managers) should be subordinated to broader, more consistent policies (administered by personnel specialists, and, naturally, from the boardroom).

All this is a particular case of a phenomenon remarked by Child, Fores, Glover and Lawrence (1983) and earlier by Fores and Glover (1978) as particularly prevalent in Britain: that the professionalisation of staff positions outside production involves a claim for decision-making autonomy which results in the imposition of the practices of the professions concerned upon the production function. In other words, personnel specialists have ascended within the global function of capital partly by exposing the inadequacies of, and at the expense of, engineers in line management.

The major crisis within the function of capital which has enabled them to do this concerned the control of labour and it resulted from the persistence of relatively full employment from the end of the Second World War until the early 1970s, although a part may also have been played by the development of capital-intensive technologies which made it necessary for employers to bargain for their workers to take a responsible attitude towards capital plant in this 'primary' sector of the labour market (Edwards 1975). Full employment created the conditions for the growth of shop steward organisation to which the response, first of academics then later of the Royal Commission, was that the techniques of industrial relations pluralism were a more realistic strategy than the bluff anti-unionism of an earlier generation of engineer/managers (Fox 1966; Flanders 1975; Donovan 1968: 264).

The appropriation by the profession of industrial relations pluralism with its assumption of permanent underlying conflicts of interest provides the perfect rationale for the curious dual relationship of personnel specialists to the control of labour. On the one hand, this obviously presents problems which must be solved at the level of day-to-day operations; and, on the other, their own organisational power and influence depend on the long-term persistence of the problem (Watson 1977: 183–9). Indeed, in Turner, Roberts and Roberts' (1977 35–9) finding that labour problems are most prevalent where personnel specialists are most heavily represented, there is even the suggestion that they may play a part in sustaining the very problems which provide the rationale for their presence. A survey by the Industrial Relations Research Unit reported by Batstone (1980) points towards a mechanism by which this may occur. By centralising and formalising company-level procedures in line with the recommendations of the Donovan report (1968), personnel managers have stimulated the development of shop steward organisation and the expectation that something was to be gained by participating in the new bargaining procedures. However, because they lacked influence on top management financial policies, personnel specialists have been unable to satisfy these new expectations. Arguably, the result has been an increased incidence of conflict with a better-organised workforce.

Another development during the years of full employment worked in favour of the personnel specialists. As part of a high-level strategy for securing the co-operation of labour, governments have introduced, from the 1960s onwards a mass of legislation offering 'individual rights' to workers on the one hand and regularising the position of their trade unions and officials on the other. Though some of these 'rights' proved more apparent than real when put to the test (Lewis 1981), the complication of the legislation provided personnel specialists with a major opportunity to supplement their somewhat indeterminate human relations skills with a genuinely codifiable and esoteric body of professional knowledge. As Thomason (1980: 33) puts it, 'The spate of employee legislation and codes of practice have enabled both the IPM and individual practitioners to acquire status enhancing power' and again 'the state response changed the balance of power as between personnel practitioners and line managers which allowed the former to enhance their discretion'. Put more crudely, personnel managers have used the threat of industrial tribunals to impose their own methods of discipline on lower line managers and to remove from them altogether the right to sack.

If the personnel profession has traditionally sought its advances within the corporate hierarchy by exposing the shortcomings of production and other line managers, with a view to taking over certain of their former roles within the global function of capital, there are signs that a different strategy is being adopted in relation to financial specialists. Recognising the corporate ascendancy of these, personnel thinkers are now seeking to present their specialist contribution to the control of labour in forms which they take to be acceptable in terms of the 'dominant utilitarian values and bureaucratic relationships' of the organisations which employ them. Thus quantitative and computerised techniques of manpower planning have been developed in answer to the criticism that personnel departments have not, in the past, provided 'hard' data (Legge 1978: 79 *et seq.*). There have also appeared the significantly labelled techniques of 'Human resource *accounting*' and the 'Industrial relations *audit*', but it is not clear whether these attempts to present personnel work as a species of accountancy are meeting with much success.

As with accountancy, the stress of competition for corporate power appears to be producing a hierarchy within the profession. There are five grades of membership in the Institute of Personnel Management, with the 'Member' grade, which numbers about one-fifth of the total, dominating the policy of the Institute and setting increasingly rigorous requirements for entry to its own ranks (Timperley and Osbaldeston 1975). However, the reported infrequency of formal qualifications amonst personnel managers in industry (Daniel and Millward 1983: 122) indicates that the creation of this hierarchy has not enabled the élite of the profession to monopolise the available top corporate positions. Though there probably *are* hierarchies within personnel practice in industry (in a case observed by the writer, such matters as interviewing, issuing warnings and even the more straightforward sackings were all handled by female subordinates), these seem to have developed in an *ad hoc* manner, unrelated to the formal hierarchy of the profession.

Though subject to negotiation and attempts at territorial expansion the role of personnel specialists in the control of labour has historically been that of delivering a suitable supply of it to operational departments and helping to motivate it or at least prevent its insurrection once it is there. Such a specialism can prosper in the corporate hierarchy only when these tasks are, or can be made to appear, sufficiently grave a problem not to be handled incidentally by other managers. Thus the logic of the personnel specialists' position demands that the control of labour, both at the individual and collective levels, should continue to pose a problem, albeit one containable by the specialist techniques possessed by them (Knights,

Willmott and Collinson 1985). Perhaps this contradiction is one reason for the rapidly changing hit-parade of psycho-sociological gimmickry deployed by the profession (the other being product differentiation under the stress of competiton amongst the associated consultants and semi-academics). These have ranged from comparatively straightforward attempts to explain to workers what they are doing and why, via insultingly childish campaigns such as 'QED' ([save a] quid each day) to highly enjoyable weekend trips on which (according to accounts given to the writer) managers and workers reach out for mutual understanding but find only a common drunkenness. In a profession with such a strong tradition of offering whatever service promises to advance or secure its own position, more will surely follow, provided, that is, it can find a way of surviving the comparative quiescence of labour imposed by the current recession.

Conclusions
The labour process perspective, which highlights the role of management in extracting surplus value from the labour process, offers far greater potential than orthodox management literature for understanding the dynamics of management control strategies. At the moment, however, this potential remains partially unrealised owing to the implicit functionalism of existing labour process accounts of managerial change. In these, successive crises within the function of capital are made to account both for the advent of new control strategies and for their nature. In contrast to this perspective, it has been argued that control strategies originate within the techniques and knowledge possessed by 'professional' groups in competition for the key positions within the global function of capital. The response of capital to its crises (which need not be specifically of control) is mediated by these professions which are poised to engage on collective mobility projects within the global function of capital in virtue of their possession of techniques which offer responses to these crises. However, if the knowledge basis of a response strategy is too accessible to outsiders, it can be implemented whilst failing as a means of group mobility, since the 'profession' may then be dispossessed of its strategy. For this reason the élites within a profession may attempt to monopolise for themselves the esoteric indeterminate aspects of professional practice whilst delegating the routine elements to subordinates, thus producing a 'horizontal fission' within the profession.

The trajectories of accountancy and personnel management prove, on examination, to be broadly consistent with this perspective. The élites of both professions have prospered within management hierarchies at the expense of engineers and production managers and have done so by developing their original techniques, or techniques 'poached' from other professions, into relatively comprehensive control strategies. It is noticeable too that the watchdogs of both professions are keenly aware that they face continuing competition for the positions which they now occupy.

All this suggests that there is a link between certain aspects of organisational politics, the process of professionalisation of managerial occupations and changes in the nature and intensity of the crises confronting capitalist enterprises. That link is the need for capital to control the labour process.

References

Abercombie, N. and Urry, J. (1983), *Capital, Labour and the Middle Classes*, London: Allen and Unwin.
ACAS (Advisory, Conciliation and Arbitration Service) (1980), *Industrial Relations Handbook*, London: HMSO.
Anthony, P. and Crichton, A. (1969), *Industrial Relations and the Personnel Specialists*, London: Batsford.
Banyard, C. (1983), 'Future Prospects for Management Accountants', *Management Accounting*, **61**, 6.
Batstone, E. (1979), 'Systems of Domination, Accommodation and Industrial Democracy', Chapter 7 in Burns, T. (ed.), *Work and Power*, New York: Sage.
Batstone, E. (1980), 'What have Personnel Managers done for Industrial Relations?', *Personnel Management*, June, 36–41.
Benston, G. L. (1977), *Contemporary Cost Accounting and Control*, London: CBI Publishing.
Berthoud, R. and Smith, D. J. (1980), *The Education, Training and Careers of Professional Engineers*, Department of Industry, London: HMSO.
Benyon, H. (1973), *Working for Ford*, London: Allen Lane, Penguin.
Boland, R. Jr (1982), 'Myth and Technology in the American Accounting Profession', *Journal of Management Studies*, **19** (1), 109–26.
Braverman, H. (1974), *Labor and Monopoly Capital*, New York: Monthly Review Press.
British Institute of Management (1972), *The Board of Directors: a survey of its structure, composition and role*. Management Survey Report no. 10.
Brookes, C. (1979), *Boards of Directors in British Industry*. Social Science Branch Research and Planning Division, Department of Employment Research Paper no. 9.
Brown, W. (1981), *The Changing Contours of British Industrial Relations*, Oxford: Blackwell.
Burchell, S., Clubb, C., Hopwood A., Hughes, J. and Nahapiet, J. (1980), 'The Roles of Accounting in Organisations and Society', *Accounting, Organisations and Society*, **5** (1) 5–27.
Calvert, M A. (1967), *The Mechanical Engineer in America 1830–1910: Professional Cultures in Conflict*, Baltimore: Johns Hopkins Press.
Carchedi, G. (1977), *On the Economic Identification of Social Classes*, London: Routledge and Kegan Paul.
Chandler, D. Jr (1977), *The Visible Hand: the Managerial Revolution in American Business*, Cambridge, Mass.: Harvard University Press.
Chandler, A. D. Jr (1980), 'The United States: Seedbed of Managerial Capitalism',

Chapter 1 in Chandler, A. D. Jr and Daems, H. (eds), *Managerial Hierarchies: Comparative Perspectives on the Rise of Modern Industrial Enterprise*, Cambridge, Mass.: Harvard University Press.

Chandler, A. D. Jr and Daems, H. (1979), 'Administrative Co-ordination, Allocation and Monitoring: a comparative analysis of the emergence of accounting and organisation in the USA and Europe', *Accounting, Organisations and Society*, **4** (1/2) 3–20.

Chatfield, M. (1977), *The History of Accounting Thought*, Melbourne, Florida USA: Krieger.

Child, J., Fores, M., Glover, I. and Lawrence, P. (1983), 'A Price to Pay? Professionalism and Work Organisation in Britain and West Germany; *Sociology*, **17**, 63–78.

Clawson, D. (1980), *Bureaucracy and the Labor Process: the Transformation of US Industry 1850–1920*, New York: Monthly Review Press.

Clegg, H. A. (1979), *The Changing System of Industrial Relations in Great Britain*, Oxford: Blackwell.

Coke, S. (1983), 'Putting Professionalism in its Place', *Personnel Management*, **15** (2), 44–5.

Cuthbert, N. H. and Hawkins, K. H. (eds) (1973), *Company Industrial Relations Policies: the management of industrial relations in the 1970s*, London: Longman.

Daniel, W. W. and Millward, N. (1983), *Workplace Industrial Relations in Britain: The DE/PSI/SSRC Survey*, London: Heinemann Educational.

Donovan, Lord (Chairman) (1968), *Report of the Royal Commission on Trades Unions and Employers' Associations*, London: HMSO, Cmnd 3623.

Edwards, R. C. (1975), 'Social Relations of Production and Labour Market Structure', Chapter 1 in Edwards, R. C., Reich, M. and Gordon, D. M. (eds), *Labour Market Segmentation*, London: D. C. Heath.

Edwards, R. (1979), *Contested Terrain: the Transformation of the Workplace in the Twentieth Century*, New York: Basic Books (page references to Heinemann edition).

Elger, A. (1982), 'Braverman, capital accumulation and de-skilling', Chapter 2, pp. 23–53 in Wood, S. (ed.), *The Degradation of Work?: skill, de-skilling and the labour process*, London: Hutchinson.

Esland, G. (1980), 'Professions and Professionalism', Chapter 7, pp. 213–50 in Esland, G. and Salaman, G. (eds), *The Politics of Work and Occupations*, Milton Keynes: Open University Press.

Flanders, A. (1975), 'Collective Bargaining: Prescription for Change', pp. 155–211 in *Management and Unions: the theory and reform of industrial relations*, London: Faber (second edition).

Fores, M. and Glover I. (1978), *The British Disease: Professionalism. Times Higher Educational Supplement*, 24 February 1978.

Fox, A. (1966), *Industrial Sociology and Industrial Relations*, Donovan Commission Research Paper no. 3, London: HMSO.

Friedman, A. L. (1977), *Industry and Labour: class struggle at work and monopoly capitalism*, London: Macmillan.

Gordon, D. M., Edwards, R. and Reich, M. (1982), *Segmented Work: Divided Workers: the historical transformation of labor in the United States*, Cambridge: Cambridge University Press.

Habakkuk, H. J. (1967), *American and British Technology in the Nineteenth Century: the search for labour-saving inventions*, Cambridge: Cambridge University Press.

Hopwood, A. G. (1974), *Accounting and Human Behaviour*, London: Haymarket.

Hutton, S. P., Lawrence, P. A. and Smith, J. H. (1977), *The Recruitment, Deployment and Status of the Mechanical Engineer in the German Federal Republic*, University of Southampton, Department of Mechanical Engineering.

Johnson, T. J. (1977a), 'What is to be known', *Economy and Society*, **6** (2) pp. 194–233.

Johnson, T. J. (1977b), 'The Professions in the Class Structure', Chapter 5, pp. 93–110 in Scase, R. (ed.) *Industrial Society: Class, Cleavage and Control*, London: Allen and Unwin.

Johnson, T. J. (1980), 'Work and Power', Chapter 11, pp. 335-71 in Esland, G. and Salaman, G. (eds), *The Politics of Work and Occupations*, Milton Keynes: Open University Press.

Knights, D., Willmott, H. C. and Collinson, D. (eds) (1985), *Job Redesign; Critical Perspectives on the Labour Process*, Aldershot: Gower.

Larson, M. S. (1977), *The Rise of Professionalism: a sociological analysis*, Berkeley, Calif.: University of California Press.

Lawrence, P. (1980) *Managers and Management in West Germany*, London : Croom Helm.

Layton, E. T. Jr (1969), 'Science, Business and the American Engineer', Chapter 2, pp. 51-72 in Perrucci, R. and Gerstl, J. E. (eds), *The Engineers and the Social System*, New York: John Wiley.

Layton, E. T. Jr (1971), *The Revolt of the Engineer: Social Responsibility and the American Engineering Profession*, Cleveland and London: Press of Case Western Reserve University.

Legge, K. (1978), *Power, innovation and problem-solving in personnel management*, Maidenhead: McGraw-Hill.

Lewis, P. (1981), 'An analysis of why legislation has failed to provide employment protection for unfairly dismissed employees', *British Journal of Industrial Relations*, **19**, 316-26.

Littler, C. R. (1982), *The Development of the Labour Process in Capitalist Societies*, London: Heinemann Educational.

Littler, C. R. and Salaman, G. (1982), 'Bravermania and Beyond: Recent Theories of the Labour Process', *Sociology*, 251-69.

McKenna, E. F. (1978), *The Management Style of the Chief Accountant*, Farnborough, Hants: Saxon House.

Mansfield, R., Poole, M., Blyton, P. and Frost, P. (1981), *The British Manager in Profile*. British Institute of Management Foundation Survey Report no. 51.

Marx, K. (1976) *Capital*, vol. I, Harmondsworth: Pelican.

Melrose-Woodman, J. (1978), *Profile of the British Manager*, British Institute of Management Foundation Survey Report no. 38.

Millar, J. (1979), *British Management versus German Management: a comparison of organisational effectiveness in West German and UK Factories*. Aldershot: Gower.

Niven, M. M. (1967), *Personnel Management 1913-63*, London: Institute of Personnel Management.

Pollard, S. (1965), *The Genesis of Modern Management: a study of the Industrial Revolution in Great Britain*, London: Edward Arnold.

Portwood, D. and Fielding, A. (1981), 'Privilege and the Professions', *Sociological Review*, **29** (4) 749-73.

Poulantzas, N. (1975), *Classes in Contemporary Capitalism*, London: Verso.

Rose, M. (1975), *Industrial Behaviour: Theoretical Developments Since Taylor*, London: Allen Lane, Penguin.

Roth, J. (1974), '*Professionalism: the Sociologist's Decoy*'. *Sociology of Work and Occupations*, **1**, 1.

Salaman, G. (1982), 'Managing the Frontier of Control', pp. 46-62 in Giddens, A. and Mackenzie, G. (eds), *Social Class and the Division of Labour*, Cambridge: Cambridge University Press.

Solomons, D. (with T. M. Berridge) (1974), *Prospectus for a profession: the report of the long range enquiry into the education and training for the Accountancy profession*, Advisory Board for Accounting Education.

Stacey, N. A. H. (1954), *English Accountancy: a study in social and economic history 1800-1954*, London: Gee and Co.

Steer, P. and Cable, J. (1978), 'International Organisation and Profit: an Empirical Investigation of Large UK Companies', *Journal of Industrial Economics*, **27**, 13–30.

Thomason, G. (1980), *Corporate Control and the Professional Association*, Chapter 4, pp. 26–37 in Poole, M. and Mansfield, R. (eds), *Managerial Roles in Industrial Relations*, Aldershot: Gower.

Thompson, G. (1978), 'Capitalist profit calculation and inflation accounting', *Economy and Society*, 7 (4), 395–429.

Timperley, S. R. and Osbaldeston, M. D. (1975), 'The Professionalisation Process: an aspiring occupational organisation', *Sociological Review*, **23**, 607–77.

Tricker, R. (1967), *The Accountant in Management*, London: Batsford.

Turner, H. A. , Roberts, G. and Roberts D. (1977), *Management characteristics and labour conflict*, Cambridge: Cambridge University Press.

Watson, T. J. (1979), *The Personnel Managers*, London: Routledge and Kegan Paul.

Willmott, H. C. (1984), 'Images and Ideals of Managerial Work: a Critical Examination of Conceptual and Empirical Accounts', *Journal of Management Studies*, **21** (3), 349–68.

Wright, E. O. (1979), *Class Structure and Income Determination*, London: Academic Press.

3 The Phoney War?
New Office Technology:
Organisation and Control

John Storey

The purpose of this paper is to assess the nature of developments in new computer-based office work and to examine the associated changes in the way work is organised. More specifically, I want to investigate the connections between these organisational and technological changes and the exercise of managerial control.

Much of the mushrooming literature on 'new technology' is highly speculative in tenor, wide-ranging in scope and prone to unwarranted bouts of optimism or pessimism (Barron and Curnow 1979; Large 1980; Evans 1982). The assumption underlying this present study is that the best approach to the problem of understanding the link between technology and social organisation can at this time be expected to derive from careful study of actual processes within specific structural contexts. A number of such studies have begun to appear (Wilkinson 1983; Buchanan and Boddy 1982; Zimbalist 1979). However, it is evident that further work is required in a number of respects. First, with regard to the large white collar sector of employment, what kind of new (micro-electronic) technology is in fact currently being introduced into the mainstream work areas – i.e. putting aside the esoterics of the fully automated electronic office? Second, in what ways have work routines and job structures been altered and with what implications for the control question? Third, how have office workers, and their unions, reacted to these changes? And fourth, what kind of theoretical scheme is appropriate in order to interpret the link between technology and control – i.e., how can the kind of variations in lost, retained or enhanced autonomy depicted in some of the above studies, be explained? The objective of this paper is therefore to begin, in an exploratory way, to consider how these questions might be approached and to present some preliminary findings.

The prime focus in this report is upon management's utilisation of, and response to, new information technology. The empirical material presented derives from case study work in three of the major composite British insurance companies. Thus, the investigations were conducted in very large and highly centralised multi-site organisations. The chosen area for study was the way 'user-managers' reacted to, and attempted to shape, the technological and organisational initiatives promoted by head office personnel. The managers studied were not direct users in the sense that they themselves accessed the computer keyboards, nor in the main did they rely heavily on data from this source. Rather, they were the process managers whose staff were now expected to transfer to the new technology with consequent shifts in tasks, controls and relationships.

The central problematic, therefore, was managerial action in making adjustments to the labour process of office work at a time when significant changes in technology were being initiated from top corporate levels (or at least with top-level support). Strategic choice on the labour process was a complex mix of influence deriving from central and branch management. In researching these processes various strands of literature offer themselves for preliminary examination – there are, for example, the kind of new technology surveys referenced above, and the conventional management of organisations literature which seeks to explain and account for managerial activity and decision-making. Early writings on management work were universalistic and explicitly prescriptive. Moreover, a great deal of the more sophisticated 'management science' writing since that time has, as Lowe (1984) points out, continued to operate with the 'primitive school's' basic assumptions of the positivistic and rationalistic models which divorce managerial practice from social context. The technicist emphasis is also retained in the popular work of Dale (1965) and Drucker (1977). And, as Willmott (1984a) argues, even the empirical studies of Mintzberg (1973) and Kotter (1982) only partially correct for the apolitical myth perpetrated in the functionalist literature. The interpersonal and inter-role conflict highlighted in these studies leaves a significant lacuna in connection with the structural forces bearing upon managers. Equally, the kind of contrasts and variety in managerial work noted, for example, by Stewart (1976, 1984) and Lawrence (1984) tend to narrow unduly the focus on what is to be understood by the term 'political'. These writers point exclusively to the micro-political conflicts endemic in organisational life – features of which senior managers are only too well aware. Hence, surveys of chief executives such as that described by Margerison (1980), easily uncover the only too well perceived importance of social-political 'skills'. Managers as social actors are themselves highly alert to these sorts of political realities. What conventional studies fail to illuminate are the less readily perceived structural realities which are the focus of the political-economy perspectives. Thus, in a study of 'managers' jobs perceptions' (Marshall and Stewart 1981), middle managers were asked about the amount of 'choice' they thought they could exercise. The majority perceived wide scope for them to bring their discretion to bear: 'Yes, it's all choice', and 'all gut feel', they reported. Perhaps most significant, however, was the statement, 'I'm free within logical boundaries' (1981: 271). It is precisely the nature and impact of these 'logical boundaries' which require further explication.

The general approach adopted here is an amended labour process theory. That is, the wider structural forces constraining strategic choice are recognised, but within these contours it is argued that greater weight should be given to seeking to understand the complexities of the social relations of production. The analytical frame derives from the interpretation of work organisation as developed by Marx, Braverman and the post-Braverman school. The critical amendments made by this last contribution (for example, as represented by the papers in Knights, Willmott and Collinson 1985) are, however, given serious weight. The neglect of worker resistance and the excessive emphasis on Taylorism as if it was the equivalent of managerial practice, were significant lapses in earlier accounts of the labour process. Further work remains to be done in locating the variety of control patterns in their contingent contexts and in exploring the actual social processes whereby control is effected and reproduced. The challenge is to develop a social science which can take account of structural and process elements in social practice (Giddens 1979; Willmott 1984b). Office workers are subject to particularly subtle, and now changing, modes of control; their responses are also complex. Case study analyses in such circumstances may therefore be particularly apposite in helping to illuminate certain persistent issues and puzzles. For example: the implications for control relationships arising out of intra-managerial conflicts, and the operation of the cluster of factors represented by the term the 'social structure of the workplace'.

This investigation is then, predicated upon the idea of a close link between technology and the control of the labour process. As Child (1985) has argued,

> New technology can play an important role in these changes to the organisation and control of the labour process. The rationales applied to investment in new technology are not necessarily focused primarily on the labour process, but the technology does carry with it a potential for change in that process. The introduction

of new technology in ways that change the labour process is therefore looked upon as the unfolding of a managerial strategy (Child 1985, p. 107).

This is of course not a stance in favour with the argument advanced by Rose and Jones (1985), but it does accord with the interpretations of strategy made by Mintzberg (1978) and Quinn (1980). The precise nature of the link between technology and control is however treated here as problematical. Informed by a reading of the early labour process literature (e.g. Braverman 1974; Edwards 1979; Zimbalist 1979), one might expect that in a broad sense the new technology would be developed and utilised in a way which fully exploited its control potential. This expectation would seem especially plausible given the current conditions of economic recession, loose labour markets and a political climate which is supportive of managerial assertiveness. It is intended here to present an empirical and theoretical report which might help to shed fresh light on this issue. More recent debate within the 'labour process literature' (this term must, perforce, be used somewhat loosely) has been more circumspect than the earlier literature cited above. Attempts have been made to gauge more precisely the extent and nature of classic Taylorist and Fordist 'solutions' to the management of the labour process problem (Littler 1985) and debate has also centred on the *explanation* for the discrepancy between classic deskilling assumptions and the measure of 'alternative' job re-design/participative work organisational forms which can be found (Kelly 1985; Ramsay 1985). These debates will be engaged when the case study material collected during the insurance research has been presented.

Before describing and analysing the observed patterns it is necessary at this point to develop the amended labour process perspective a little by paying regard to two interlocking dimensions of organised work: control and response. The nature of the capital-labour relationship is built upon the paramountcy of capital in the last instance. Labour, especially in a collective form, may create a measure of autonomy under this regime, but when this is exercised in a manner which impedes the accumulation process to an extent where it becomes more profitable to relocate, even discounting for sunk costs, then labour's resistance is likely to be curtailed. Moreover, well before such limits are reached, labour's autonomy is in any case squeezed. The struggles between competing potential usages of capital engenders a force, fluctuating in intensity, towards the more 'efficient' (i.e. profitable) utilisation of labour.

But within this capital-labour context there operate certain key variables which confound a simple thesis of an incipient tendency towards deskilling. It is important that these be given serious attention. For, as we shall see, the patterns of control and response in the office situations reported here reveal significant departures from what might be expected if relying on a simple model of the real subordination of labour. White collar workers historically comprised a relatively privileged stratum in the social structure (see, for example, Westergaard and Resler 1975, p. 76). They erstwhile enjoyed a superior position in market, status and work condition terms (Lockwood 1966). This was especially so for many insurance clerks (Barnard 1948; Supple 1970). Those who worked for the Royal Exchange Assurance, for example, in the nineteenth and early twentieth centuries 'were by no means average members of a homogeneous clerical labour force. They were near the top of a complex hierarchy ... sharing with staff of other long-established insurance offices, of the Bank of England and of the better Civil Service Departments, a standard of living, a level of responsibility, and a status, which strongly differentiated them from the mass of clerical employees' (Supple 1970, p. 377).

Since that time, however, significant changes have occurred, not the least of which have been the massive increase in the number of white collar workers both absolutely and relatively, the large influx of females, the routinisation of much of the work and now, the far-reaching developments in the technology with which they work. Just such a combination of changes has been reported in the United States as producing a 'factory-isation' and 'proletarianisation' of the insurance workforce (de Kadt 1979; Glenn and Feldberg 1979). And in Britain, also, the old-style patriarchal relations of control characteristic of the social office is being 'transformed' by the new technology, report Barker and Downing (1980). The growth of unionisation in the insurance workforce in the 1970s was explained by Crompton (1979) as in large measure a consequence of the changed class position of these workers. She writes: 'changes in the class situation of the insurance clerk are of crucial importance in the explanation of the apparently sudden increase in union membership' (1979, p. 429).

The current drive to effect large-scale technological change in the insurance industry might be expected therefore to accentuate these kinds of developments. This is especially so if one notes that the first stage of computerisation in the industry between 10 and 20 years ago was largely confined to centralised electronic data processing. Nowadays the new (miniaturised) technology is allowing technological change to penetrate to the very desk-top of the clerk. Yet, as will be reported in detail, the interesting point about control and resistance in this industry is the apparent extent of restraint. It might even be described as a 'phoney war'.

In seeking to explain the findings, recourse will be made to the amended labour process model. As I have argued elsewhere (Storey 1983), the nature of the managerial role must be fully taken into account when exploring labour control. Abstract capital 'interests' are interpreted and effectuated by managers in a far from straight-forward and unproblematical fashion. Management scientists and Bravermanites alike have tended to attribute an exaggerated degree of formal rationality to managerial action. In reality much of it is misguided, self-interested, half-hearted, short-term and inchoate. In addition, management, while easily labelled a 'hostile totality' (Hyman 1976, p. 92) is in fact fissured both vertically and horizontally. Middle and lower level managers have their own positions as employees to protect and this may well undermine their unambiguous devotion to the task of rationalising and cutting their organisations to the bone. And between managers, the various specialisms generate alternative and competing versions of organisational priorities. At one point in time the emphasis may be upon accountancy and cost savings, at another time on 'efficiency' and customer service; at yet another time the emphasis may shift to marketing.

The scope for variability, experiment and 'slack' will be likely to differ between industries. Job contracts painfully established in the motor industry, for example, may be quickly dissipated in the face of international competition. In relatively protected markets there is opportunity for a greater tolerance for less severe regimes and cultures. The insurance industry in Britain may be one such instance where a relatively benign culture has often obtained. In terms of hours of work, salary and holiday entitlement, the leading insurance companies from early days 'offered prospects for salaried employment which were difficult to match outside the fields of highly trained professional or managerial work' (Supple 1970, p. 383).

And within these companies today the organisational climate frequently reflects that of the 'social office'. Weddings and other like occasions are assiduously marked by collections, cards, presents and parties. Sports and social events are promoted. The managerial style is often relaxed – though one can find marked exceptions to this generalised depiction.

The control-reaction dimensions thus require further probing. It may be rightly echoed that, in general terms, labour represents for management an uncertain resource. The degree of uncertainty varies, however, between different circumstances. The active recalcitrance of the labour force cannot be assumed. The patterns of response to the variety of control devices are quite varied. The observation that 'How much work gets done every hour or every day emerges as a result of the struggle between workers and capitalists' (Edwards 1979, p. 16) must not be taken too literally. For various reasons, including social location and socialisation, workers may bring a large measure of co-operation to their tasks (cf. Burawoy 1979; Knights and Collinson, 1985).

One immediate purpose here then is to explore the relationship between these methods of control and the kinds of response actually evoked. The standardisation of work through bureaucratic and technological modes of control might be expected to erode the measure of willing participation. A time of rapid technological change in the labour process of office work should therefore afford an opportune moment at which to investigate the complex dynamic of control and response.

The organisations selected for investigation contained workforces finely divided both horizontally and vertically. The pattern of their work has been increasingly subject, over a fairly lengthy period now, to greater routinisation – much of this being allied to the changing technology of administration. Such developments would presumably be detectable in objective conditions and subjective responses. The new technology confirmed here as currently being injected into the work routines of these employees might be expected to be deployed in such a way as to reinforce these trends. The control possibilities associated with this technology are significant. The choices facing management in implementing and using such technology have, however, also been emphasised. The organisation and management of the labour process in a sector of employment in many respects the exemplar of modern capitalism, might be thought to reveal some lessons of wider application.

This project has, to date, been essentially based on case studies of three major British composite insurers: Hightech, Midtech and Lowtech. The study is focused at the main administrative processing level and, for most companies, this means the branch office. This term may be misleading: a 'branch' here denotes what is in reality a regional processing centre, each employing approximately 100 staff. It is at this level that the main tasks of processing proposals, endorsing existing policies and the handling of claims are accomplished (in the non-life categories of business).

British Insurance : Context and Practice
The insurance industry comprises a vital sector of the economy. It employs approximately a quarter of a million people, has a premium income of £20,000 million and enjoys a strategic location in the cycle

of capital accumulation. In recent years, profitability has been largely derived not directly from underwriting but from investment income. Under recessionary conditions the commercial insurance market in particular has proved resistant to increases in premium yet at the same time outgoings to meet claims are difficult to control. Greater attention has accordingly been directed to operating costs, the largest part of which are salaries. There has been considerable restructuring, branch and district offices have been closed, but technological change has permitted the throughput of the merged workloads.

There is significant concentration in the industry: a dozen or so large 'composite' companies transact the full range of insurance business – life and non-life. These companies, such as General Accident, Commercial Union and Legal and General, maintain office structures extending from headquarters to large branches in the main cities. Smoothing out the differences between the companies, just over half the staff are on average represented by trade unions. The ASTMS (Association of Scientific, Technical and Managerial Staffs) is the most significant body; it is the sole or chief negotiating partner in the Norwich Union, Legal and General, Royal, Pearl, General Accident and Zurich. Apex and BIFU also have a stake, however, in the industry. Thus BIFU is significantly represented in the Guardian Royal Exchange, Eagle Star and Phoenix. Bargaining is conducted mainly at company level.

The labour process in insurance had traditionally been clerical and 'professional'. In the case of the former, centrally devised procedures and standardised documentation ensured a uniformity in data handling. The utilisation by this industry of the early commercial mainframe computers and DP departments, fostered a further drive in this direction. The coteries of 'professional' staff at branch level comprised branch managers who in the main reached this status via the inspectorate-sales function, and a small number of so-called 'underwriters' whose function was to calculate premiums and accept or reject proposals on the larger and more complex categories of business. In each case, the examinations of the 'professional' body had to be tackled and invariably the staff selected for this status-category of work were male. Recent developments in the labour process associated with new micro-electronic technology have modified this traditional pattern. The composite insurance companies have been at the forefront of technological change in office systems. Essentially, however, this amounts to the installation of desk-top visual terminals (VTs). Noticeably the new technology of the automated office had hardly extended further: even the much vaunted word processor was absent from these offices. Teleconferencing and managerial on-line information systems are as yet not to be found. Yet the scale and significance of the wholesale introduction of VTs on to the desks of the hitherto pen-and-paper clerks should not be underestimated.

The three companies reported here had each devised a different pattern of processing the common tasks of handling the non-life, general insurance business studied in this report. The VT hardware was essentially similar but its utilisation varied in important ways. Hightech had a sophisticated 'intelligent', interactive on-line system. New policy proposals and amendments to existing policies were all entered directly by branch office staff. Documentation, including new policies were machine-printed at the branch and posted direct to the customer or, more usually, to the broker. This 'single-key-stroking' was not attained by Lowtech who used their VDUs only for calling-up and viewing customer files and policy details. Calculations and documentation were then accomplished in traditional fashion and forwarded, by post, to head office. Branch staff had then to await the return of this documentation before they could continue to action it. Midtech used its VTs for viewing existing policies but it could create new files for the purpose of processing new proposals. In all cases the insurance clerks continued to be responsible for dealing with telephone enquiries from brokers and customers. Apart from isolated exceptions therefore, these companies had avoided creating a new category of 'VDU operators' at branch level.

Changes and Consequences
In making comparisons between these cases, perhaps the first simple point to be noted is that in terms of physical presence the technology in all instances is, superficially at least, the same. That is, a casual visit to any one of these offices would entail a largely similar encounter with VDUs comprising screens and keyboards. Further exploration would reveal a printer and, in two instances, a local processing unit – i.e. a microcomputer mediating with a remote mainframe. The real differences therefore, concern the interrelated factors of the amount of time spent at the VDU, the proportion of clerical tasks executed on it and the organisation of work relating to it. Underlying these differences, of course, is the diversity of software. As we have already noted, some systems are interactive and allow the full repertoire of information input, storage computation/manipulation and retrieval. Others merely permit access to a data-base for viewing purposes.

The range of changes and consequences associated with the types of technological innovation may be usefully grouped under five headings: the division of labour; job characteristics; technological monitoring; organisation re-structuring; and productivity.

Figure 1   Branch organisation chart

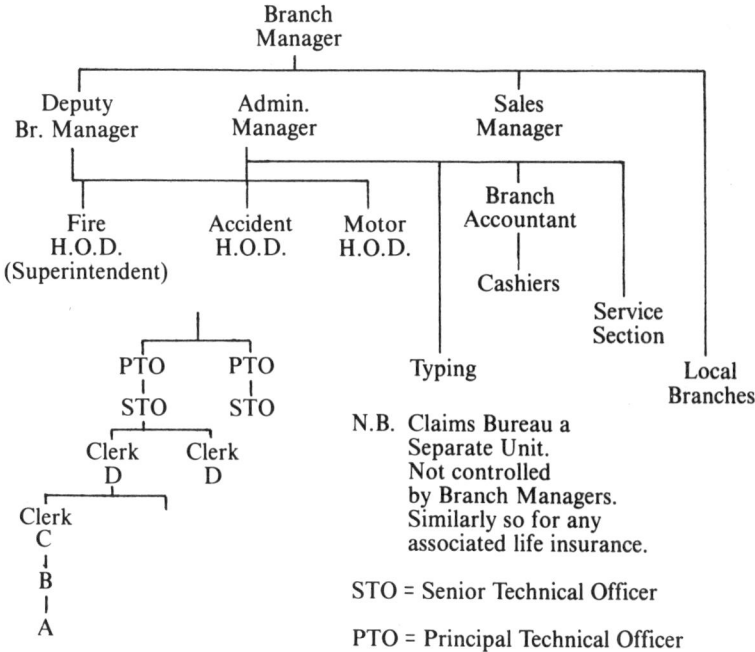

N.B. Claims Bureau a
Separate Unit.
Not controlled
by Branch Managers.
Similarly so for any
associated life insurance.

STO = Senior Technical Officer

PTO = Principal Technical Officer

Source: Insurance Company Branch Documents

(i) *Division of labour*
The division of labour is an organisational choice which appears to be associated with, but not determined by, the extant technology. Labour was segmented both vertically and horizontally. The organisation chart from one of the branches shows a vertical division into nine levels (see Figure 1). This was also typical of the other two companies.

The horizontal division of work is only hinted at by the chart. It shows three underwriting departments: Fire, Accident and Motor, but within each of these was a still more refined sub-division of task. Thus work was split in diverse ways – between private accident and commercial liability; between motor-cycle policies and automobile policies; between business deriving from various large brokers; alphabetically by customer name; by district office served, and so on. In addition, the work was divided in shades of complexity between the different grades of staff – thus clerks grade A and B would receive only the most routine work. This proved to be significant, for when asked in interviews what distinguished a 'good day' from a 'bad day' at work, the majority referred to the former having obtained when 'a really difficult case' had been tackled – and significantly again – when a customer with a particular problem had been 'helped'.

Yet it should be noted that the fragmentation of task had not been advanced anywhere near as much as would have been technologically possible. Thus in Hightech the new 'intelligent' distributed computer facility had been accompanied by only minor adaptations to the previously existing system. In the motor department the main division was between those clerks processing new business proposals and those amending existing policies. The batch work-allocation system meant that an assorted work programme was compiled after a sifting process beginning with the sorting of mail into departments (motor, accident, claims etc.). This was followed by a more detailed sorting by the head of department. The work then underwent a further sifting by a Grade D clerk (Figure 1) who diverted 'tricky cases' upwards to the Senior Technical Officer and Principal Technical Officer, and who compiled a varied 'mix' of tasks for allocation to the remaining clerks. These clerks then called up details of the relevant policy on a VDU, amended as per written instructions and awaited the eventual return of the batch with an interspersed copy of the print-out. The same clerk then posted and directed the print-out to the broker or customer and the amendment slip was disposed of. Meanwhile, at intervals during the day, the cycle was interrupted by telephone enquiries – usually from brokers or other intermediaries. To respond to these the clerk called up the relevant policy on the screen and tried to resolve the issue immediately. In consequence, there was a degree of variety in the work resulting from its mode of organisation. The company has intuitively resisted the temptation – so far at least – to 'rationalise' further.

Management's utilisation of the new office technology with regard to the division of labour was thus, up to this point in time, remarkable for its caution. This arose in part because central management had, as a top priority, the implementation and de-bugging of the system. Second, branch managers had, to a certain extent, ameliorated some of the initial organisational impacts by permitting their administrative managers to make organisational readjustments in order to ensure an acceptable transition. And third, none of the competitors had as yet devised second-phase models where the technological systems had actually been designed to do something more than replicate the tasks of the pre-mechanised system.

(ii) *Technology and changes to job characteristics*

As noted earlier, the kind of changes in office technology being examined here have been claimed by some writers to result in the factoryisation and proletarianisation of office work. Certainly clerical work does seem to have absorbed more 'mechanistic' principles (Vinnicombe 1980, p. 9) but in many respects the worst aspects have, in British insurance composites, been avoided again, at least for the time being. Using a job characteristics framework derived from an amalgam of Hackman and Oldham (1980, 1974) and from the Tavistock Institute (Emery 1963) it may be suggested that in terms of key dimensions – variety, task identity, optimum work cycle, autonomy, feedback of results, preparation and auxiliary tasks –– many of these clerical jobs have to this point not changed so very dramatically. In so far as the jobs studied were routine and degraded this was in large measure a consequence of a process begun much earlier. There was no instance, in any of the departments studied, of machine-pacing. The pre-programmed 'pages' once keyed would remain on the screen over long periods if the clerk so chose. The avoidance of the specialist VDU operator option has been noted. In consequence, at *branch* level the new technology agreements typically limiting continuous work on a VDU to two hours have been of little relevance. One reason for lack of a major change in job characteristics is that work was already geared to a coded and systematic form in order to meet the requirements laid down during the mainframe computer phase 15 to 20 years ago. Since that time, further standardisation has occurred with even more coded 'dataform' activity. A second factor may be that managements are playing a clever tactical game. Thus one important 'finding' has been what has *not* happened. There seems to be a policy to soften the impact of the new systems. Hence evidence was found of clerks who were clearly underemployed. Management may be waiting until all sections come on-line before seeking to push-up workloads and make redundancies. Where significant changes to working practices have been instituted they have been seen by the clerks as resulting in 'mixed blessings'. Thus the most evident change is the elimination of the need to get up from one's 'work station' to retrieve files. This has removed a chore which provoked a good deal of frustration. It has been a development almost universally approved of by the clerks. Yet at the same time there is now less reason or opportunity for mobility in the office; social relations could now easily be curtailed. Once again, however, the observation periods revealed a very tempered supervisory restriction on 'social visits' around the office.

While this account fairly reflects the situation facing the majority of staff covered by this study, there were certain exceptions – as, for example, the part-time female in Midtech Motor department who was effectively a VDU operator. All the routine entry work was stockpiled for her arrival and as my perusal of the records revealed, she completed prodigious amounts of work – nearly always exceeding the numbers of policies processed by the majority of full-time staff (who were, however, answering telephone enquiries and processing rather more complex cases).

(iii) *Technological monitoring*
In one of the companies (Hightech), the computer demands that a personal identity code be entered. Against this is automatically logged the number of transactions completed and the number of aborted transactions. Reports on these are sent monthly by head office to the branch manager. So far, little action has been taken on the strength of such information. Its main utilisation was to warn staff (collectively) of the unacceptably high proportion of aborted transactions – i.e. where the sequence of screen 'pages' had been commenced but for some reason abandoned before the task had been taken to completion. There were a number of reasons why such an incidence of 'wasted work' might arise. Frequently it was because a telephone enquiry had been received soon after the sequence had been commenced. In such a case the clerk would clear the screen in order to call-up the troublesome policy. Alternatively, it occurred because a clerk entering a new policy had realised part-way through that certain necessary information was unavailable – i.e. the paper proposal was incomplete. The rules stipulated that documentation was to be thoroughly checked prior to commencing the program in order to avoid this eventuality, but in practice clerks 'took chances' following no more than a rather cursory inspection. The existence of the technological monitoring and reporting was, it transpired, 'semi-public knowledge' as the manager had indeed estimated. About half the clerks were apparently unaware of it and seemed unconcerned or were resigned to the idea when it was put to them. Management's tactic seemed to be to have the availability of the facility known whilst being seen to do little with it.

Monitoring and control, however, also took other forms. There was, for instance, much reliance on traditional direct supervision. Each of the underwriting departments in each of the three companies was constructed on open-plan principles. The departmental head or superintendent presided in each instance over the whole room or over his (for it was he in all cases) territory in a multi-department large room. The desk was always situated so that a single glance would permit surveillance of every member of the department – a feat that would be impossible if private offices were to be used. And then each of the subsidiary grades: PTO, STO and D grade clerks, would, in turn, have responsibility for the general 'order' of his or her own section.

Quantity and quality controls were also mantained in a more systematic manner. Irrespective of whether the computer kept a count, the second-in-department also usually maintained a desk-drawer, 'informal' written record of weekly throughput by each clerk. This was built up from daily records of the various grade D 'allocation clerks'. Information gleaned from these sources will be presented later under the section concerning consequences and productivity.

Quality control checks were usually more formally constituted. The methods of conducting these were stipulated by auditors from head office. Typically the required approach was rather rigid, being built on 'scientific' statistical sampling principles.

Usually it was the PTO grade or the Superintendent who was responsible for the exercise. In Hightech the rules were followed rather assiduously given that it involved the PTO in checking one piece of work (i.e. comparing the written request from the broker with the completed amendment as shown on the subsequent print-out) from every batch of ten. If a mistake was detected then the rule required a further piece be selected from a stipulated location in the same pile of work, and so on. Clerks (quietly) complained in the interviews that this checking process 'held up' their work. It should be noted that this daily scrutiny was supplementary to the computer facility that identified certain kinds of error, and to the checks run by head office and by the brokers who received the work. Midtech had a rather similar quality control procedure – though not quite so intensive. In fact, in one department where the staff had an average tenure of eight years the monitoring had, unofficially, been all but abandoned.

(iv) *Organisational Restructuring*
This was a further control option. The companies had considerable leeway in controlling the size of the workforce. The mere *possibility* of 'new technology' could be utilised as a negotiating and disciplinary device. The wider organisational restructuring which was occurring immediately preceding and concomitant with the introduction of new technology has led to quite startling branch closures and mergers. The withdrawal from the local network expansion plan undertaken by Commercial Union is quite well known. The reduction in general business occasioned by the recession has left that company particularly exposed. Each of the companies reported here is in fact

closing district and branch offices and transferring its work to the remaining branches. The new technology has enabled these companies to cope with this kind of rapid restructuring. Lowtech had reduced its number of district offices (the local level which feeds business to the branches for processing) from 500 to 270 in just two years (1981–3). In addition, the number of branches had also been cut by half over a 15-year period.

Internal to the branches, where the main processing is accomplished, a further level of restructuring is taking place. In a trend largely common to most of the insurance composites, the new distributed computer processing is permitting the merger of the hitherto divergent departments (Barras and Swann 1983). The emergent pattern is for just two underwriting departments – personal lines and commercial. And within these, in turn, policies are becoming more comprehensive – i.e. there is a trend towards omnibus policies covering whole categories of risk. Such packages can save the company considerable expense in that, for instance, just one visit from an inspector is required to a commercial premises to permit cover for fire risk, employer liability, commercial vehicles and so on. Equally, policy records are simplified in that just one policy number attaches to each client. The consequence of this development will be a reduction in the number of departmental superintendents and a consequent diminishing of career opportunities. On the positive side, it could, if choice was so exercised, allow a greater variety of work for the clerks dealing with these more complex policies. Merging of departments in this manner is made possible only because the standardised rating of risks has radically reduced the need for expert and knowledgeable underwriters making individual judgements. Equally, the electronic processing of this standardised data makes the handling of one category of business very much like another. Third, the speed at which the transactions can take place means spare capacity is created. Finally, the need for a detailed division of labour in product terms and in supervisory terms is attenuated when task requirements appear as prompts on the screens.

(v) *Productivity*
This is a notoriously difficult phenomenon to define and assess. Here nothing more than a few indices of alteration to throughput will be attempted. Interestingly, the staff tended to follow management in emphasising the improved 'quality of presentation' as the key impact of the computer system. It is hard to imagine that the massive investment would have been undertaken simply to secure this objective, but the group ideology ensured that this was the initial

rationale to spring to mind when confronted with the simple question: 'What's the outcome?'

Measures of performance were gathered for individual clerks and for sections undertaking similar operations, before and after the branch computer systems were introduced. In Lowtech, specialist Head Office work-study charts were examined. These revealed, for example, that the processing of a new motor policy at branch level had an 'allowed time' of 0.46 of an hour in 1981.

The new timings conducted in 1983 after the branch computer system was introduced reduced the 'allowed time' to 0.32 of an hour. As noted earlier, this 'saving' at the point of production actually understates the overall turnaround time for a job, given that the waiting for postal communication from head office is now eliminated. In another respect, however, the saving is only notional for, the main if not the sole use of this data was to calculate staffing levels. In practice these levels were open to negotiation.

At Hightech, measures were made available (from the Superintendent's handwritten desk-drawer book) of the numbers of folders which were actually processed per clerk before and after branch computerisation. Using this source of data the level of 'productivity' begins to look more ambiguous. The consensus among allocation clerks was that the average throughput in the pre-computer days had been one folder of 10 workpieces per clerk per day. The Senior Technical officers reported an overall estimated increase from 1 batch per day to 2.5. But the actual throughput for 7 operators/clerks was as shown in Figure 2:

Some of the factors referred to earlier suggest reasons for this uneven flow. The main one usually raised by the clerks themselves, was the

Figure 2   Amount of actual paperwork processed before and after branch-on-line computerisation

| | | *Average completed folders per day* |
OPERATIVE	*1983*	*1981*
1	1.94	1.02
2	0.62	0.66
3	2.50	1.36
4	1.1	0.90
5	2.3	1.19
6	4.86	3.10
7	1.37	1.20

Source: Calculations from branch records

unpredictability of telephone work. But irrespective of that, it is worth noting that the best performers pre-branch computerisation, were outperforming the average *post*-computerisation operatives. Another point arising from the above data is the wide margin of variance in performance which is currently tolerated.

The Change Process and the Role of the Unions

Unions representing insurance workers have not been unmindful of the potential implications of these technological changes. Thus one union states: 'Those aspects of the new jobs which provide variety, stimulation, new knowledge, skills and responsibility must be emphasised to ensure that the majority of office workers do not become a deskilled substratum of machine minders.' (APEX, 1980 p. 49.)

But in practice in this aspect of job content and even more so in the objective of 'sharing the benefits' by, for example, reducing working hours, union *aspirations* have far exceeded actual achievement (see also Manwaring 1981 and Williams and Moseley 1982). A stark contrast can be made between trade union model agreements and everyday activity.

In the case of two of the companies, ASTMS had negotiated a new technology agreement, and in the third, BIFU was close to concluding a similar document. In this last instance, the agreement may just be signed as the major branch on-line computer system reaches completion! In the former cases, ASTMS had managed to secure a no compulsory redundancy clause. Returning again to the theme of transition, however, it must be noted that the clause is renegotiable annually. Whether this central plank of the new technology agreement will survive after the end of the change-over period, during which time co-operation is at a premium, may be open to some doubt.

The importance of the remaining parts of the new technology agreements must also appear contentious. In terms of content they fell a long way short of the aspirations contained in many draft 'model' agreements (see, for example, APEX 1980). The provisions for 'sharing the benefits' were noticeably absent or very thin. Hours had not been reduced nor salaries increased.

Much attention had, on the other hand, been given to specific issues and standards relating to health and safety. Eyesight and ergonomic questions relating to VDU operation were, in contrast, usually afforded close attention. Indeed, branch managers had in each case been eager to demonstrate their co-operation on such matters. In the interviews they were even prepared to accede to the idea that the preponderance of union activity on these aspects was in fact rather welcome and was symptomatic of union helplessness in other regards. Notable also was the fact that in each of the three companies the great majority of the staff interviewed (85 per cent) did not know whether or not their company was signatory to a new technology agreement.

The variety of work patterns and organisational forms revealed in these three companies, each of which is engaged in very similar tasks and characterised by similar features such as staff numbers and area of location, serves only to re-emphasise the degree of choice underlying technological development and utilisation. That particular choice in the insurance industry has, so far, been almost entirely exercised by management. Union influence on these sorts of questions appears to have been minimal.

Discussion

The main issue identified at the start of this paper concerned the control-response interplay. Technology, it was agreed, could be used as a control device either in itself or when allied to other, for example, bureaucratic, approaches. The first question which was posed related to the nature and extent of actual deployment of the observed new technology in the insurance sector. The paper has contained a report on this issue which reveals an uneven application but one which nonetheless indicates very significant levels of deployment having occurred or about to occur in the major composites.

The question of the impact on work organisation and control has been shown to be complex. The capital-labour relationship is complicated by variation in managerial strategies. This point bears directly on our central theme. The main finding concerns the failure fully to exploit the control potential of the technology. In large measure these companies have 'soft-pedalled'. This is so, in so far as the full control rigour made possible by the adopted technology had not been pursued. Hence, for example, the Babbage principle, which could have been manifested by creating a stratum of full-time 'VDU operators', was not followed. Similarly there is an evident measure to which a number of staff are underemployed as a consequence of the new system but some of these companies seem in no hurry to correct this.

There are a number of possible explanations for this relative lack of rigour on the control front. As noted, managers had their own vested interests to protect. Branch managers' remuneration and prestige are linked to the size and turnover of the branch; departmental managers may also be assumed to be reluctant to automate and then lose their sections through merger. An account of 'soft-pedalling' which was built on such factors would have some validity. In itself, however, it is unsatisfactory.

The composite insurance companies are in the main large centralised entities. The ability of particular branch managers to maintain serious resistance to a centrally-inspired systems reform must be open to doubt. This is especially so at a time when some branches face closure. Moreover, the method of introducing new technology in these companies tends to be carefully planned and, most important of all, is conscientiously *piloted* in selected branches.

An alternative account could refer to the distinctive cultural tradition generally prevailing in these leading companies. Many insurance workers themselves made reference to the 'benign' organisational climates. A number of ASTMS officials referred to one of these companies in particular, as a 'soft touch'. It is not being suggested here that these companies are representative. Indeed, work recently commenced in a fourth company indicates the existence of a very different managerial style in at least one of the major composites. The point rather is that at the moment there is such scope for variation in the organisation and control of the labour process. Nevertheless the paternalistic mode must itself be accounted for; in no small measure the lack of control rigour emerges from the fact that given present staff orientations, senior managers have few reasons for adopting a severe disciplinary style.

In addition, a third hypothesis could be advanced. The branch-based micro-electronics technology is, it must be remembered, not only new but still in a stage of implementation. During this interim period it would be foolish to jeopardise co-operation just at the time when it is a commodity at a premium. If this is the strategy then, so far, it has in the main been largely successful. Despite the foreshortened career ladders – also a concomitant of the new technology – staff had, in the offices studied, not only *not* resisted the technological change, but they had also maintained a degree of commitment to their work which went well beyond mere compliance. Thus, while I would concur with the points made by Knights and Collinson (1985) in their 'corrective' to Burawoy, it ought to be noted that just as English engineering workers can retain a highly conflictual orientation despite engagement in the 'making out game', so too can other 'deviant' cases be found where workers display a marked measure of co-operation – a phenomenon which equally requires explanation.

These findings clearly provoke certain questions for both conventional and labour process theorising on management and work control. The positivistic, rationalistic models quite evidently miss a great deal of the complexity of managerial activity. Equally, the inter-personal, political-social-skills perspective itself leaves significant gaps. It de-emphasises important structural constraints upon management practice. These are brought into particular focus by the labour process perspective. The distinctive labour process of the insurance office, fostered during a period when the cutting edge of capital accumulation was directed towards transforming work processes in factories, is now displaying tentative signs of alteration. But it is important to note that the signs are only tentative. The assumed, and indeed frequently alleged, transformation of the office under conditions of new technology are revealed by this research in insurance to be subject to some important qualifications. The extent and type of change in managerial control is taking place in a very cautious manner in most of the major composites. The attenuated utilisation of the control potential inherent in the kind of new technology being introduced may well be altered when the change process is more fully implemented. Nevertheless, it must be acknowledged that until this interim-period hypothesis is sub-stantiated, the findings reported here do leave open certain questions which could prove important for the further development of labour process theorising.

Those critics of Braverman who find his reference to Taylorism as the 'explicit verbalisation of the capitalist mode of production' unhelpful in the quest to interpret empirically-based studies (e.g. Kelly 1985, p.31), are to be supported in their attempt to construct a more theoretically adequate account. Kelly argues that 'changes in the organisation of work in the post-war period cannot be accounted for by examining only the capital-labour relationship in the labour process. It is the degree of *disarticulation* of the moments in the circuit of capital ... which provides the key to understanding why some firms sought to redesign jobs in ways that apparently conflicted with Taylorist principles' (1985, p.33). This echoes Littler and Salaman's point (1982) that developments in the labour process cannot be understood by restricting one's analysis to the level of the labour process – the point of production. It remains a valid observation. Ramsay's (1985) criticism of Kelly's positive-sum control assumptions and of his belief that job enrichment (and by extension other similar management initiatives) has no intrinsic quality favouring capital or labour, is in part based on his stark observation that empirical studies confirm that workers have gained little from job enrichment schemes. This, he says, should not occasion surprise: it accords with a general theoretical stance which notes that management design schemes in order to serve the needs of capital, and although 'management may not be omnipotent', they nevertheless 'do have extensive resources' (Ramsay 1985, p.74).

This discrepancy of position between Kelly and Ramsay seems to me to express a persistent and crucial issue in current labour process theorising and debate. It is an issue particularly pertinent to the theme of this present volume – i.e. the *management* of the labour process (though ironically both Kelly and Ramsay seem to locate themselves outside the 'labour process perspective'). There is insufficient space here to analyse their positions fully. However, operating rather more readily from within a labour process framework, one might question the theoretical adequacy of relying on a 'cycles' analysis of participation and of management-labour relations; and equally, while concurring with Kelly that certain initiatives (participation, job enrichment, productivity bargaining, new technology) might, in the abstract, have a measure of indeterminacy in their consequences, this observation on its own is insufficient. The stance I would urge, based upon a dialectical analysis (Storey 1983; 1985), and upon the kind of empirical findings reported here, would be one that allows due weight to management's ultimate structural location. This location typically permits a certain measure of experimentation but nevertheless continues to reward actions consonant with a general ideological presumption equating 'efficiency' with a *delimited* scope for worker 'disruption', 'unreliability' and 'discretion' over effort, method or output. Circumstances may arise when certain managers judge it appropriate to refrain from pressing the full logic of this ideology, but a persistent undercurrent reminds them that any such remissions must always be rescindable. Attempts to discern a shift in the balance of advantage when faced with a phenomenon such as new technology must therefore be necessarily tentative. The phase of engagement might well turn out to be just the 'phoney war' preceding a more decisive campaign.

References

Abercrombie, N. and Urry, J. (1983), *Capital, Labour and the Middle Classes*, London: Allen and Urwin.

APEX (1980), *Automation and the Office Worker*, Report of the Office Technology Working Party, Association of Professional, Executive, Clerical and Computer Staff, London.

Barker, J. and Downing, H. (1980), 'Word Processing', *Capital and Class*, no. 10, Spring.

Barnard, R. W. (1948), *A Century of Service: Prudential Assurance Company, 1848–1948*, London: Times Publishing.

Barras, R. and Swann, J. (1983). *The Adoption and Impact of Information Technology in the UK Insurance Industry*, London: The Technical Change Centre.

Barron, I. and Curnow, R. (1979), *The Future with Microelectronics*, London: Pinter.

Braverman, H. (1974), *Labor and Monopoly Capital: The Degradation of Work in the Twentieth Century*, New York: Monthly Review Press.

Bright, J. (1958), *Automation and Management*, Boston: Harvard.

Buchanan, D. and Boddy, D. (1982), *Organisations and the Computer Age*, Aldershot: Gower.

Burawoy, M. (1979), *Manufacturing Consent*, Chicago: University of Chicago Press.
Child, J. (1985), 'Managerial Strategies, New Technology, and the Labour Process' in Knights et al. (eds) (1985), op. cit.
Crompton, R. (1979), 'Trade unionism and the insurance clerk', *Sociology* 13 (3).
Crozier, M. (1971), *The World of the Office Worker*, Chicago: University of Chicago Press.
Dale E. (1965), *Management Theory and Practice*, New York: McGraw-Hill.
Drucker P. (1977), *Management*, London: Pan.
Edwards, R. C. (1979), *Contested Terrain : The Transformation of the Workplace in the Twentieth Century*, London: Heinemann.
Emery. F. E. (1963), 'Some hypotheses about the ways in which tasks may be more effectively put together to make jobs', London: Tavistock Institute of Human Relations.
Evans, C. (1982), *The Mighty Micro*, 2nd edition London: Gollancz.
Giddens, A. (1979), *Central Problems in Social Theory*, London: Macmillan.
Glenn, E. and Feldberg, R. L. (1979), 'Proletarianizing clerical work : Technology and organisational control in the office' in A. Zimbalist (ed.) op. cit.
Hackman, J. R. and Oldham, G. R. (1980), *Work Design*, New York: Addison-Wesley.
Hackman, J. R. and Oldham, G. R. (1974), *The Job Diagnostic Survey - an instrument for the diagnosis of jobs and the evaluation of job redesign projects.* JSAS Catalogue of Selected Documents in Psychology, 4 (148), Ms. N.810.
Hyman, R. (1976). 'Trade unions, control and resistance', in The Open University, *Politics of Work and Occupations*, course unit 14, Milton Keynes: The Open University Press.
Institute of Personnel Management, (1983), *How to Introduce New Technology : a Practical Guide for Managers*, London: IPM.
Jarrett, D. (1982), *The Electronic Office*, Aldershot: Gower.
Kadt, M. de, (1979), 'Insurance – a clerical work factory' in A. Zimbalist (ed.), *Case Studies on the Labor Process*, New York: Monthly Review Press.
Kelly, J. (1985), 'Management's Redesign of Work' in Knights et al. (eds), (1985) op. cit.
Knights, D., Willmott, H. and Collinson, D. (eds) (1985), *Job Redesign: Critical Perspectives on the Labour Process*, Aldershot: Gower.
Knights, D. and Collinson D. (1985), 'Redesigning work on the shopfloor: a question of control or consent?', in Knights et al. (1985) op. cit.
Kotter J. P. (1982), *The General Managers*, New York: McGraw-Hill.
Large, P. (1980), *The Micro Revolution*, London: Fontana.
Lawrence P. (1984), *Management in Action*, London: Routledge and Kegan Paul.
Littler, C. (1982), *The Development of the Labour Process in Capitalist Societies*, London: Heinemann.
Littler, C. (1985), 'Taylorism, Fordism and Job Design' in Knights et al. (eds), (1985), op. cit.
Littler C. and Salaman, G. (1982) 'Bravermania and Beyond: Recent Theories of the Labour Process', *Sociology*, 16 (2), 251–69.
Lockwood, D. (1966), *The Blackcoated Worker*, London: Allen and Unwin.
Manwaring, T. (1981), 'The trade union response to new technology', *Industrial Relations Journal*, 12, 4.
Margerison, C. (1980), 'How chief executives succeed', *Human Resource Development*, 4, 9.
Marshall, J. and Stewart R. (1981), 'Managers' job perceptions: opportunities for, and attitudes to choice', *Journal of Management Studies*, 18, 3.
Mintzberg, H. (1973), *The Nature of Managerial Work*, New York: Harper and Row.
Mintzberg, H. (1978), 'Pattern in Strategy Formation', *Management Science*, 24, 934–48.
Mumford, E. (1981), *Values, Technology and Work*, The Hague: Nijhoff.
Nichols, T. and Beynon, H. (1977), *Living with Capitalism: Class Relations and the*

Modern Factory, London: Routledge and Kegan Paul.

Otway, H. and Pelton, M. (eds) (1983), *New Office Technology: Human and Organisational Aspects*, London: Pinter.

Quinn, J. B. (1980), *Strategies for Change: Logical Incrementalism*, Homewood, Ill.: Irwin.

Ramsay, H. (1985), 'What is Participation For? A Critical Evaluation of Labour Process Analyses of Job Reform' in Knights et al. (eds), (1985) op. cit.

Rose, M. and Jones, B. (1985), 'Managerial Strategy and Trade Union Responses in Work Reorganisation Schemes at Establishment Level' in Knights et al. (eds), (1985) op. cit.

Stewart, R. (1976), *Contrasts in Management*, Maidenhead: McGraw-Hill.

Stewart, R. (1984), 'The nature of management? a problem for management education', *Journal of Management Studies*, **21**, 3.

Storey, J. (1983), *Managerial Prerogative and the Question of Control*, London: Routledge and Kegan Paul.

Storey, J. (1985), 'The Means of Management Control', *Sociology*, **19** (2), 193–211.

Supple, B. (1970), *The Royal Exchange Assurance: A History of British Insurance 1720–1970*, Cambridge: Cambridge University Press.

Vinnicombe, S. (1980), *Secretaries, Management and Organisations*, London: Heinemann.

Westergaard, J. and Resler, H. (1975), *Class in a Capitalist Society*, Harmondsworth: Penguin.

Whisler, T. (1970). *The Impact of Computers on Organisations*, New York: Praeger.

Wilkinson, B. (1983), *The Shopfloor Politics of New Technology*, London: Heinemann.

Williams H. and Moseley, R. (1982), 'The Trade Union Response to Information Technology: Technology Agreements' in M. Bjorn-Anderson, M. Earl, O. Holst, and E. Mumford, (eds), *Information Society: For Richer, For Poorer*, Amsterdam: North Holland.

Willmott H. (1984a), 'Images and ideals of managerial work', *Journal of Management Studies*, July ,**21**, 3.

Willmott H. (1984b), 'Making sense of managerial work -- a critique and a proposal', paper presented to the BSA Annual Conference, University of Bradford, 2–5 April.

Zimbalist, A. (ed.), (1979). *Case Studies in the Labour Process*, New York: Monthly Review Press.

4 Management Objectives in Technical Change*

David A. Buchanan

Points of Departure

Braverman's (1974) picture of the evolution of the labour process assumes that industry and commerce are run by a homogeneous managerial cadre which pursues consistently the imperatives of capital accumulation. Braverman further argues that because of the exploitative nature of the employment relationship, managers assume that they are dealing with a refractory workforce who do not willingly display loyalty, commitment and effort. The managerial response is thus characterised by a preoccupation with control which is operationalised in applications of scientific management and in technical process innovations which together progressively deskill labour and reduce dependence of work systems on human intervention and control.

This chapter argues that Braverman's assumptions are oversimplified generalisations in three respects. First, managers pursue a wide range of objectives; not all managers are closely wedded to the capitalist imperative in their decision-making. Second, developments in technology trigger a management decision-making process in which various managerial objectives are translated into work and organisation structures. Third, contemporary information and computing technologies potentially enhance operator control of the work process and increase management dependence on operator skill, knowledge and experience.

The impact of technical change on the labour process is influenced by prevailing patterns of management objectives. These objectives are shaped by the wider social and organisational structures within which managers function. The decisions which determine the organisation and control of the labour process are made and influenced by middle

*I would like to thank Howard Rose, David Knights and Hugh Willmott for their comments on earlier versions of this paper.

and junior managers who often work at a distance from the capitalist imperative. They pursue a range of objectives, related to personal careers as well to corporate policy. Their 'operative goals' (Perrow 1961) are not alway consistent with the pursuit of profit and capital accumulation.

It is therefore necessary to develop an understanding of the nature, formation, transformation and operationalisation of management aspirations, particularly at the organisational levels where decisions affecting the labour process are taken. Central to this understanding is the fact that managers are themselves controlled by other managers.

It is not the intention of this chapter to replace economic or technical determinist accounts of the nature of the labour process with some form of managerial determinism. The aim is to focus attention on the diverse and complex nature of the management decision-making process as it affects the organisation and control of work. This position is similar to that of Reed (1984) who is also critical of Braverman's simplified view of the relationship between capitalist imperatives and management aims and structures, and for whom management decision-making is a social process with political and moral dimensions which are not wholly subordinated to the single-minded pursuit of administrative and technical necessities.

This argument is based on research into the implications of new information and computing technologies for the organisation and experience of work, the role of management and organisational performance (Buchanan and Boddy 1983a). The main steps in the argument, detailed in the following sections, are as follows. First, technology has no effect on an organisation independent of the objectives behind its use. Second, the impact of technical change is mediated by management decisions about reorganisation to accommodate technical change. Third, the managerial preoccupation with control objectives is dysfunctional in performance terms. Fourth, managers who introduce technical change pursue an inconsistent mix of objectives. Finally, management decisions and objectives are influenced by the control and reward system within which they themselves function.

Technology is a Trigger Variable with Enabling Characteristics

Proposition: Technology has no independent effects on an organisation.

The implications of technical change depend on why and how new technology is applied – contingent on the objectives of managers in organisational positions from which they define why and how technologies are used. These new technologies bring with them no new 'technical necessities' (Friedman 1983). This proposition is supported by the findings of Warner et al. at Henley (see Sorge et al. 1982; 1983), Wilkinson (1982; 1983) at Aston, Evans (1982) in European companies, and by our Scottish studies (Buchanan 1982).

Braverman argues that process innovation leads to progressive elimination of human skill, cheapening of labour, and transfer of control over the labour process to management (e.g. 1974, p. 212). This argument follows from Braverman's assumptions about management objectives and the adversarial employment relationship. Thompson has more recently argued that 'the latest forms of new technology' extend the scope of deskilling and management control and enhance these long-term trends (1983, p. 215). But there is evidence which suggests that the objectives that managers pursue are not as consistent as Braverman assumes and that the implications of technical change are not as straightforward and homogeneous.

Technical innovations *trigger* a decision-making process in which management objectives are translated into organisation structures and systems. The capabilities of new technologies are not determining but *enabling characteristics*, which open up new opportunities for products, services, processes and forms of work organisation. These characteristics may also create new forms of constraint on managerial action. There is a research tradition which has consistently indicated that hierarchical control and deskilling of labour are not the inevitable consequences of technical advance (from, e.g. Rice 1958 to Davis and Taylor 1976).

The implications of a technical innovation thus depend on how managers perceive and decide to exploit its enabling characteristics. The varied devices in the loosely defined category of information and computing technology have the following enabling characteristics in common:

information capture	They gather, collect, monitor, detect and measure.
information storage	They convert numerical and textual information to binary, digital form and retain it in some form of memory from which the information can be retrieved.
information manipulation	They can rearrange and perform calculations on stored information.
information distribution	They can transmit and display information electronically, on screens and on paper.

Figure 1
Technical Change: The Management Decision-making Process

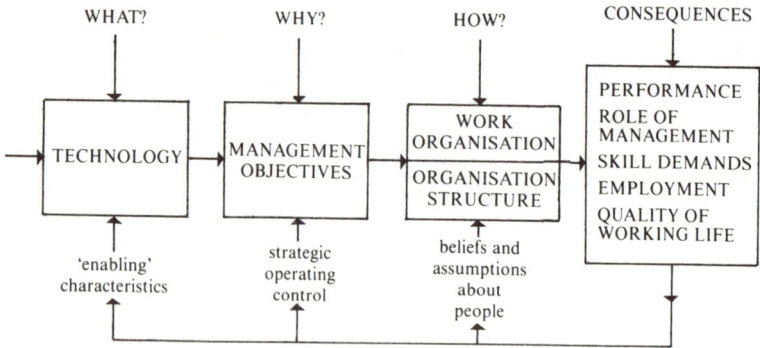

| WHAT? | WHY? | HOW? | CONSEQUENCES |

TECHNOLOGY → MANAGEMENT OBJECTIVES → WORK ORGANISATION / ORGANISATION STRUCTURE → PERFORMANCE / ROLE OF MANAGEMENT / SKILL DEMANDS / EMPLOYMENT / QUALITY OF WORKING LIFE

'enabling' characteristics — strategic operating control — beliefs and assumptions about people

Source: Buchanan, 1983

But as the purpose of the information handling capabilities of computing technologies is usually to effect control over physical work operations (such as typing, machining or draughting), *control technology* is perhaps a more appropriate label than information technology. Developments in technology are essentially developments in the way in which operations are controlled (Bright 1958; Braverman 1974; Bessant et al. 1980).

Management Choices Matter more than Machinery

Proposition: The effects of technical change are mediated by management decisions about the reorganisation of work, the design of control systems, and changes to organisation structure.

Technical change is usually accompanied by changes in work design, organisation structure and associated control systems. It has been asserted that managers have organisational choice (Trist et al. 1963; Buchanan 1979), strategic choice (Child 1972), or design space (Bessant 1983) in reorganising work to accommodate technical change. The resultant combination of technical and organisational changes determines the outcomes for performance, the role of management, and operator skill and knowledge requirements (see figure from Buchanan 1983).

Contrary to Braverman's argument, these new technologies can *complement* human skills. They can however dispense with the need for human intervention in work processes and create *distanced*, deskilled and demotivating roles. Information technology can also make individual performances more *visible* by disseminating performance information rapidly around an organisation (Boddy and Buchanan 1982). The following illustrations demonstrate how these possibilities are achieved through management's organisation choices.

Complementarity

Ciba-Geigy is a multi-national producer of specialist chemicals. The company has a site near Glasgow and this study concerned one plant where computer controls were being developed. The plant made a range of blue pigments on four continuous process lines (see Buchanan and Bessant 1985). The process was run by one control room and one plant operator. Information on the state of the process was presented in the control room on video and digital displays, trend recorders, equipment status lights and a printer. The computer control loops were mostly automatic, but when a process variable went beyond its set limit, an alarm sounded in the control room and process control passed to the operator. If the operator's actions were not effective, the computer shut down sections of the plant or the entire process depending on the nature of the fault.

The control room operator adjusted the process through a keyboard or by instructions to the other operator who patrolled the plant and could visually inspect the process. The computer sensors could become fouled and give inaccurate alarms. No alarm was given when items of equipment or sections of the process that were not directly monitored became faulty. The plant operators were not supervised and they rotated jobs daily. Management saw this as a successful experiment. The labour productivity of this plant was twice that of comparable conventional plants on the site.

The minimum training time for these operators was one year. They had responsibility and discretion and their actions had a significant impact on plant output. They retained a key controlling role and exercised a high degree of skill and knowledge to perform their role effectively.

The operators had to understand the process, the product, the equipment and the nature of the computer controls. They used their experience, judgement and intuition to over-ride the computer controls when they knew they were not functioning correctly. The number of interdependencies in the process was high, the speed of events was faster than in batch production, and the operators were thus under pressure to respond rapidly to problems. They had to be able to interpret the *pattern* of information from the computer and from the visible and audible condition of the process to trace the source and cause of deviations and to decide what action was necessary.

The computer could not effectively control the process without skilled human intervention. The organisation of work gave the operators experience that allowed them to develop knowledge of the process and to use that knowledge to control the process with the help of the computer system. This is an example of *complementarity* between operators and computing technology. Complementarity is a feature of the *relationship* between operator and equipment; the term is not used here to refer to a type of skill or a property of either the individual or the technology.

Frustrated complementarity

Y-ARD is a marine engineering consultancy whose product is technical reports for clients. Reports are usually long, complex, have more than one author and are revised several times. (See Buchanan and Boddy 1982.) When the word processing system was installed in 1981, the eleven video typists were grouped in two word processing centres, taking them away from the small groups of report authors with whom they had worked closely.

The technology of word processing did not dictate this organisational arrangement. Management wanted to be able to control more closely the flow of work to and from the typists. Each centre thus had a supervisor, and a co-ordinator was also appointed to oversee the groups' activities. The output of the typists in pages per day was six times higher with word processing than with conventional typing and the number of typists was reduced. The manager responsible for the centres felt that the application was successful on these criteria.

But the authors were dissatisfied with the system. They spent more time correcting proofs and the waiting time for typing had not been reduced. The typists did not know the authors whose work they typed and could not use their knowledge of individual styles and preferences. Rather than check problems with authors, typists would 'have a go' as correction was easier than finding the author in the 15-storey building. The typists could not show authors alternative layouts for documents. The authors were not aware of the capabilities and constraints of the equipment, made unrealistic demands on the typists and did not make full use of the system.

The reorganisation that accompanied the introduction of word processing gave management the control over typing they sought. But it created a comparatively ineffective typing service. The typists could have remained with their author groups. The typists could have been allocated to specific author groups while still in the pool as this would have retained contact between authors and typists and would still have enabled typists to cover for each other and share peak loads. The control that management achieved, however, was established through the reorganisation of work, and not through the 'control' capabilities of the word processing equipment. This is an example of *complementarity frustrated* by an inappropriate form of work organisation. Four years after the system was introduced, in 1985, the typists were still pooled in their supervised centres.

Distancing
United Biscuits started to computerise their biscuit dough mixing in the early 1970s (Buchanan and Boddy 1983b). The computer controls replaced the mixing of dough in open vats supervised by craftsmen bakers or 'doughmen'. The recipe for each biscuit type was stored on punched paper tape and recipe changes required the programming and punching of new tapes. When the tape was read into the computer, the controls fed quantities of flour and water to the mixing vessels. The doughman (management preferred 'mixer operator') started the mixer on a computer instruction and emptied the finished mix into a hopper 20 minutes later. Doughmen used to hold positions of status, supervised other manual workers and had considerable mobility in the factory. They now worked alone at one location. The mixing machine was enclosed. The mix was interrupted two or three times for the doughman to add small quantities of other ingredients or 'sundries' such as salt and other chemicals difficult to add automatically.

In 1980, a microprocessor based device called a 'recipe desk' was installed to replace the old computer system. Recipe adjustments could be made quickly and easily using small thumbwheels on the desk panel and programming skills were no longer required. When the mixing control computer was first installed, a computer room group was set up to program and operate it. The recipe desks were installed in the computer room.

The computer controls deskilled the doughman's job although the need for human intervention had not been overcome. Previously, he could see, hear and feel the dough as it mixed and could when necessary add ingredients to adjust the quality. This was no longer possible and the result was that the mixer operators had poor understanding of the process and equipment, could not visualise the consequences of their actions, could not trace sources or diagnose causes of equipment faults, and developed no knowledge or skills that could make them promotable.

This created several problems. Specialist maintenance was required, the mixer operators became bored, apathetic and careless and rejected responsibility for breakdowns, and management lost a source of supervisory recruitment. This *distanced* role may be characteristic of work in 'nearly automated' production systems where traditional skills are replaced and where the work experience does not give operators the skills and motivation to carry out residual but key functions effectively. Management had not considered the options of giving the recipe desks to the doughmen, allowing job rotation, or the formation of autonomous line teams.

Visibility

Biscuit packets have to be close to their stated weight to comply with consumer protection legislation and to reduce costs. In 1979, United Biscuits began to replace electromechanical with microprocessor controlled weighing machines. The old devices accepted packets that were at or above the required weight and rejected underweight packs. But they could not record packet weights. The electronic check-weigher recorded the weight of every packet and removed the need for a half-hourly manual check.

The weight of every packet was displayed on the wrapping machine and the operator could within limits adjust the number of biscuits put into each packet to compensate when necessary. The packet weight information was also displayed graphically on a video display unit for the ovensman and was updated every two minutes. The computer system was also programmed to produce regular production performance analyses for management.

The wrapping machine operator and ovensman now had more information than they had previously and this enabled them to control the process more effectively. The proportion of excess biscuit wrapped was halved. When packet weights went beyond the ability of the wrapping machine to compensate, the ovensman made appropriate adjustments to the oven controls.

This was a complex task as action to correct one feature of a biscuit, such as its thickness or 'bulk', affects other features, such as moisture content and colour. This is thus another example of complementarity.

But any errors by the wrapping machine operator or ovensman appeared within two minutes on the video display terminal which passing managers could see, and on analyses of performance over each shift. Their work had thus become more *visible* as more people could see more quickly the effects of their actions. This made it difficult to deny responsibility for errors. Complementarity in this case was thus accompanied by a tightening of management control over both the workflow and operators. The degree of visibility is dependent on managerial choices over the organisational distribution and use of computer-captured information.

Control versus Performance

Proposition: A preoccupation with control is dysfunctional in terms of operator skill, motivation and performance.

The enabling characteristics of information or 'control' technologies create opportunities to introduce tighter control and stricter discipline over workflow and workers, with adverse consequences for operator skill. But pressures to retain and enhance human skills and to increase worker control over the labour process, arise from four observations. First, these technologies are expensive and mistakes in their use can be correspondingly costly. Second, the interdependence or integration which computing technologies allow between previously discrete stages of workflow means that errors can escalate and spread faster. Third, if computing technologies reduce employment, those who remain in whatever 'residual' positions may have comparatively key roles. Fourth, effective operation of many computerised devices depends on skilled operator 'feel' or intuition based on experience with the equipment and its functions.

Several other commentators have reached the conclusion that skills replacement and reduced operator control are not generally useful approaches to the effective and safe operation of technically sophisticated equipment. Noble (1979) describes how the design of numerically controlled machine tools has been conditioned by the desire to reduce or eliminate operator discretion in the machining process. But he also demonstrates how quality machining requires 'close attention to the details of the operation and frequent manual intervention', and notes how this 'reintroduces the control problem for management' (p. 43). Noble points out that managerial intentions in introducing new technology are 'subverted' by shop floor realities (p. 45). The complexity and 'invisibility' of the functions of computer based devices, and the high costs of error, place a premium on skilled and motivated human intervention. As Noble pointedly explains, 'What will a machine operator, 'skilled' or 'unskilled', do when he sees a \$250,000 milling machine heading for a smash-up? He could rush to the machine and press the panic button, retracting the workpiece from the cutter or shutting the whole thing down, or he could remain seated and think to himself, "Oh look, no work tomorrow".' (Noble 1979, p. 44.)

Perrow (1983) describes several entertaining and frightening instances of the disastrous effects of failing to take into account the need for user comprehension in the design of high technology systems. His illustrations are drawn mainly from computer automation in aircraft, ships and nuclear power generation but have a wider applicability. The process control operators at Ciba-Geigy know for example that a particular sensor detects bubbles on the surface of viscous liquid entering a vessel before the liquid itself reaches the probe. When the alarm sounds, they override it because they know that the vessel is not about to explode. They use their knowledge of the plant to maintain continuous production in circumstances where the computer controls would automatically shut the plant down.

The preoccupation with control can override these considerations and lead managers to use the introduction of new technology as an opportunity to reorganise work in ways that improve management control at the expense of the autonomy, discretion, skill and performance of the direct user. In the Scottish studies, resistance to technical change was encountered in one instance only, from managers who felt that the new equipment would weaken their control over their areas of responsibility. Clegg and Dunkerley (1980) argue that this preoccupation creates a 'vicious circle of control'; the perception that tighter management control is required leads to deskilled and unmotivated workers who then behave in ways that reinforce the inital perception. Knights and Roberts (1983) also document examples of similar 'self defeating' management actions.

Attempts to exploit the management control possibilities of new technologies thus contradict the need for skilled operation for safe and effective performance. This need may be difficult to stifle. The users of computerised devices often develop an intuitive or tacit understanding of equipment and processes that managers and supervisors who do not operate the equipment cannot have. These trends affect the role of first-line supervisors who become dependent on operator understanding of equipment and processes. The capability of computing technologies automatically to capture, analyse and distribute performance information may erode the role of middle-line management.

Computing technologies provide their operators with additional resources which strengthen their position in what Giddens calls the 'dialectic of control'; complex technologies allow their operators to broaden their autonomy and create larger 'spaces of control' (Giddens 1982, p.197). The ability of management to extend control over the labour process and the ability of operators to resist management control are thus both potentially enhanced by modern technical innovation (see also Purcell et al. 1978).

Middle Management as a Subversive Activity

Proposition: Managers pursue an inconsistent mix of strategic, operating and control objectives.

Braverman argues that the accumulation of capital, 'dominates in the mind and activities of the capitalist, into whose hands the control over the labour process has passed' (1974, p. 53). The research evidence demonstrates that managers pursue a range of objectives that are more or less loosely connected to the capitalist imperative. Wilkinson (1983, p.19) argues that managers are not capitalist actors but, 'political beings with particular interests and having particular positions of power'. Our Scottish studies generally support Wilkinson's conclusion that, 'most of the important decisions about technology – from its choice to the establishment of detailed working practices – are taken deeply within organizations' (1983, p. 97). The middle and junior managers who take these decisions work at a distance from the capitalist imperative and are influenced also by political and moral considerations (Roberts 1984).

As Willmott (1984) however notes, Braverman's labour process perspective promotes the understanding that, despite local aberrations, the logic of management action is ultimately constrained by the rules of the capitalist game which declare simply that no surplus means no company which means no job for the manager. This thesis is insensitive in two respects. First, it does not consider the extent to which 'rule bending' by individual managers within the ultimate constraints can make a significant difference to the nature of the labour process and the experience of work. Second, it does not consider the extent to which rule bending both reflects and shapes longer term trends in the transformation of capitalist relations through technical changes of the kind examined here, and through wider social and political developments such as shared ownership, profit sharing and industrial democracy.

The reorganisation that accompanies technical change reflects the diverse objectives that managers decide to pursue. This proposition is supported by the findings of Francis et al. (1982) at Imperial College and McLoughlin (1983) at Southampton. The Scottish studies suggest that managers pursue three broad sets of objectives. *Strategic objectives* concern external, economic, market and customer oriented objectives. *Operating objectives* concern internal, technical, performance oriented criteria. *Control objectives* concern management desires to reduce human intervention in the control of equipment and processes, to replace people with machines, to capture and analyse more performance information faster, and to reduce uncertainty and increase predictability in production operations.

Strategic thinking was characteristic of senior management. Operating concerns were characteristic of middle and financial management. The main concern of middle and junior line management was control. This split in management perceptions of the objectives of technical change suggests that senior managers believe that technical change is strategy oriented, middle management justify technical investment on strategic and operating criteria, while middle and junior line managers apply new technologies in pursuit of control objectives.

Wilkinson (1983, p. 82) similarly notes that while productivity arguments are used to justify investment in new technology, performance analyses are rarely available to show whether the expected benefits were achieved. Explanations of organisational choice in terms of performance or efficiency are thus inadequate. Such considerations – the 'ideology of efficiency' – are used to 'preserve or create desired organizational arrangements' (Wilkinson 1983, p. 93). This supports Child's (1984) 'political contingency approach' which suggests that organisational arrangements are determined by individuals or groups within management who are in positions of power from which they can select the organisational alternatives that they prefer, such preference often being dependent on a range of criteria in addition to 'organisational effectiveness'.

The key decisions that affect organisational performance are those concerning the reorganisation of work that accompanies technical change. Some middle and junior line managers apparently translate their control objectives into organisation structures in ways that *subvert* strategic and operating goals. The additional performance information, and the increased visibility and distance of operators, result in frustrated complementarity, frustrated operators, and performance levels that are lower than expected. Some managers thus appear to be prepared to accept unnecessarily poor performance from applications of new technology which in other respects maintain their organisational status. Marglin (1976) similarly argues that the popularity of Taylorist techniques relies on their perceived effectiveness in ensuring a continued high status role for the entrepreneur or capitalist in the production process.

But 'management' is a heterogeneous group and not all managers can be described accurately as either entrepreneurs or capitalists. Many managers *can* see the folly of Taylorism, and the human, technical and financial advantages in having skilled and motivated people in control of work processes. Many managers *are* sensitive to accusations of arbitrary and exploitative control. John Storey (1983) argues that workers' feelings of exploitation *can* be consistent with the desire to produce competent work performance. Braverman's assumptions about the unitary capitalist nature of management objectives, the effects of technical innovation and the refractory nature of labour are not generally accurate. The critical questions thus concern the ways in which managers exercise organisational choice with respect to the introduction of technical change. We need a better understanding of the nature, formation and expression of management objectives.

The Limitations of Strategic Choice

Speculation: Organisational decisions that accompany technical change are influenced by managers' experience and interpretation of the control and reward systems within which they function.

Why are some managers prepared to subvert the strategic possibilities of new technology in the pursuit of control objectives? The forms of control to which individual managers are subjected condition the premises on which they make the organisational decisions that accompany technical change. Individual managers have vested interests or 'stakes' in applications and outcomes of technical change in their organisations. These stakes differ between management levels and functions and are not necessarily consistent with the overall performance goals of the organisation. Lamborghini (1982, p. 153) thus comments that, 'the process of change appears to be slowed down by management's reluctance to implement drastic changes which could have a negative effect on their own future'.

It is necessary at this point to make a distinction between (formal) organisational objectives and (personal) managerial aspirations. The latter concern the individual's projected personal career and its relationship to the organisational control and reward systems within which it may progress or founder. It may be that for many middle managers, personal aspirations have a more powerful influence over decisions concerning technical change than organisational objectives.

Control theory suggests that people simply seek to perform well on the criteria on which their performance is assessed. Controls focus attention on specific *targets* (Boddy and Buchanan 1984). Where the controls on middle and junior managers are related to narrow, short-term partial productivity and local capacity and output measures, reorganisation decisions tend to be influenced by short-term, control-oriented, parochial, technical and low-risk aspirations. Some managers are rewarded for achieving stability or incremental improvement on a narrow range of performance measures. They are encouraged not to 'rock the boat' and rely on traditional 'organisational recipes' when faced with novel circumstances created by technical change. They may in addition be encouraged to defend decisions and make them work, as notions of learning from experience imply prior admissions of failure which are unacceptable. The prevailing informal norms for managerial behaviour as well as formal reward systems thus condition management decisions and organisational choices.

The managers of an automated chemicals processing plant can choose to run it with closely supervised and unskilled operators who can easily be replaced and whose goodwill and co-operation are not essential to production. In the case examined here, plant managers were concerned with the continuity of output and that arrangement would have been less effective in achieving that goal. The managers of a biscuit-making factory can choose to make line operators responsible for computerised process controls, and to establish autonomous line teams. In the case examined here, management were preoccupied with automating the process to eliminate labour costs and human errors and created deskilled and monotonous jobs. With the application of word processing, management created a hierarchy to control the work of their video typists more closely. They rejected the choice of locating typists with their authors, which could have produced a more effective typing service but which would have increased management dependence on typists to advise on layout and determine priorities. These organisational choices were made by middle and junior managers whose sights were focused on the expectations of their colleagues and their immediate career prospects, not by senior managers concentrating on the long-term company strategy. It is thus the immediate controls on management behaviour which influence organisational choices more than ultimate capitalist imperatives, by specifying the local 'targets' to be achieved.

This analysis is reflected in the comments of several recent critics of British management who blame the British education system and culturally defined attitudes to work, industry and management for poor performance (e.g. Mant 1977; Brown 1977; Brittan 1978; Carter 1981). This is also similar in some respects to the psychological analysis of Dixon (1976) who blames managerial ineffectiveness on personality factors (which are allowed expression in particular organisational contexts). There is also evidence that compared with their Japanese colleagues, British managers concentrate on short term tactics and not on long-term strategy (Brown 1983).

Where the controls on and expectations of middle and junior managers are related to broad, long-term contributions to organisation strategic objectives, reorganisation decisions tend to be influenced by long-term, strategy-oriented, organisational, socio-technical, high performance aspirations. Some organisations encourage competition, change, innovation, high performance, experimentation and learning from experience. Managers who 'rock the boat' and try new solutions are not penalised when things go wrong. This latter approach emphasises high performance and implies recognition of the need for worker autonomy and control. This approach is broadly reflected in two recent statements of 'best capitalist practice' – *The Pursuit of Excellence* by Peters and Waterman (1982) and 'intra-preneurialism' from Norman Macrae (1982).

This analysis is in contrast to Braverman's account of the determination of the nature of the labour process. The research outlined here suggests that forms of work organisation which encourage worker contribution to corporate strategy, to capitalist imperatives, are more likely to be characterised by direct worker control of the labour process. Contemporary applications of computing and information technology appear to encourage this development.

These suggestions are speculative, based on the continuing research outlined above and on numerous casual conversations with (particularly younger and junior) managers who have identified constraints on their decision-making with respect to the technical and organisational changes that they wish to introduce. The reward structures at middle and lower levels of line management are often connected to capitalist goals in loose, fragmented and unco-ordinated ways which encourage the pursuit of individual and sectional interests at the expense of the achievement of the formal goals of the organisation with respect to capital accumulation.

Conflicts of interest between the needs of the company and the aspirations of its managers are less rare than Braverman and subsequent commentators on the labour process debate have been able to admit. There are instances, for example, of data processing sections in large organisations developing applications of computer systems which ensure the continued power, status and growth potential of the section, but which are notoriously inappropriate and ineffective in operation. But this is anecdotal evidence only and indicates a possible direction for further research.

A major implication of this argument for the labour process debate is that *organisational choice* (or strategic choice or design space) *does not exist* or that it exists only in the knowledge that to exercise such choice may subvert the individual manager's career. Formal and informal controls and norms condition management action and decision-making. The organisational control and reward systems that impinge on managers may in part reflect and be reinforced by cultural notions of the individual career and achievement, and psychological needs for security, order and avoidance of ambiguity. The point is that these control and reward systems do not simply reflect the financial imperatives of the capitalist enterprise. A current research task therefore is to identify how these reward systems are established and how they shape the nature of the labour process.

References

Bessant, J. (1983), 'Management and manufacturing innovation: the case of information technology' in G. Winch (ed.), *Information Technology in Manufacturing Processes: Case Studies in Technological Change*, London: Rossendale, 14–30.

Bessant, J., Braun, E. and Moseley, R. (1980), 'Microelectronics in manufacturing industry: the rate of diffusion', in T. Forester (ed.), *The Microelectronics Revolution*, Oxford: Blackwell, 198–218.

Boddy, D. and Buchanan, D. A. (1982), 'Information technology and the experience of work' in L. Bannon, U. Barry and O. Holst (eds), *Information Technology: Impact on the Way of Life*, Dublin: Tycooly International Publishing, 144–57.

Boddy, D. and Buchanan, D.A. (1984), 'Information technology and productivity: myths and realities', *Omega*, **12**, (3).

Braverman, H. (1974), *Labor and Monopoly Capital: The Degradation of Work in the Twentieth Century*, New York: Monthly Review Press.

Bright, J. (1958), *Automation and Management*, Boston, Mass.: Harvard Business School Division of Research.

Brittan, S. (1978), 'How British is the British Sickness?', *Journal of Law and Economics*, **21**, October, 245–68.

Brown, H. P. (1977), 'What is the British predicament?', *Three Banks Review*, **116**, December, 3–29.

Brown, M. (1983), 'The might of Japan is cut down to size in looking-glass war', *Sunday Times*, 16 October.

Buchanan, D. A. (1979), *The Development of Job Design Theories and Techniques*, Farnborough, Hants.: Saxon House.

Buchanan, D. A. (1982), 'Using the new technologies: management objectives and organizational choices', *European Management Journal*, **1** (2), 70–9.

Buchanan, D. A. (1983), 'Technological imperatives and strategic choice', in G. Winch (ed.), *Information Technology in Manufacturing Processes: Case Studies in Technological Change*, London: Rossendale, 72–80.

Buchanan, D. A. and Bessant, J. (1985), 'Failure, uncertainty and control: the role of operators in a computer integrated production system', *Journal of Management Studies*, **22** (4), October.

Buchanan, D. A. and Boddy, D. (1982), 'Advanced technology and the quality of working life: the effects of word processing on video typists', *Journal of*

Occupational Psychology, **55** (1), 1–11.

Buchanan, D. A. and Boddy, D. (1983a), *Organizations in the Computer Age*: *Technological Imperatives and Strategic Choice*, Aldershot: Gower.

Buchanan, D. A. and Boddy, D. (1983b), 'Advanced technology and the quality of working life: the effects of computerized controls on biscuit-making operators', *Journal of Occupational Psychology*, **56** (2), 109–19.

Carter, C. (1981), 'Reasons for not innovating', in C. Carter (ed.), *Industrial Policy and Innovation*, London: Heinemann, 21–31.

Child, J. (1972), 'Organization structure, environment and performance: the role of strategic choice', *Sociology*, **6**, (1), 1–22.

Child, J. (1984), *Organizations: A Guide to Problems and Practice*, London: Harper and Row.

Clegg, S. and Dunkerley, D. (1980), *Organization, Class and Control*, London: Routledge and Kegan Paul.

Davis, L. E. and Taylor, J. C. (1976), 'Technology, organization and job structure' in R. Dubin (ed.), *Handbook of Work, Organization and Society*, Chicago: Rand McNally, 379–419.

Dickson, N. F. (1976), *On the Psychology of Military Incompetence*, London: Futura.

Evans, J. (1982), 'The worker and the workplace' in G. Friedrichs and A. Schaff (eds), *Microelectronics and Society, For Better or For Worse: A Report to the Club of Rome*, Oxford: Pergamon, 157–87.

Francis, A., Snell, M., Willman, P. and Winch, G. (1982), 'The impact of information technology at work: the case of CAD/CAM and MIS in engineering plants' in L. Bannon, U. Barry and O. Holst (eds), *Information Technology: Impact on the Way of Life*, Dublin: Tycooly International Publishing, 182–94.

Friedman, A. L. (1983), 'Managerial, organizational and industrial relations implications of advances in data processing and information technology: survey of research', London: Economic and Social Research Council.

Giddens, A. (1982), *Profiles and Critiques in Social Theory*, London: Macmillan.

Knights, D. and Roberts, J. (1983), 'Understanding the theory and practice of management control', *Employee Relations*, **5** (4) (whole issue).

Lamborghini, B. (1982), 'The impact on the enterprise' in G. Friedrichs and A. Schaff (eds), *Microelectronics and Society, For Better or For Worse: A Report to the Club of Rome*, Oxford: Pergamon, 119–56.

McLoughlin, I. (1983), 'Problems of management control and the introduction of new technology: the case of TOPS', University of Southampton New Technology Research Group Working Paper.

Macrae, N. (1982), 'Intrapreneurial now', *The Economist*, 17 April, 47–52.

Mant, A. (1977), *The Rise and Fall of the British Manager*, London: Macmillan.

Marglin, S. (1976), 'What do bosses do?: the origins and functions of hierarchy in capitalist production' in A. Gorz (ed.), *The Division of Labour: The Labour Process and Class Struggle in Modern Capitalism*, Brighton: Harvester, 13–54.

Noble, D. F. (1979), 'Social choice in machine design: the case of automatically controlled machine tools' in A. Zimbalist (ed.), *Case Studies on the Labour Process*, New York: Monthly Review Press, 18–50.

Perrow, C. (1961), 'The analysis of goals in complex organizations', *American Sociological Review*, **26**, 854–66.

Perrow, C. (1983), 'The organizational context of human factors engineering', *Administrative Science Quarterly*, **28** (4), 521–41.

Peters, T. J. and Waterman, R. H. (1982), *In Search of Excellence: Lessons From America's Best Run Companies*, New York: Harper and Row.

Purcell, J., Dalgleish, L., Harrison, J., Lonsdale, I., McConaghy, I. and Robertson, A. (1978), 'Power from technology: computer staff and industrial relations', *Personnel Review*, **7** (1), 31–9.

Reed, M. I. (1984), 'Management as social practice', *Journal of Management Studies*, **21** (3), 273–85.

Rice, A. K. (1958), *Productivity and Social Organization*, London: Tavistock.

Roberts, J. (1984), 'The moral character of management practice', *Journal of Management Studies*, **21** (3), 287–302.

Sorge, A., Hartmann, G., Warner, M. and Nicholas, I., (1982), 'Computer numerical control applications in manufacturing' in L. Bannon, U. Barry and O. Holst (eds), *Information Technology: Impact on the Way of Life*, Dublin: Tycooly International Publishing, 99–113.

Sorge, A., Hartmann, G., Warner, M. and Nicholas, I. (1983), *Microelectronics and Manpower in Manufacturing*, Aldershot: Gower.

Storey, J. (1983), 'After Japan/after Braverman: a consideration of management control, management science and social science', Nottingham: Trent Business School Occasional Paper Series no.3.

Thompson, P. (1983), *The Nature of Work: An Introduction to Debates on the Labour Process*, London: Macmillan.

Trist, E. L., Higgin, G. W., Murray, H. and Pollock, A. B. (1963), *Organizational Choice: Capabilities of Groups at the Coal Face Under Changing Technologies*, London : Tavistock.

Wilkinson, B. (1982), 'New technology and human tasks: the future of work in manufacturing industry' in L. Bannon, U. Barry and O. Holst (eds), *Information technology: Impact on the Way of Life*, Dublin: Tycooly International Publishing, 158–65.

Wilkinson, B. (1983), *The Shopfloor Politics of New Technology*, London: Heinemann Educational.

Willmott, H. C. (1984), 'Images and ideals of managerial work: a critical examination of conceptual and empirical accounts', *Journal of Management Studies*, **21** (3), 349–68.

5 The Labour Process in the State Welfare Sector

Christine Cousins

The labour process debate has paid scant attention to the growth and importance of the state as employer in the post-war period. Consequently, there has from this perspective, been little written on the management of state agencies and changes which have occurred in the organization and control of state work.

The theme of this paper[1] is to point to structural properties of state modes of organisations which may differentiate them from capitalist organisations and condition worker and management strategies. The paper is concerned with the state welfare sector and examines changes in the organisation and control of work in one specific state service in Britain, the NHS. This analysis is located within a framework which considers that although labour processes in state and private sectors are similar, each is governed by a different criterion of rationality. In this regard, the analytic distinctions drawn by Offe, in conjuction with Habermas and O'Connor, between the different modes of rationality governing state and private sectors, are discussed and applied to the empirical example of the NHS.

An analysis of state labour processes should include consideration of the relation of state production of goods and services to both the capital accumulation process and the democratic processes. It is in relation to both accumulation and legitimation that the state's activities have become the source of new contradictions and political divisions in the 1970s and 1980s. Such an analysis should also, as Fryer (1983) has argued, take into account the rapid growth of state employment, trade unionism and the rationalisations and reorganisations of work which have incorporated Taylorist and other principles of labour control.

A further feature of state employment is that it involves a wide range of work activity, skills, autonomy and pay levels. Whilst it is a major employer of middle management, professional and semi-professional workers, the state sector also has one of the largest concentrations of women, migrant and part-time workers in low paid and low status work. These latter groups and some semi-professionals have proved vulnerable to the extension of managerial controls, although, the lack of set work routines, variability of work and the fragmentation of the workforce limits the scope for rationalisation and control. On the other hand, some welfare professionals retain considerable degrees of technical autonomy, the ability to define and determine clients' needs and treatments, and a role in policy determination. The work process of these professional providers cannot therefore necessarily be seen as analogous to that of industrial workers, nor even subject to the deskilling and loss of control of technique which Braverman and others have described as central to the proletarianisation of wage-workers.

Empirical evidence on the management of this heterogeneous labour force is to be found in the more conventional academic disciplines, such as organisational analysis, and public administration. A number of such studies, however, have been concerned with prescribing the most 'rational' or 'efficient' mode of organising and managing state agencies, and have themselves been influential in the design of 'appropriate' management structures and the hierarchic forms which were imposed on state welfare organisations in the 1970s.[2] Other writers, though, have rejected this 'managerial' model and influenced by perspectives developed in organisation sociology, have focused instead on a model of the organisation as a plurality of competing groups and coalitions. Organisational structure and policies are then perceived as the outcome of a political process from which a dominant coalition emerges and succeeds in imposing its preferences and values on the organisation (Child 1972, Hunter 1980, Alaszewski and Haywood 1980, Ham 1981).

A view of the organisation as a political, negotiated process has been of especial value in drawing attention to the different ideologies and sources of power actors bring to their work situation and to the policy-making process, and the ways in which different groups can influence or resist managerial choices. Such studies have also shown that formal management arrangements often have a limited influence on work processes. Burns, in a perceptive study of NHS hospitals, found that much of the work was accomplished by a collaborative system[3] which was not 'subject to, or the consequence of, sets of instructions and specific routines laid down by management' (1981, p. 4). Other studies have found that the 'power of managers in the NHS to effect change is very limited' (Haywood and Alaszewski 1980, p. 149), since the medical profession is able to define the purpose of the health services and control the actual delivery and general development of services (cf. also Hunter, 1979 and Ham, 1981). However, although these approaches are empirically valuable and are sensitive to the complexities of management in organisations which contain groups with quite different rationales, there is a tendency to neutralise the environment of the state's activities and to ignore the structural constraints implicit in the state's role in a capitalist economy.

In the labour process literature, on the other hand, the link which Braverman has drawn between the imperatives of capitalist accumulation and managerial control structures has recently been regarded as too 'automatic, unmediated and unproblematic' (Salaman 1982). Wood and Kelly (1982), and Salaman (1982) argue, for example, that management is not, as Braverman implies, homogeneous, omniscient and conspiratorial, but that the internal differentiation of management generates sectional groups with their own interests, identities and objectives. Drawing on pluralist studies, these authors suggest that processes of internal bargaining and conflict between these groups will mediate between system requirements and the labour process as Braverman describes it (Armstrong; Chapter 1; Storey, Chapter 2; Buchanan, Chapter 3). Other writers have developed more historically and empirically informed accounts of management practices by documenting the ways in which different structures and types of managerial control have varied by plant, industry, over-time and cross-nationally (Littler 1982, Gospel and Littler 1983, Friedman 1977). But almost all of these studies concern themselves with the private manufacturing sector of the economy and few have considered the different economic and organisational context of state managers.

There are exceptions though – for example one treatment of 'non capitalist state activities' is to be found in those discussions of the class location and work situations of state service workers as unproductive workers (Carchedi 1977, Crompton and Gubbay 1977, and Crompton and Jones 1984). In these schemes, state employees are regarded as being as oppressed as employees in privately owned enterprises, (even though the latter produce surplus value and the former do not), since the work of both is controlled and supervised by management.

Both state and private sector workers are subsumed under the authority of employers by virtue of the fact that they sell their labour power and surrender the creative capacity of their labour. Crompton and Jones note that although it may be theoretically incorrect to describe state service managers as capitalists, 'they are nevertheless constrained to act as "capitalists" in respect of the organization and control of their labour force' (1984, p. 214). Although this analysis seemingly makes the concept of surplus value redundant, it is correct in pointing to similarities in the labour processes of state and private sector workers. In the post-war period, forms of capitalist rationality have been introduced into state organisations and state managers are required to act, as do those in the private sector, according to principles of cost efficiency and productivity in order to contain costs. But, as it is argued later in this paper, state managers are not just constrained to 'act as capitalists' but are also subject to a non-market rationality which does have consequences for state managers and workers.

A further view of state management is to be found in the now considerable literature, from a Marxist or neo-Marxist perspective, on the role of the state under conditions of advanced capitalism. These discussions are mainly theoretical in treatment and in social welfare provision have focused on the structural constraints that shape state intervention. Writers such as O'Connor (1973), Gough (1979) and the CSE State Group (1979) have analysed the contradictions generated by the development of the state's welfare activities. In this respect Gough has argued that whilst the Keynesian welfare state helped sustain the economic and social relations of capitalism, it generated contradictory tendencies, namely, 'the exacerbation of class conflict over the distribution of the national product, and the undermining of the production of the surplus product' (1983, p. 472). In turn, these contradictions have given rise to the restructuring[4] of the welfare state which is explained by Gough as the 'state acting in the long-term interests of capital' (1979, p. 141). Gough recognises, however, that re-structuring is restricted by the prior and existing organisations of the welfare state and by the interest of the professionals, trade unions and clients' movements thus affected.

The CSE Group also attempt to show that 'management structures within the state apparatus have been developed in order to maintain long-term ideological domination and effective day to day control, so that the long-term interests of capital in general are furthered' (1979, p. 122). They note, however, that 'the state has no magic way of knowing what is in the interests of capital'. 'For there is a certain arbitrariness in the rules and norms that guide the management of state agencies. Unlike the private sector they are not subject to the law of value' (pp. 21–2).

The view that state managers simply act in accord with the interests of a 'far-sighted capitalist class or as the automatic functional response of the political system to the needs of capitalism' has been challenged by Theda Skocpol (1980, p. 200). In her study of the US

New Deal she agrees that neo-Marxist analyses are more promising than others for explaining political conflict and transformation within advanced capitalism, but she considers that 'state organizations have their own structures, their own histories and their own patterns of conflict and impact upon class relations and economic development' (1980, p. 200). In other words, state management is embedded in a political apparatus with its own mode of rationality.

The different organisational logics or modes of rationality governing state and private sectors have been recognised by writers such as O'Connor (1973), Habermas (1976) and Offe (1976). In privately owned enterprises, management acts in ways which serve and legitimise the form of property for which they work, i.e. they are governed by the logic of maximising profits. Habermas notes, for example, that in the private sector there are clear and finite parameters which surround capital and labour relations, the social consequences of which are bankruptcy and unemployment. In the state welfare sector this logic does not apply. The provision of services is governed by non-market criteria and parameters, for example, public policy-making and budgetary decisions. Policy formation, however, takes place in the context of a diffusion of objectives between political concerns, interest group demands, professional and other provider groups as well as budgetary constraints. Consequently there are no clear criteria that can be applied in the assessment of efficiency or effectiveness, as the state's activities 'cannot be calculated in monetary terms, since they are not sold on a market' (Offe 1975a, p. 139). Rather, the thresholds or parameters of the state's activities are those of legitimation, 'irrational or inefficient decisions by state administrators may result in social disorganization or deprivation but these consequences are not strictly quantifiable ... it depends on the population as to what are regarded as tolerable disruptions to social life' (Frankel 1979).

Because of discrepancies in rationality between state and private sector organisations, Habermas and Offe contend that the state cannot act as a 'class-conscious political organ' which is able self-consciously and effectively to plan for the reproduction of capital. Rather, because the state has to operate according to its own administrative logic, and cannot directly control private investment or production, it has a deficient planning capacity, characterised by a vacillation of policies, a 'muddling through' and a 'reactive avoidance of crisis'.

By differentiating between labour processes in private and state sector organisations Habermas, Offe and O'Connor are able to distinguish different relations of production in each social formation.

The theoretical difficulties which surround discussion of state workers in labour process theory (although not in Braverman's work) namely, that state workers are unproductive workers who do not produce surplus value, are overcome in the writings of these theorists. For as Frankel (1979) remarks, critical theorists move beyond the debate about productive or unproductive labour to consider state labour as not only reproducing capitalist social relations but also as negating them.

Habermas and Offe claim that advanced capitalism cannot be understood solely in terms of exchange relations of capital and wage labour, but that productive state activity itself brings into being new and additional forms of social relations of production. Yet, although the commodity form depends upon the extension of these productive state activities, the latter nevertheless tend to undermine the dominance of the capital relation and thus, the conditions on which their survival depends. Not only do productive state activities exacerbate the fiscal crisis of governments, but the state itself can become the possible focus of political and social conflict over the way in which societal resources should be utilised.

It would seem then that critical theorists have important insights to offer on the 'contradictory role which present states have to sustain' (Frankel 1979) which includes their role as employer. In addition, Offe has been one of the few writers to provide a theory of the capitalist state which also considers its internal mode of operation. The following discussion is therefore an attempt to relate the theoretical propositions of the critical theorists to the empirical example of the organisation and control of work in the NHS in Britain.

The paper is divided into three sections. The first section examines the links which Offe has drawn between a theory of the capitalist state; public policy making and the state's internal mode of organisation. Developing the view that the state has a limited capacity for rational administration, Offe argues that the state's key problem is how to 'devise' modes of internal organisation which will be 'adequate' both to meet pressures from the requirement to sustain the accumulation process and those of certain non-capitalist interests represented through the political process. Moreover, Offe spells out the mechanisms by which the administrative activities of the state do not necessarily always guarantee that the interests of capital will be secured, as the state is also dependent on the compliance of organised professional and labour élites. The implications of these propositions are considered first, for the structuring of work and divisions of labour amongst the professional provider groups in the NHS (Section

I (ii)), and second, for the rationalisation of labour in the NHS, which were part of attempts to devise 'appropriate' or 'adequate' forms of work organisation in the state welfare sector, in the 1960s and 1970s (Section I (iii)).

The second section of the paper considers the sector model developed by O'Connor, Habermas and Offe, which differentiates the economy into private and state production sectors. Using this sectoral model it is possible to distinguish the different modes of rationality governing each sector, the 'different rates of productivity, levels of worker bargaining power and levels of overtly political determination of wage levels' (Dunleavy 1980a, p. 382). One interpretation of the growth and militancy of state service sector workers in the 1970s is, therefore, as an aspect of their structural location within a sector which is governed by non-market criteria. This analytic framework is then applied to both the emergence and the consequences of militant trade unionism amongst health workers in the 1970s.

The third section of the papers examines Offe's analysis of the structurally contradictory position of the state's welfare activities, government's attempts to resolve these contradictions and lastly (and the most criticised aspect of his thesis) the limits to state policy making. These arguments are then related to the current restructuring of work in the NHS.

Section 1

(i) Internal organisation of the state and policy formation
Offe distinguishes different modes of state intervention as allocative and productive state activities. In allocative activities the state possesses the authority to allocate resources acquired from taxation, for example, social security payments or protective tariffs to industry. Under conditions of advanced capitalism, however, allocative policies have to be augmented by productive activities which individual capitals are incapable of creating, finding them too risky or costly. Productive activities such as the health, education and social services, and research and development require some physical input in the nature of raw materials, capital investment and labour (1975a).

For Offe, explanations of social policy must take into account both 'demands' from the 'political processing of class conflict' and 'system requirements' of the accumulation process. The key problem for social policy formation, however, is the extent to which modes of internal organisation of the state apparatus can be devised which make compatible these two poles of the 'needs' of capital and labour (1984).

Offe (1975a) suggests that the state's allocative and productive activities are capable of being organised in accordance with three modes of operation.

First, the bureaucratic mode which arises when state resources are allocated in a routine way, applying pre-determined rules through hierarchical structures.

Second, the purposive-rational mode, planning inspired by technical rationality, such as cost-benefit analysis, performance indicators and control by objectives.

Third, the democratic mode of political conflict and consensus.

Offe argues that none of these three logics of policy production provide an adequate structural basis for the state to reconcile its contradictory pressures of accumulation and legitimation. Bureaucratic modes, although suited to allocative state activities, are too routinised, rigid and ineffective for the state's productive activities. This is intended as a critique of the Weberian thesis; namely 'the superior efficiency of bureaucratic structures', which in Offe's view is only of limited relevance to the organisation of many state activities.

In the second mode, however, the criteria of rationality governing state organisations creates a number of obstacles to the application of purposive rationality. Such techniques are similar to those in industrial commodity production, but whereas private industry has clear criteria of effectiveness and efficiency, the state does not possess 'unequivocal, uncontroversial or operational cues as to what the goals of its productive activities should be'. In addition, the resources required for long-term planning attempts interferes with the prerogatives of the accumulation process, or conversely, the well-known problem of state welfare programmes being blocked by limitations on state spending.

Lastly, the democratic process of political conflict/consensus, as a mode of organisation, can lead to unlimited demands by working-class and non-capitalist interests which become subversive to the balance between the state and the accumulation process. At the level of local government this is a useful argument for, as Saunders has shown, the state is here relatively responsive to popular demands (1983). It is for the reasons suggested by Offe that the dynamic of state production has 'shifted through increasing concentration and scale, to the regional and central levels of the system' (Cawson and Saunders 1983).

The inadequacy of these three modes of operation imply that it is difficult for the state to devise forms of internal organisation which make compatible political demands and the requirements of capital accumulation. Hence the vacillation of governments between a number of strategies in the management of state services, reorganisations, efficiency drives, privatisation and centralisation.

The 'structural selectivity' of the state, however, means that there is no guarantee that these internal modes of organisation will either secure or serve the interests of capital or the interests and needs of unorganised and marginal groups. In a variant of corporatist theory, Offe suggests elsewhere (1972) that those groups representing institutionalised interests, fractions of capital, organised labour and professional élites, who are able to make the most effective contribution to the avoidance of risks, are granted 'structurally determined privileges'. The state selectively intervenes, so that these groups are able to define the scope of 'realistic' issues and demands, which are then filtered through political and administrative processes. As a consequence, general social interests which are not institutionally organised, and peripheral groups and depressed areas which do not generate dangers to the system, are excluded from access to political decision-making. Moreover, a new technocratic concept of politics becomes relevant where public policy-making is not directed to the solution of 'correct and just vital reforms', but to the 'conservation of social relations which claim mere functionality as their justification' (Burris, Chapter 6). Offe points here to the repressive character of the state, in which the articulation of a wide range of democratic interests and needs are excluded and depoliticised.

(ii) The division of labour in the NHS

As Cawson (1982) has noted, Offe's analysis of allocative and productive state activities and their organisational forms is of value in explaining the differences in political process in various social policy areas. For example, whilst allocative policy is most effectively administered through a bureaucratic organisation, 'the production of welfare services involves the collaboration of professional providers in the determination of goals' (Cawson 1982). The production of welfare services is 'adequate', not because it conforms to pre-determined rules and procedures, as in allocative activities, but because it leads to certain results or policy goals.

But as we have seen, there is no simple relationship between goals, organisational activity and final outcomes or quality of welfare services. Moreover, clients themselves do not, as do customer preferences in the private market, create demands, for these are largely defined and controlled by the professional providers. Lacking clear criteria of their own state administrators have, therefore, depended on the professional providers' judgement as to what are adequate resources and types of treatment. Not only has this meant that the professional provider groups have had an expansionary impact on state welfare budgets, but also that the interest of the more powerful professions have been privileged (Armstrong, Chapter 1). This mutual compliance and dependence between the state and the professional provider groups has been important in the structuring of work and divisions of labour, as well as in the determination of social policies.

Occupations pursuing professionalising strategies have sought the co-operation and legal backing of the state in their attempts to gain a monopoly of control over areas of knowledge, recruitment and training. Historically, the medical practitioners achieved a monopoly position during a period when state machinery for regulating and controlling medical care was weak (Parrys 1977). By the end of the nineteenth century, nursing reforms were incorporated and subordinated in a technical, social and sexual division of medical labour dominated by doctors. Ideological claims of responsibility for the patient and authority in the diagnostic relationship have further ensured that emergent allied health occupations have developed under the control and direction of medical practitioners.

Medical hegemony was ratified by the privileged position the profession retained after the negotiations which created the NHS. Here the BMA was able to achieve favourable terms and conditions of employment, a crucial role in policy determination, the right to define and take medical decisions and an acknowledgement that 'health auxiliaries must remain under the supervision and tutelage of the general medical profession' (Bevan, quoted in Armstrong 1976). More recently though, medical hegemony has been challenged by the re-organisation of administrative structures designed to shift power away from doctors. Additionally, there have been increased pressures on the medical profession from the para-medics (reflecting changes in health policy and technology) and the new unionism.

Vulnerable to both medical and managerial controls, nurses have also pursued strategies of professional control and closure. By seeking state sponsorship in their professional aspirations, however, nursing élites have contributed to the self-stratification of work processes and labour markets. In their attempts to resist the intrusion of untrained labour, nursing élites created a hierarchical 'grade system' of trained and untrained nurses, with corresponding opportunities for promotion.[5]

Yet, nurses, as a profession, have never been able to gain control of recruitment, which the state, in its use of the power to license practice, has retained, 'keeping open a plentiful supply of cheap labour' (Bellaby and Oribabor 1980). Nursing élites were also instrumental in the co-option of nursing structures into management in the 1960s, further weakening the links between nursing grades, and dividing nurses into those orientated to management and those committed to clinical nursing.

(iii) Rationalisations of labour in the NHS

The movement to economic planning and measures to increase labour productivity in the 1960s brought major reorganisations and rationalisations of labour in the state service sector. It was argued that capital investment and reorganisation would bring economies of scale, which, with effective management techniques, would increase the efficiency and productivity of labour.

This technocratic rationality was manifested in the design of 'appropriate' organisational structures, a faith in 'experts' to provide technical solutions and a reliance on techniques such as scientific management, cost-benefit analysis and programme budgeting (Klein 1983, Draper and Smart 1974).

In the NHS the new rationalism was to be found in the capital investment programme of the 1962 Hospital Plan which concentrated advanced technology, skilled manpower and new management techniques in the large District General Hospitals. Crucial to later developments, were attempts to increase labour productivity by directing scientific management techniques to the largest occupational groups, nurses and ancillary workers. Eventually, scientific management principles were extended to the 1974 reorganisation of the NHS, which, through the co-option of doctors and (for the first time) nurses into 'consensus management' teams, were designed to promote greater managerial controls and accountability of front-line staff, as well as providing an organisational setting for planning decisions.

The application of a 'foreign' rationality to nursing structures and the management of ancillary workers created the preconditions for increased trade union membership and organisation. For nurses, the implementation of the Salmon Report imposed hierarchic, bureaucratic controls on nursing structures. Nursing work was further divided by the hiving-off of management roles above ward level and the removal of unskilled work to auxiliaries or ancillary workers, leaving ward level staff with a loss of control over previous work practices. Imposed on the pre-existing 'grade system', this bureaucratisation of work reinforced the sense of disillusionment experienced by many rank and file workers[6] towards the lack of promotion opportunities, pay and conditions of work and exclusion from 'élitist' professional associations (Carpenter 1977).

A direct impetus to trade unionism, however, came from the

introduction by the National Board for Prices and Incomes in 1967, of work-study and incentive schemes aimed at productivity increases amongst ancillary workers (Manson 1977). The NBPI recommendations that the low pay of the ancillary workers could be increased by self-financing productivity schemes have led to increased management controls, and the re-deployment of fewer staff on re-structured jobs. But the productivity schemes, which were later often instigated by unions rather than an indifferent management, brought groups of workers together for the first time, and encouraged the emergence of shop stewards and local collective bargaining. The necessary conditions of increased trade union organisation and consciousness at a local level were therefore established prior to the 1973 national dispute, which, in turn, also increased union membership, conciousness and activity (Manson 1977, Dimmock 1977).

The application of technical rationality in the NHS since the 1960s has not been uniformly successful. As a means of containing costs, preventing industrial unrest, or of promoting rational planning, managerialism has been ineffective. Policies have been subverted, resisted or have had unintended consequences, as, for instance, the increased costs of bureaucratisation or growing trade union activity and organisation (discussed in greater detail in the next section).

One consequence, however, has been the development of health care in technocratic, hospital-based 'cure' modes of treatment, of benefit to the prestigious medical specialities at the expense of other areas of health care such as prevention or the chronically ill. The use of performance indicators, 'throughputs' of patients, and other 'efficiency' criteria is more easily applied and measured in the high technology sector of medicine, which in turn, has attracted more resources (Manson 1979). Since the mid 1970s government planning priorities have been to promote the redistribution of resources, more equitably between the client groups and types of medicine. But a shift to the more 'caring' functions of health, as, for example, the elderly or mentally ill groups, would be to affect the balance of power between the diagnostic and curative medical profession and the caring semi-professions. The privileged position of the doctors as the direct providers of health care and as the primary decision-makers has, however, ensured that this shift in health care has been marginal (Hunter 1980, Haywood and Alaszewski 1980).

Section 2

(i) A sector model
Habermas, Offe and O'Connor have developed a sectoral model

which enables them to comprehend the different relations of production according to the forms of organisational logic governing state and private sectors. These sectors are (i) a private monopoly sector, (ii) a private competitive sector, (iii) a state service sector (iv) Dunleavy (1981a) and Thompson and Beaumont (1978) further divide the state sector to include a public corporation sector, (v) Habermas and Offe add a 'residual labour power sector' consisting of the state dependent population.[7]

By differentiating the economy into state and private production processes these writers have analysed the contradictions generated within and between the sectors. For example, Habermas, Offe and O'Connor have suggested that in the private monopoly sector wage levels are determined by quasi-political bargaining structures between strongly organised trade unions and the corporations. The monopoly sector's structural position as a price-maker, and the small share of its total costs accounted for by labour costs, enables it to grant union wage demands by passing on price increases, or by generating higher levels of productivity. As a consequence these writers claim that conflict within the private monopoly sector has been partially immunised and displaced into other sectors of society. Particularly important here have been conflicts over the determination of wage levels of state workers, which in seeking comparability with private sector workers have contributed to the growth of state sector unions.

The state sector's labour-intensive nature, the ambiguities of calculating productivity increases and the relatively low gains of productivity that are possible mean that, for any given level of inflation, the costs of the state sector will rise relative to the private sector. The mechanisms of the relative price effect are exaggerated by increased wage levels as a result of militant actions of state workers. In turn, rising relative costs of the state sector is one of the factors affecting the fiscal strains of governments. Gough has usefully summarised the other factors affecting the growth of public expenditure as; population changes, new and improved services and the growth of new social needs as a result of the 'diswelfares' of economic progress (1979). The result is the tendency for state expenditure to increase more rapidly than the means of financing it. For O'Connor the source of this fiscal crisis is the discrepancy between the growing socialisation of capital and social overhead costs by the state, and the continuing, private appropriation of profits (1973).

(ii) The emergence of militant trade unionism in the NHS
In Britain, control of wage costs in the labour intensive NHS was

effectuated partly by means of rationalisations of labour, but also by the centralised Whitley system of collective bargaining. Prior to the 1970s, the Whitley system depoliticised the employment relation enabling governments to keep tight controls on pay levels and insulating local management from workplace bargaining. The workforce was largely acquiescent, weakly unionised and orientated towards professionalism or a 'public service' ethic (Dimmock 1977, Sethi and Dimmock 1982, Bosanquet 1979).

However, state intervention in the 1960s and 1970s, to regulate incomes and industrial relations in order to promote capital accumulation, had a significant impact on work relations and trade unionism in the state service sector. By the late 1960s the cumulative effect of government income policies, inflation and high wages amongst some key groups of private sector workers led to a sense of grievance and perceived discrimination by state service workers. As Dunleavy shows, 'In the public services, a fundamental shift in industrial attitudes and behaviour took place during the labour government's Prices and Incomes Board and Conservatives' (n-1) incomes policy. In the five years 1969–1974 more than seven times as many public service workers went on strike as in the whole of the previous twenty years'. (1980b). In the NHS the implementation of an income policy in 1972–4 was the direct cause of the first national pay disputes amongst ancillary workers and nurses.

Industrial relations legislation in the 1970s also influenced the growth and character of trade unionism in the NHS. Although the legislation was initially corporatist in intention, designed to strengthen trade union organisation in the private sector and so subvert the militancy of its rank and file, the effect in the NHS was to expand and strengthen shop floor organisation and local collective bargaining. The legislation encouraged and formalised the appointment of shop stewards, workplace bargaining and established explicit procedures at local level with respect to discipline, dismissal and grievances. The effect was 'more militant tactics, more collective discipline amongst workers, more skilled negotiations at local levels and more awareness of trade union consciousness. The second effect was that of encouraging membership and collective action' (Berridge 1977). Professional associations had no choice but to adapt trade union methods of recruitment, organisation and activity (Dyson and Spary 1979).

The growth of union memberships in the NHS during the 1960s and 1970s was especially rapid.[8] The factors affecting this increase have already been outlined; the restructuring of nursing and administrative work 'creating a mass of workers whose career mobility was blocked'

(Carpenter 1982), the impetus to ancillary workers' unionisation by the introduction of scientific management techniques, government income policies and comparability with private sector workers, and industrial relations legislation which encouraged shop floor organisation. Women accounted for the majority of this increase in trade unionism,[9] reflecting their growing employment in low paid and low status work during this period.

The ancillary workers' strike in 1973 is considered to be a watershed in industrial relations in the NHS. Its major effect was to change attitudes between management and workers at hospital level. Thereafter the nature of the employment relation changed, the vocational, public service ethic and 'obligation of loyalty' on the employees' side became a more instrumental orientation with an emphasis on the case nexus (Berridge 1977). The ancillary workers' strike, although concerned with pay, also raised issues of control, which were later to spill over into conflicts over private practice and pay-beds, challenging not only state policies, but also the power of the doctors (Manson 1977). At the same time the employment relation of other occupational groups became more politicised as their subsequent militancy involved governments more directly. For state workers, issues of pay, working conditions and the object of their work, can become politicised in a way that they do not for private sector workers (Frankel 1979, Fairbrother, Johnston 1982). Nevertheless, for many state sector workers, despite rapid growth of union membership and politicisation of activity, it is unlikely, as argued in the next section, that they have succeeded in pushing back the 'frontiers of control' in the 1980s.

Attempts to contain costs in a labour intensive service industry, either through rationalisations of work, income policies or the regulatory processes of Whitleyism, have instead contributed to the rising relative costs of the state service sector by increased costs of bureaucratisation and wage raises gained as a result of militant action (Gough 1979, O'Connor 1973). The greater strength of state service sector trade unionism has enabled workers to resist more effectively, especially at a local level, subsequent government policies. But these activities have also heightened a climate of opinion in which state workers and the state dependent population are seen as unproductive burdens on wealth creation. Dunleavy (1980b) has noted that in addition to the increased incidence of taxation there are a number of ideological elements in the conflicts of interests between the different sectors, including the scapegoating of 'welfare scroungers' and state sector workers, especially those are seen to take industrial action against the 'national interest' as in the 'winter of discontent' in 1979.

Section 3

(i) The limits of state policy making

For Offe the significance of the expansion of productive state activity is that it brings into being new and additional (decommodified) forms of social relations of production. Yet, although the commodity form depends upon the extension of these productive state activities, the latter nevertheless, tend to undermine the dominance of the capital relation and thus, the conditions on which their survival depends. State productive activities not only exacerbate the financial problems of government, but open up the state to possibilities of political and social conflicts over state resources themselves.

One of the ways in which this potential conflict can be defused is through the application of technical rationality, in which political issues or practical problems are transformed into technical problems and solutions. In this way state management is given more scope in its attempts to increase the efficiency of its internal organisations. Offe avers, however, that because of the mode of rationality which governs state organisations, the state is unable to achieve efficiency according to its own criteria (because there is no way to determine whether efficiency or effectiveness has been advanced, and increases in efficiency are usually at the expense of effectiveness) (1975b). In Offe's view, state policies are efficient or effective only to the extent that they succeed in putting individuals in a position to find employment of their labour power, or profitably invest their capital. To this end we find governments pursuing strategies of 'administrative recommodification', (regulations and financial incentives, public infrastructure and neo-corporatist institutions). But these measures still tend to be costly for state budgets and still 'take place under social arrangements which are themselves external to commodity relationships'. Further strategies therefore include the re-privatisation of public goods and services, motivated not only by the need to relieve the burden of taxation, but also to remove state productive activities from the political arena.

Writing in 1975, Offe claimed that policies of recommodification, privatisation and retrenchment of public expenditure can only serve to undermine the basis of mass loyalty and de-politicisation on which the state depends. In particular the increased visibility of the dual reference of the state's productive activities, to the commodity form on the one hand and to use values on the other hand, can create problems of legitimation. Legitimation problems occur when expectations that a government will 'contribute to common and individual welfare and other desirable ends' fail. Offe contends that when the discrepancy between the promise and actual experience of welfare services, 'cause attitudes of frustration over false promises', then there is a possibility of the undermining of acceptance of the state's legitimacy (1975b).

Offe's concept of legitimation should, however, be treated with circumspection.[10] Whilst it may yet be the case that governments ultimately have to guarantee legitimation as well as conditions of profitability, recent government policies which have not produced desirable or material outcomes have not been accompanied by a withdrawal of mass loyalty from political authority. Nor has the 'pauperism' of depressed areas and groups led, as Habermas and Offe suggest in their earlier articles, to potential zones of conflict. Instead, it has been left to state workers to protest against government policies, but their resistance can be contrasted with a widespread public tolerance, or at least ambivalence, with regard to the impoverishment of state welfare services.

(ii) Some recent government policies and the NHS

Recent restructuring of the NHS, as other welfare services, has included increased centralised controls, the statutory requirement that health regions keep within their 'cash limits' and increased performance monitoring of the regions through, for instance, performance indicators and 'efficiency savings' included in budgets. Restrictions on budgets had affected the quality of health care before the manpower cuts and actual reduction in budgets in 1983. These cuts have quickened the pace of closures of wards, hospitals and rationalisations of labour, although there are wide discrepancies between authorities.[11]

As Manson has argued, many of the effects of these policies on health services, and conditions and content of work and employment, do not stem solely from recent short-term policies, but 'from long-term policies either deriving from plans for expansion or from problems that arose in this expansion' (Manson 1979).

Of particular importance are the contradictory effects of incompatible policies – for example, strategies of rational planning in a period of overall limits in reductions in expenditure (Offe 1975a). Radical critiques of health care, such as the 'inverse care law' or the diminishing returns of high technology medicine (which as we have seen were promoted by the application of technical rationality in the NHS in the 1960s) were incorporated into government planning policies in the 1970s. Such policies seek to redistribute resources more equitably between geographical areas (RAWP) or between client groups and types of medicine. But the implementation of the RAWP formula, has resulted in cutbacks and closures of hospitals and wards, in some of the 'richer' regions, which also have pockets of social deprivation.[12] The recent financial and manpower cuts have also meant that health authorities have economised by postponing improvements in care for the elderly, handicapped and mentally ill groups, government priority groups since the mid 1970s.[13]

The rapid growth and density of unionism in the NHS has led to an increase in workplace organisation, the number of shop stewards and, as we have seen, the politicisation of union activity, but the limited empirical evidence available suggests that these changes have probably had little impact on the unions' ability to control job content or job loss or to affect relative pay levels (e.g. Bosanquet 1982 and Ogden 1984.)[14] The response to unionisation, however, has been to strengthen the resolve of management, both at local and central levels, to reassert what was perceived as a loss of managerial prerogative.[15] At central level this has involved more punitive policies which have been directed at actual or potential sources of conflict and resistance. At the end of the largest and most unified dispute of health service workers in 1982, came a directive to contract out domestic, laundry and catering services. The trade unionism of ancillary workers is directly challenged by privatisation as are their levels of pay and conditions of work. As a managerial strategy, privatisation may prove to be a most coercive form of labour control, reversing any gains of the ancillary workers in the last decade (see e.g. Paul, 1984).[16]

Recent central management attempts to impose more coercive forms of control highlight, however, certain tensions which are present in state welfare work. Whilst state work does represent, as the critical theorists claim, a form of production liberated from the commodity form, this view ignores the 'factory-like' logic of state institutions (Keane 1978). As Keane has argued, state production is a highly ambiguous development. Forms of social inequality are perpetuated and developed for both workers and clients, for instance, the persistence of low paid work, gendered and radical divisions of labour, and forms of stigmatism and dependency induced by professional and bureaucratic definitions of clients' 'needs'.

Moreover, the introduction of technical rationality into state welfare organisations creates pressures of bureaucratisation and intensification of work which, as Weber identified, are as coercive as those in private sector organisations. In this context, the distinction drawn by Offe between bureaucratic and purposive-rational modes of organisation, as discussed earlier, is less clear cut than he suggests. The application of purposive-rationality, as for instance scientific management schemes in the NHS, can themselves lead to bureaucratic modes of organisation. More recently reductions in staffing levels and the use of performance indicators and other 'efficiency' criteria have intensified work practices and work relations in the NHS, as in other welfare services.

Conclusion

This paper has argued that the theoretical framework developed by critical theorists can provide a useful starting point for the analysis of state labour processes. The critical theorists and neo-Marxist writers discussed above have viewed the state's role, and the increase in state employment, in post-war capitalist societies as a major transformation of those societies. State workers and employees, they argue, add a new dimension to class relations in which they are not directly implicated in conditions of exchange between capital and labour, but are both external yet dependent on the capital-wage-labour nexus (see also Therborn 1984). Additionally, state organisations and state policies for the distribution and provision of its goods and services are said to have become an 'arena of struggle' as they have been opened by increased political demands and conflicts. However, whilst some writers such as O'Connor and Gough have contributed to our understanding of the outcomes of the contradictory relationship of the state's activities to the monopoly and competitive sectors, for example, the growth of the welfare (and warfare) state, the fiscal crisis of the state and subsequent restructuring, they have not seen their task as involving a detailed analysis of state labour processes. It is here that the work of Offe is important, for he provides a framework which links a theory of the capitalist state to its internal mode of organisation.

Applying the ideas developed by Offe to a specific state labour process, the NHS in Britain, it was argued that they provided; first, a means of analysing the hierarchical division of health labour and the dominant position held by the medical profession (through selective privileging and sponsorship by the state and the pursuit of that sponsorship by other occupational groups), and second, an analysis of the ambiguities facing state managers in devising 'appropriate' forms of control in an organisation governed by non-market criteria yet dependent for its resources on capitalist production. In conjunction with the views of O'Connor, consideration was also given to the increasing unionisation and politicisation of state workers and the ways in which 'their special conditions of exchange' exacerbated the economic and social crises of the 1970s. Finally, Offe's arguments relating to the limits of the state's policy making capacity were discussed; namely, that fiscal crisis and politicisation tendencies lead to pressures for the recommodification of certain state activities, which together with the state's inability for rational planning, suggest the possibility of an eventual legitimation crisis. It was argued, however, that these latter propositions might seriously underestimate central managers' capacity for directing coercive forms of control at potential sources of resistance within the state apparatus.

A further research agenda would need, therefore, to incorporate not only the type of societal level analysis set out above, but also focus more directly upon forms of work control, in a way that would include themes only touched on briefly in this paper – such as the proletarianisation thesis and gendered and racial divisions of labour.

Notes

1. This paper is intended as a contribution to the analysis of a labour process which is outside the sphere of capitalist production. It does not however deal with all the important issues and questions raised by Braverman's work nor the subsequent debate. In particular the paper does not focus on the deskilling thesis nor the implications of state work for class relations, nor is its main concern with sexual and racial divisions of labour in state welfare work. With respect to the NHS, there exist a small number of studies in these areas, for example, Bellaby and Oribabor (1977, 1980) on nurses; Doyle (1981) on migrant workers; Gamarnikow (1978) and Carpenter (1977) on the sexual division of labour. But as Fryer (1983) has remarked for 'a continuation of Braverman's work in the public services' there remains 'a substantial programme of research'.

2. For example, the publications and consultative activities of the Brunel Institute of Organization and Social Studies, see E. Jacques (1978) and R. Rowbottom et al. (1974). For commentaries see Whittington and Bellaby (1979) and Draper and Smart (1974).

3. For Burns the collaborative system was sustained by 'commitment, trust and habits of mind and conduct inculcated by training on the job' (1981, p. 31).

4. Restructuring of the welfare state here refers to 'policies to secure more efficient reproduction of the labour force, a shifting emphasis to the social control of destabilising groups in society, raising productivity within the social services and the reprivatisation of parts of the welfare state' Gough (1979, p. 141).

5. These include Register of trained nurses, 1919, creation of SEN grade in 1943, and the new grade of untrained nursing auxiliaries in 1958. Although GNC has controls over standards of nurse training, the health authorities control recruitment of labour.

6. During the 1950s and 1960s the composition of the nursing labour force changed to include more unqualified and SEN grade nurses, and more part-time and married women workers amongst both trained, semi-trained and untrained grades (Briggs Report, 1973).

7. These sectors are briefly (i) a private monopoly sector, characterised by highly capital intensive productions, organised sales markets, national and international operations, strong unionisation and high wage rates, (ii) a private competitive sector, characterised by small firms which are price takers in competitive markets, labour intensive, low levels of productivity improvement, low wages rates, low unionisation and employment instability. (iii) A state service sector which is labour intensive, low levels of productivity improvement except by employment growth, political determination of wage rates, and in Britain centralisation of wage bargaining. (iv) Dunleavy (1981a) and Thompson and Beaumont (1978) further divide the state sector to include a public corporation sector, which consists mainly of

nationalised industries, similar to private monopoly sector in that they are governed to some extent by market principles, but greater political determination of wage levels, pricing policy and investment programmes. (v) A residual labour power sector consisting of the state dependent population, which is also in part a source of reserve labour and a secondary labour market. See also Offe (1976); O'Connor (1973); Habermas (1976); Dunleavy (1980a) and Thompson and Beaumont (1978).

8. For example, COSHE's membership increased from 54,241 in 1960 to 211,415 in 1978. During the same period NALGO increased from 273,644 to 709,331 and NUPE from 197,648 to 693,097. The latter two also recruit outside the health service (Source: P. Fairbrother, 'Working for the State' WEA).

9. The proportion of women members in COSHE increased from 39 per cent in 1950 to 75 per cent in 1978, in NALGO from 31 per cent in 1950 to 45 per cent in 1978, and in NUPE from 30 per cent in 1950 to 66 per cent in 1978. Hunt (1982) shows that the increase of women's membership of TUC unions accounted for nearly all of the increase between 1958 and 1968, and almost the same proportion as men's between 1968 and 1978.

10. Held (1982) argues in his criticisms of Habermas's concept of legitimation crisis that 'the worthiness of a political order to be recognised is not a necessary condition for every relatively stable society ... what matters most is the approval of the dominant groups'. Held further argues that there is a lack of consensus regarding the significance of the social order. People's experiences at work and elsewhere are fragmented and atomised: there exists a 'dual consciousness' which supports a pragmatic acceptance and partial understanding of the social totality.

11. The *Guardian*, 18 January 1984.

12. The Oxford RHA, worst affected by RAWP, has experienced a collapse of planning for future growth and now plans for service reductions.

13. The *Guardian*, 18 January 1984.

14. For non-medical workers, management control manning levels and work content to a much greater extent than other public services (Bosanquet, 1982). A recent study of job loss in local government and the NHS suggests that in the early 1980s management were largely unhindered in implementing changes in working conditions. Lack of union resistance was explained by the way in which management achieved job loss, that is, through job erosion, of which the unions were simply not informed (Fatchett and Ogden 1984).

15. With respect to industrial relations at a local level, Trainer found that this has occurred through management initiatives to institute a 'web of procedure agreements to provide a framework by which control of work relations could be achieved' (Trainer 1983).

16. Further centralisation of the management structure is also to be implemented as set out in the Griffiths Report. This report recommends a stronger line, chief executive style of management, and is intended to tackle not only the inability of managers to manage (in that they are essentially reactive and lack influence in relation to the medical profession) but also those aspects of the present structure – for instance, consensus management teams, and the complex consultative machinery, which can subvert, resist or delay central management policies.

References

Armstrong, D. (1976), 'The decline of medical hegemony: A review of Government reports during the NHS', *Social Service and Medicine*, **10** (3/4), 157–63.

Bellaby, P. and Oribabor, P. (1980), 'Determinants of occupational strategies adopted by British hospital nurses', *International Journal of Health Services*, **10** (2), 291–309.

Bellaby, P. and Oribabor, P. (1977), 'The growth of trade union consciousness among general hospital nurses', *Sociological Review*, **25**, 801–22.

Berridge, J. (1977), *A Suitable Case for Treatment: a case study of industrial relations in the NHS*, Milton Keynes: Open University Press.

Bosanquet, N. (1979), 'The search for a system' in N. Bosanquet (ed.), *Industrial Relations in the NHS*, London: King Edward's Hospital Fund.

Bosanquet, N. (1982), 'What is the impact of trade unionism on the NHS.' Health Services Manpower Review.

Braverman, H. *(1974), Labor and Monopoly Capital*, New York: Monthly Review Press.

(The Briggs Report) (1972), *Report of the Committee on Nursing*, London: HMSO.

Burns, T. (1981), *A Comparative Study of Administrative Structure and Organizational Processes in Selected Areas of the National Health Service*, SSRC Research Report.

Carchedi G. (1977), *On the Economic Identification of Social Classes*, London: Routledge and Kegan Paul.

Carpenter, M. (1982), 'The labour movement in the NHS: UK' in A. S. Sethi and S. Dimmock, *Industrial Relations and Health Services*, London: Croom Helm.

Carpenter, M. (1977), 'The new managerialism and professionalism in nursing' in M. Stacy et al. (eds) *Health and the Division of Labour*, London: Croom Helm.

Cawson, A. (1982), *Corporatism and Welfare*, London: Heinemann.

Cawson, A. and Saunders P. (1983), 'Corporatism, competitive politics and class struggle' in R. King *Capital and Politics*, London: Routledge and Kegan Paul.

Child, J. (1972), 'Organizational structure, environment and performance: The role of strategic choice', *Sociology*, **6** (1) January.

Child, J. et al., (1983), 'Microelectronics and the quality of employment in services', paper presented to the British Association for the Advancement of Science.

Crompton R. and Gubbay, J. (1977), *Economy and Class Structure*, London: Macmillan.

Crompton, R. and Jones, G. (1984), *White Collar Proletariat: Deskilling and Gender in Clerical Work*, London: Macmillan.

CSE State Group, (1979), *Struggle over the State: Cuts and Restructuring in Contemporary Britain* London: CSE Books.

Dimmock, S. J. (1982), 'Incomes Policy and Health Services in the UK' in A. S. Sethi and S. Dimmock, *Industrial Relations and Health Services*, London: Croom Helm.

Dimmock, S. J. (1979), 'Dilemmas of medical representation – a view', in N. Bosanquet (ed.), *Industrial Relations in the NHS*, King Edward's Hospital Fund.

Dimmock, S. J. (1977), 'Participation or control? The workers' involvement in management' in K. Barnard and K. Lee (eds), *Conflicts in the NHS* London: Croom Helm.

Doyal, L., Hunt, G., Mellor J. (1981), 'Your life in their hands: migrant workers in the NHS', *Critical Social Policy*, **1** (2).

Draper, P. and Smart, T. (1974), 'Social science and health policy in the UK: Some contributions of the social sciences to the bureaucratization of the NHS', *International Journal of Health Services*, **4** (3), 453–70.

Dunleavy, P. (1980a), 'The political implications of sectoral cleavages and the growth of state employment: Part I, The analysis of production cleavages', *Political Studies*, **28**, 364–83.

Dunleavy, P. (1980b), 'The political implications of sectoral cleavages and the growth of state employment: Part II, Cleavage Structures and Political Alignment', *Political Studies*, **28**, 527–49.

Dyson R. and Spary, K. (1979), 'Professional Associations' in N. Bosanquet, (ed.), *Industrial Relations in the NHS*, King Edward's Hospital Fund.

Fairbrother, P. (1982), *Working for the State*, London: Workers' Educational Association.

Fatchett, D. and Ogden, S. G. (1984), 'Public Expenditure Cuts and Job Loss: A Union

Response', *Journal of Management Studies*, **21** (2).

Frankel, B., (1979), 'On the state of the state: Marxist theories of the state after Leninism', *Theory and Society*, 7.

Friedman, A. (1977), *Industry and Labour*, London: Macmillan.

Fryer, B. (1983), 'Managerialism, deskilling and trade unionism in the public services', paper given at the 1983 Conference on the 'Organization and Control of the Labour Processes', UMIST.

Gamarnikow, E. (1978), 'Sexual division of labour – the case of nursing' in A. Kuhn and A. M. Wolpe (eds), *Feminism and Materialism*, London: Routledge and Kegan Paul.

Gospel, H. F. and Littler, C. R. (1983), *Management Strategies and Industrial Relations*' London: Heinemann.

Gough, I. (1979), *The Political Economy of the Welfare State*' London: Macmillan.

Gough, I. (1983), 'The crisis of the British welfare state' *International Journal of Health Services*, **13** (3).

Griffiths Report, 1983, NHS Management Inquiry, DHSS.

Habermas, J. (1976), *Legitimation Crisis*, London: Heinemann.

Habermas, J. (1971), 'Technology and science as ideology' in Habermas, *Toward a Rational Society*, London: Heinemann.

Ham, C. (1981), *Policy Making in the National Health Service*, London: Macmillan.

Hayward, S. and Alaszewski, A. (1980), *Crisis in the Health Service*, London: Croom Helm.

Held, D. (1982), 'Crisis tendencies, legitimation and the state' in J. B. Thompson and D. Held (eds), *Habermas: Critical Debates*, London: Macmillan.

Hunt, J. (1982), 'A woman's place is in her union' in J. West (ed.), *Work, Women and the Labour Market*, London: Routledge and Kegan Paul.

Hunter, D. J. (1980), *Coping with Uncertainty*, Chichester: Research Studies Press.

Jacques, E. (1978), *Health Services*, London: Heinemann.

Johnston, P. (1980), 'Democracy, public work, and labour strategy', *Kapitalistate*, **8**.

Keane, J. (1978), 'The legacy of political economy: thinking with and against Claus Offe', *Canadian Journal of Political and Social Theory*, **2** (3).

Klein, R. (1983), *The Politics of the NHS*, London: Longman.

Klein, R. (1982), 'Performances, evaluation and the NHS: A case study in conceptual perplexity and organizational complexity', *Public Administration*, **60**, Winter.

Larson, M. S. (1980), 'Proletarianization and Educated Labour', *Theory and Society*, January.

Littler, C. R. (1982), *The Development of the Labour Process in Capitalist Societies*, London: Heinemann.

Manson, T. (1977), 'Management, the professions and the unions in M. Stacey (ed.) *Health and the Division of Labour*, London: Croom Helm.

Manson, T. (1979), 'Health policy and the cuts', *Capital and Class*, 7.

National Board for Prices and Incomes, (1967), 'Report No. 166: The Pay and Conditions of Ancillary Workers in the NHS', London: HMSO.

O'Connor, J. (1973), *The Fiscal Crisis of the State*, New York: St. Martin's Press.

Offe, C. and Ronge, V. (1982), 'Thesis on the theory of the state' in A. Giddens and D. Held (eds), *Classes, Power and Conflict*, London: Macmillan.

Offe, C. (1975a), 'The theory of the capitalist state and the problem of policy formation' in L. Lindberg et al. (eds) *Stress and Contradiction in Modern Capitalism*, Lexington: D. C. Heath.

Offe, C. (1975b), 'Legitimacy versus efficiency: Introduction to Part III' in L. Lindberg et al. (eds) *Stress and Contradiction in Modern Capitalism*, Lexington : D. C. Heath.

Offe, C. (1976), '"Crisis of crisis management": Elements of a political crisis theory', *International Journal of Politics*, VI, (3).

Offe, C. (1976), 'Political authority and class structures' in P. Connerton (ed.), *Critical*

Sociology, Harmondsworth: Penguin.

Offe, C. (1983), 'Some contradictions of the modern welfare State', *Critical Social Policy*, 7–16.

Offe, C. (1984), 'Social policy and the theory of the state' in C. Offe (ed. J. Keane) *Contradictions of the Welfare State*, London: Hutchinson.

Parry, N. and J. (1977), 'Professionalism and unionism: aspects of class conflict in the NHS', *Sociological Review*, 25, 823–41.

Paul, J. (1984), 'Contracting out in the NHS', *Critical Social Policy*, Summer, 10.

'Report of the Committee on Senior Nursing Staff Structure' – (The Salmon Report) (1966), London: HMSO.

Rowbottom, R. Hey, A. and Billis, D. (1974), *Social Service Departments*, London: Heinemann.

Salaman, G. (1982), 'Managing the frontier of control' in A. Giddens and G. Mackenzie (eds), *Social Class and the Division of Labour*, Cambridge: Cambridge University Press.

Saunders, P. (1983), *Urban Politics, a sociological interpretation*, London: Hutchinson.

Sethi, A. S. and Dimmock, S. (1982), *Industrial Relations and Health Services*, London: Croom Helm.

Skocpol, T. (1980), 'Political response to capitalist crisis: Neo-Marxist theories of the state and the case of the new deal, *Politics and Society*, **10** (2).

Therborn, G. (1984), 'The prospects of labour and the transformation of advanced capitalism' *New Left Review*, **145**, May/June.

Thompson, A. W. J. and Beaumont, P. B. (1978), *Public Sector Bargaining: a study of relative gain*, Farnborough: Saxon House.

Trainer, R. (1983), 'The Management of Industrial Relations', Health Services Manpower Review.

Whittington, C. and Ballaby, P. (1979), 'The reasons for hierarchy in Social Service Departments: A critique of Elliott Jacques and his associates', *Sociological Review*, **27** (3).

Wood, S. and Kelly, J. (1982), 'Taylorism, responsible autonomy and management strategy' in S. Wood (ed.) *The Degradation of Work*? London: Hutchinson.

6 Management Control and Worker Resistance in the National Coal Board: Financial Controls in the Labour Process*

Trevor Hopper, David Cooper, Tony Lowe, Teresa Capps, Jan Mouritsen

Introduction to the Themes

Through a detailed analysis of financial planning and control practices in the National Coal Board, this paper seeks to reinforce several recent attempts to integrate studies of the labour process with the process of producing surplus value. Our study of financial control in the NCB[1] involves not only a study of internal systems, processes, ideologies and practices but also an understanding of how these systems and practices produce outcomes which fit in with current preoccupations of the British state, and its concerns to facilitate the realisation of surplus value for British capitalism. It illustrates the need to synthesise the analyses of Baran and Sweezy (1966) and Braverman (1974) on the lines of Gordon et al. (1982) and Burawoy (1985). Specifically we focus on three broad themes that seem to represent lacunae in much of the literature on the labour process.

One major theme concerns accounting and financial controls within the enterprise and their influence on managerial control more generally. In doing so we emphasise both control and contradiction in the labour process. This focus is illustrated in the following interchanges which highlight how control at the point of production may be irrelevant for understanding the valorisation process:

> *Colliery trade union official to researchers:* It's pathetic to watch the deputies (supervisors), they're wandering around with nothing to do ...it's the chargehand (elected official) and the men that run things underground.

*We gratefully acknowledge the financial support of the ESRC (then the SSRC) and the co-operation of the managers and workers in the National Coal Board. We also acknowledge the assistance of Tony Berry and Peter Ferguson who were involved in parts of the investigation, and of Hugh Willmott, who made valuable comments on an earlier draft. However, only the authors can be held responsible for the errors in this paper.

Colliery manager quoting the same Trade Union official when the latter came to him requesting a copy of the Monopolies and Mergers Commission (1983) report on the National Coal Board (NCB): 'But they won't close our pit if it's making a profit, will they?'

As the first quotation indicates, miners have at times been successful in struggles for control of operations. This success may even extend to successful resistance and control over information flows and technologies. However even this 'worker control' has contradictions within it: resistance may be associated with a segmentation and fragmentation of the workforce. The second quotation indicates that a focus upon struggle underground and at the point of production carries the danger of overstating the significance of such struggles when assessing the influence of labour control over colliery workings and the industry generally. For example, planning, both locally and nationally, is typically the preserve and perceived prerogative of management (Edwards 1983). In this paper we particularly emphasise that accounting, through its espousal of particular reporting structures, its patterns of segmental reporting, and modes of calculation, is a significant plank in efforts to manufacture subjectively the compliance of labour. Its presumed neutrality and objectivity reinforces particular understanding of how the industry is, and should be, managed. The paper takes issue with such presumptions by drawing attention to ideological aspects of accounting, its relationship to particular interests, and its mediation through processes of resistance. What is 'profit' and what is 'loss' is contestable (Berry et al. 1985b) but such considerations are typically not seen by workers as the object of conflict.

A second theme concerns the use of controls as an important component by which capital has attempted to control the activities of enterprises. This has involved not only internal mechanisms which are intended to control subordinate managers, as well as workers, and thereby to produce as much surplus value as possible, but also mechanisms whose rationale is to facilitate the realisation and appropriation of this surplus value to owners of capital. The state has been heavily implicated in the development of accounting and financial control practices (Hopwood et al. 1979; Armstrong 1985). Developments in the NCB and in the nationalised sector of the British economy more generally illustrate the role of the state in encouraging specific (and historically, variable) forms of management control and in encouraging the recognition of surplus value in specific parts of the economy.

Lastly, a third theme concerns the importance of class relationships for an understanding of accounting and financial control within the labour process. Rather than provide a monistic or deterministic explanation, the paper argues for a dialectical approach to control (Storey 1983) in which factors such as technology, cultures, professional rivalries and markets for labour and products are incorporated.[2] A simple capital-labour dichotomy is deemed inappropriate, not least because it fails adequately to recognise the ambivalent position of management within class structure and the consequences of this for controls (Crompton and Jones 1984; Wright, 1976). The control of controllers is problematic.

Empirical studies of management (e.g. Mintzberg 1973, Kotter 1982) have tended to take the individual manager as the unit of analysis, ignoring institutional structures (including ownership structures and taken-for-granted views of the world). In so far as politics are considered, they are depicted as tensions between sub-group goals, within essentially unitary structures of organisations. The possibility that managements behave politically, rather than technically, owing to the inherent contradictions of their positions or tasks within the general mode of production tends to be ignored (Willmott 1984). Thus deviations from 'rational' procedures tend to be explained through individual failings, pathologies or local rivalries.

In contrast, this paper argues that managerial resistance to, manipulation of, and non-compliance with, accounting systems (e.g. Dalton 1959; Dew and Gee 1973; Mintzberg 1975) is connected to management's own ambiguous position within class conflicts and to managers' attempts to cope with conflicting pressures. Studies of the labour process have tended to ignore the complexities of such managerial reactions, often minimising the relative autonomy of managements, their freedom of action, and cleavages within management. Accounting studies, on the other hand, almost entirely neglect the possibility of class-related behaviour by management and the role of accounting in the production and reproduction of organisation and society.

These three themes – the ideological aspects of accounting and financial control, the significance of the state, and the contradictions within management – are addressed in the three main sections of this paper. The first, focusing on struggles for control underground, indicates the nature and extent of worker resistance, and can thus be seen as a fairly conventional case study of control at the point of production. The second section illustrates the significance of financial controls in management's attempts to control the labour process. Here we emphasise the apparently perverse ways in which financial controls can be used to enhance ambiguity in the face of competing managerial perceptions of what is the most profitable strategy for the NCB:

responding to the logic of markets or to the logic of production. The final section of the paper explores the role of the state in the management of enterprises and the nationalised sector of the economy. The state's concern with the adoption of financial control systems represents, we suggest, a concern to secure surplus value in specific locations of the economy.

Struggles For Control Underground

Control of Operations

Even the most cursory examination of the history of mining (e.g. Hall, 1981; Fine et al. 1983; Pollard 1965), reveals continual conflict between management and miners, and the difficulty of maintaining management control. Whilst studies of mining as diverse as Trist et al. (1963), Handy (1981), Gouldner (1954) and Douglass and Krieger (1983) illustrate the complex interactions between technology, wage payment systems and social strutures, it is nevertheless clear that it is virtually impossible for management to rely on direct surveillance as a major means of operational control. Workers are geographically dispersed underground and many operations are almost unobservable, taking place in cramped and poorly lit conditions. Underground workers are therefore in a position to control their own activities. The mechanisation of face work (especially the cutting and conveying of coal and the use of power supports) gave miners increased job control and probably increased skill requirements, particularly in machine handling and routine maintenance (Yarrow 1979).

The formal management hierarchy underground is to an extent mirrored by systems of control operated by the miners themselves. From direct observations of underground workings, interviews with managers and conversations with trade unionists and miners, it was evident that there is a continuous struggle between the systems of the managers and the miners for day-to-day control of underground operations. It was apparent that for much of the time the pacing and allocation of work resided with the men, co-ordinated through elected chargehands, rather than with direct supervision. For example, during observations of delays (stoppages) at the coal face, deputies were rarely directly involved with rectifications. It was clear from the tone and content of the language that they were neither welcomed nor expected to participate.

The production emphasis of colliery management reinforced the control of underground operations exercised by miners. Whilst they may or may not be mystified by higher management's concern for abstracted notions such as profit or returns, the overt emphasis of the miners is on physical performance indicators, which are directly understandable in terms of day-to-day practices (and pay). Physical indicators of performance, notably metres cut, machine working time, output per manshift and total production are emphasised as the key to efficient operations. The emphasis on physical indicators, the working knowledge of miners of the relationship between work practices and these indicators, their social cohesion, spatial differences, working conditions underground and methods of coal extraction all strengthen the ability of miners to control production. Managerial control is also lessened by the problematic loyalty of first-line supervision to management, given their recruitment from, and lingering loyalties to, miners. This is reinforced by their continual contact with miners as opposed to their sporadic contact with higher management.

Control of Information
Since management has relatively little direct control over operations, they are reliant upon information coming from pit bottom. But detailed reliable information is not always forthcoming, partly owing to resistance on the part of miners, and partly owing to its implications for payment systems. This is compounded by the unreliability of reports from first-line supervision. Given strong trade unions and solidarity underground, close supervision and control through orders and disciplinary procedures is not feasible. In short, the uncertainty of operations which confronts management and which is due to the difficulties and variability of production, is compounded by the uncertainty attached to information on distant and relatively inaccessible workings. However, an absence of operational control and uncertain operational information does not in itself imply an absence of management control. To gain a 'picture of reality' multiple information sources are cultivated at all levels of management. Just as the undermanager cross-checks stories of engineers and deputies, comparing them with various official reports, so higher level management develops a network of contacts and information sources. Determining what is happening is a major preoccupation of senior management and consumes much of its time. Such knowledge, however imperfect, permits a modicum of simple control (Edwards 1979) such as using the allocation of overtime opportunities and deployment to jobs as a means of rewarding co-operative behaviour.

Bureaucratic control through incentives and standards?
Traditionally management has sought to control in mining through the wage structure rather than direct supervision (Krieger 1983). Internal sub-contracting was used during the Industrial Revolution

(Goffee 1981; Pollard 1965) and has been utilised as late as the inter-war years. Piece-rates may be seen as a natural extension of such methods and were widely used until the National Power Loading Agreement of 1966, which stipulated a five-year transition to uniform national day wages for face workers. However, significantly, after a bitter and complex internal union struggle the scheme was abandoned, district by district, under pressure from managements who were disappointed by the low gains in productivity, and by those miners who worked pits with favourable geology and who could earn high piece-rates. Since 1978 the industry has turned to a mixture of a national wage agreement on basic rates and localised productivity deals. But as Krieger (1983) demonstrates, whilst the logic of productivity schemes and piece-rates is intended to provide management with control of output without its having to bother with detailed work practices, direct supervision or elaborate formal controls, the reality of the differing wage payments systems has been rather different. Ever since nationalisation, the NCB has found that the unanticipated consequences of the various wage payment systems has overwhelmed the anticipated effects which have been so carefully assessed and considered by NCB management. Using Gidden's concept of the dialectic of control (1981), Krieger shows how the introduction of the national wage agreement of 1966 appeared to offer management greater centralised, bureaucratic control. Yet at the same time, this bureaucratic control was mediated by variable regional work practices and resulted in greater national unity and militancy amongst miners.

The abandoning of centralised bureaucratic control through wage payment systems has been paralleled in some respects by the failure of another supposed mechanism of bureaucratic managerial control. In the 1950s, the NCB, along with many other large British enterprises, introduced a system of standard costing. Many writers (eg. Solomons 1968) have shown how standard costing systems were originally developed by engineers at the same time as Taylorism and indeed that can be regarded as the extension of scientific management into the financial domain. Standard costing systems create conceptions of an ideal level and means of production by an ideal worker and by comparing actual performance with the ideal or standard performance, it is possible to assess individuals and individual production units. In the case of coal mining, the standard costing system was also extended to a system whereby the financial performance of individual production faces could be assessed. The logic of such systems is that as long as the financial performance is deemed appropriate (i.e. actual performance is as good as, or better than, the standard expected) detailed supervision and control of work practices need not be in direct managerial control.

Just as with the incentive systems, NCB management has, despite the commitment of considerable resources to try to ensure their success, disbanded standard costing systems and attempts to measure the financial performance of individual faces. The reasons for the failure of scientific management (i.e. standard costing) are clouded in confusion. The NCB annual report of 1958 ascribed its 'failure' to difficulties in obtaining accurate data from underground personnel, who resisted control. Also it was suggested that valid standards could not be produced in an industry where workings are neither predictable nor uniform and where mechanisation quickly dated standards. However, such explanations would seem to apply equally to physical and financial standards, yet the former have been used continuously, whilst the latter have been abandoned. Ascribing failure to the difficulty of obtaining information underground may not be entirely satisfactory and, as will be examined later, inter-professional rivalries may have been significant (Armstrong 1985). Accounting innovations introduced by the Finance Department of the NCB appear to have been successfully undermined by mining engineers and line management, who preferred to use their own methods of physical controls.

The Technological Threat?
Management control methods are not stable and the inadequacies and failures of 'bureaucratic' controls have been associated with a rise in management hopes for 'technical' controls. Currently at some collieries management control is being extended through technology, especially the Mine Operating System (MINOS). The rate of cutting and machine breakdowns are critical to the pace and variability of mining work. MINOS has the potential to provide management centrally with information on aspects of mining work through a system of monitoring devices and mini-computers installed in coal face machines and operating from a central control room. Its potential for restructuring work and altering power relations underground has been noted and challenged by union-sponsored researchers (Burns et al. 1983).

However, the management vision of accurate direct information through technology is problematic. This became apparent even in our somewhat unsystematic observations of the control room and the discretion allowed to operators to decide the 'cause' of deviations from physical plans. The control room represents an attempt, through modern technology, to gather detailed formal information on underground workings in an impersonal manner. Computerised information on matters such as ventilation, conveyors and output are fed directly to the surface where they can be controlled. All conversation on intercoms underground, including the face, can be picked up here. In addition, underground close-circuit television monitors the conveyors, which in turn can indicate whether face machines are operating. Whilst traditional systems rely on verbal reports of face delays regarding deviations and their causes, computer-controlled systems may record face machinery delays directly. Thus, *prima facie*, the control room provides a means of impersonally gathering detailed data for management control.

However, in our researches, it was apparent that this is an oversimplification, for in some instances the struggle for control had extended to the control room. For example, control room operators were sometimes highly politicised and loyal trade unionists, a finding that mirrors the tendency of face workers to be more involved in union affairs than other miners and workers. Local trade union officials frequently spent much time in the control room. Similarly it was noted that stageloaders, the underground workers who are critical in transmitting information from the face to the control room, were similarly loyal. In one pit studied, the colliery manager was clearly concerned to limit access to the control room, to try and curb 'manipulation' of data, albeit with limited success. The point of interest is that modern information systems (introduced as neutral management decision aids but clearly also intended to overcome labour resistance to detailed control) can themselves be objects of struggle and resistance.

Implications for the analysis of the labour process underground
Several points pertinent to the analysis of labour processes are raised by the descriptions above. First, the form of control is problematic and reflects continual resistance, in this case by miners to controls over operations. Such behaviour is highly significant in shaping the form of control exercised. Second, such struggles extend to the control of information. Consequently, information may be as great a source of uncertainty to management as are the operations themselves. Third, simple classificatory schemes of the development of controls (e.g. Edwards, 1979) do violence to the complexity of control. In the NCB case, control is achieved by a mix of direct, bureaucratic and technical controls. Controls of various sorts are subject to change and amendment due to alterations in managerial strategies, patterns of resistance, unanticipated consequences upon their introduction and not least of all because of changes within the mode of production.

Fourth, as will be examined later, areas of autonomy created by miners may not necessarily be counter-productive to managerial aims. Managers still have some ability, despite surprises, to manipulate the reward system. With sporadic checks, much of the production, coal getting, process can be treated as a 'black box'. This is because senior managers may achieve control through the system of physical and financial planning which has traditionally been a managerial prerogative (Edwards 1983). Although management may value 'control' for its own sake (Buchanan and Boddy 1982), a concentration on the control of work tends to draw attention away from the relationship between control of the labour process and the production of surplus value. Focusing on the latter requires an analysis of the distribution of power within the industry and more generally within the economy.

Management and the Integration of Control
Superficially, as the Monopolies and Mergers Commission Report (1983) documents, the NCB might be regarded as an exemplary Weberian bureaucracy, employed to rational ends. Government determines objectives; long-run plans are specified in tripartite agreements such as 'Plan For Coal'; there is a carefully specified hierarchy with defined roles; certain managerial positions are required by statute to possess specific qualifications; the timetables of the numerous committee meetings are determined well in advance; and throughout the industry there exists a detailed, uniform and well-understood system of planning and control.

Yet when the management control systems are investigated, such initial impressions give way to a recognition of the complexity of practices. In particular, financial information may not only illuminate the organisation and enhance management control. It may also become an obfuscatory practice which may both facilitate and undermine alternative conceptions of what is effective management.

The formal management structure
The control system of the National Coal Board has been described as 'a hierarchical, top-down MBO system based on physical performance indicators' (Berry et al. 1985a). In terms of Edward's classification it might be described as bureaucratic, with elements of technical control, especially at colliery level.

To elaborate, upon nationalisation the NCB adopted a highly centralised administrative structure with a line of command running through the 'spine' of the industry from the Board, through Divisional Boards and Area Managers to Colliery Managers. Hence the underlying philosophy adopted by the Board regarding organisational structure was that of 'line and staff'. The line was the production or mining aspects of the organisation and the staff functions were Manpower and Welfare, Industrial Relations, Marketing and Finance. This basic philosophy still exists. The structure has been elaborated by several organisational changes, notably in 1955 and 1967. The NCB is now basically a three-tier organisation comprising headquarters (HQ), Areas and, finally, Collieries, with the colliery manager and the Area Director accountable personally and directly to the next tier for achieving the objectives laid down for them in the management by objectives (MBO) system. Further, the headquarters (in the form of the Board) is accountable to its sponsoring ministry, namely the Department of Energy. This organisational structure emphasises the strength of the line and the power of the mining engineers (who man the line).

Under the MBO scheme each level of management in the line (Board, Area and Colliery) has a set of responsibilities. All three levels have long-term plans (up to 20 years) and medium-term plans (five years horizon), both of which are reviewed annually. In addition, colliery action programmes exist for each colliery and set out the physical objectives (eg. output, manpower, productivity, production faces, development work and equipment requirements) for the next 18 months. These are used as the basis of the financial budgets for both the colliery and, in aggregate (and after revision) for the Area. A series of weekly, monthly and quarterly accountability meetings are held to review, revise and develop plans for the next period(s).

This formal picture can be contrasted with our observations of how control actually operated in the NCB in 1982–4. The first set of observations emphasises the development of self-contained units within the organisation and is discussed in the rest of section three. The second set relate to investment in information systems and is examined in section four, on the state.

Loose coupling as a managerial control strategy

The major impression, explained more fully in Berry et al. (1985a) was that the NCB managed its business through a loosely coupled management control system. The decoupling occurs functionally, whereby Corporate Policy, Finance, Marketing and Industrial Relations are relatively detached from Production and Engineering. The former functions are, broadly speaking, handled by HQ whereas the latter are the major concern of Areas and the collieries.

Each part of the NCB maintains its own identity and separateness. Whilst parts are somewhat responsible to one another, relationships appear to be relatively infrequent, weak in terms of mutual effects, and slow in mutual response. Decoupling enabled the NCB to manage varying types and degrees of complexity—most notably production, technical, political and economic—by sealing the first two types from the problems arising from the latter two. This may be at the expense of short-run efficiency but the decoupling significantly reduces the complexity of the management task and thereby facilitates longer-run control of the labour process. The remainder of this section illustrates this strategy with reference to the operation of financial controls, namely capital budgeting, strategic planning, accountability meetings, line-staff structural relationships and colliery accounts.

Official procedures for reviewing investment plans are carefully documented and insisted upon. HQ produces highly sophisticated planning and investment models (Plackett et al. 1982). In practice, however, budgeting was initiated and appeared focused on Areas—where plans were carefully assessed in terms of technology and production expertise, but where there was rather rudimentary financial expertise. Timing and framing of submissions was carefully monitored. For example, the manner in which an investment proposal was classified ('labour saving', 'increasing productivity', 'increasing production', 'safety', etc.) was regarded as a crucial factor in its approval and considerable discussions centred on how to sell (through the appropriate choice of classification type) the proposal. Bower (1970) found similar processes occurring in US private industry. Further, in the process whereby Areas had to submit their proposals to HQ for approval, great sensitivity was placed on producing a sanitised proposal free from blemishes of ambiguity, and that it was submitted 'at the appropriate moment'. The sensitivity was focused, however, rather more on the political and technical ramifications and little concern was placed on producing a supporting financial statement, which was a somewhat *ex post* financial rationalisation (with cash flows etc. 'estimated' so that the desired outcome was produced). It is significant, we feel, that almost no emphasis was placed on identifying, and financially evaluating, alternative investment proposals. The best alternative identified by the mining engineers tended to be the only proposal that was likely to be fully costed. As one engineer involved in capital investment indicated, in relation to the timing of submissions to HQ: '(We start talking) when we decide. We don't hang out our dirty washing there. We only submit when we are sure that we want it and it will go ahead. We can't just make financial decisions, for we are a very political industry.'

Areas have only limited authority to initiate investment proposals. National headquarters carry out strategic management and especially financial planning (often in collaboration with the Department of Energy, a point to which we will return later). The strategic model at HQ consists of a Mining model (supply curves), an Energy model (demand curves), a Matching model, and a DCF model (Plackett et al. 1982). But no one at Area level mentioned or seemed to be aware of the strategic model or the detailed marginal analysis associated with it, both of which might be used for internal management. At Area level, long-run reviews of pits were not based on prospective returns on capital, but on premises of workable capacity supported by rudimentary contribution analysis. Similarly we could find no explicit translation of strategy at national level to collieries, where longer-run planning appeared to be concentrated on geologically feasible capacity and accountability on the twelve-month budget.

Accountability of collieries to Area is focused upon budgeted physical and financial targets, compared to actuals. However, observations indicated that financial and marketing information was cursorily examined in a ritualistic fashion in contrast to the careful consideration of physical factors (e.g. machine delays, mine layouts, and geology). As it was explained to us, 'If you get production right, then finance falls into place', and 'Finance and accounting must not get in the way of managing'.

In contrast, financial matters are highly significant at HQ, especially in relationship to government, where it seems that issues of finance limits, cash resources and marketing opportunities dominate. Yet at Area level, marketing and finance personnel and considerations tended to enter budget processes at very late stages. The discontinuity between finance and operations was underlined by relationships between accountants. Professionally qualified staff were located at Area HQ whereas within collieries the only accounting presence was clerical staff who were responsible to colliery managers and who had little expectation of promotion. Significantly, in the Area we studied, the finance department employed a former colliery cost clerk to interpret and explain the concerns of collieries to Area office.

Further evidence to support the impression of loose coupling came from the computation of accounts at colliery level, especially with respect to revenue, overheads, and the treatment of capital. Such accounts are important in translating marketing and financial criteria to a colliery level. Marketing is a centralised activity in the NCB and sales revenue is imputed to colleries by a formula matching price to quality. The formula is relatively arbitrary, particularly when production becomes inventory, which is stored by the customer or centrally. However, by recording all output at a notional selling price, the accounts reinforce the divorce between operations and marketing problems. Neither collieries nor Areas work with contribution statements; whilst this can be explained by the unwillingness to allow accounting reports to *ex ante* decide what is controllable or not, the resulting confusion about colliery profits points to a lack of significance in accounting reports *per se*. This is reflected in the treatment of capital at a local level. Neither Area nor collieries keep balance sheets. In so far as capital charges enter accounts they do so by historic accrual accounting in the calculation of depreciation. The large capital investment in Areas and collieries did not seem to be a major concern of managers. Further, a widely reported and frequently mentioned indicator of colliery performance is output per shift. Yet this measure of productivity does not take the level of investment into account. The consequence of this particular form of accounting is that labour is recognised as a cost but investment in capital is not. Thus labour-intensive modes of working will appear to be costly (and frequently unprofitable) whilst capital intensive modes of working will appear to be cheap (and also score highly on measures of labour productivity). Such 'accountings' tend to correspond with a pre-disposition towards technical innovation and 'super-pits' which is prevalent amongst mining engineers and indicates that financial accounts can be orientated to supporting technical rather than economic arguments (Williams and Haslam 1985).

Explanations for loose coupling
The above arguments illustrate the strategy of decoupling used to handle contradictions in the management of the labour process in the NCB. Decoupling is used to keep parts of the NCB separate from others and thereby to localise and contain contradictions in the demands placed on the NCB by markets and finance on the one hand and technological considerations on the other. That is to say, the various parts of the NCB (and these 'parts' can represent hierarchical, spatial or functional sub-units of the organisation) may be relatively isolated from, and independent of, one another. Each part can ignore uncertainties, contradictions and conflicts which the other parts are assumed to manage. Loose coupling implies that such uncertainties, contradictions and conflicts are localised and their effects rarely significantly affect other parts of the NCB. Decoupling is essentially an operational strategy, concerned to deal with short-term un-certainties and conflicts. We are not suggesting that managers do not make strategic choices but that within such broad choices, decoupling practices may be used to handle contradictions that arise from the chosen strategy. This broad explanation for decoupling may be elaborated by considering four interrelated reasons for decoupling:

managing different complexities; problems of disseminating information; coping with ambiguity and securing legitimation; and managerial
cleavages and resistance. The subsequent analysis will briefly outline
the first three factors (for more detail see Berry et al. 1985a) and
concentrate on the fourth.

But before proceeding with these explanations it is important to
note that we will, at the end of this section of the paper, show that the
strategy of decoupling may have consequences other than 'merely'
managing contradictions. In particular we will emphasise that the
financial accounts may be used to separate parts of the NCB but they
may also provide a coherent (if partial) discourse for the organisation
as a whole.

The first explanation for loose coupling which we consider is that it
has enabled the NCB to manage different types of complexities,
namely production and technical, as opposed to political and
economic, by sealing each from the problems of the other. Thus the
uncertainties of finance, markets and relations with government,
other state corporations, and bodies such as the TUC and CBI are the
province of HQ, whereas the major production uncertainties are held
at Area level. In such a manner local management can negotiate with
labour emphasising continuity of production and markets, whilst HQ
negotiates with external bodies on the future of coal and the
consequent shape of the industry, relatively untroubled by local
problems. As explained in Berry et al. (1985a) such a system may be
effective for managers in a benign environment, but it experiences
major problems when sharp discontinuities occur. At such times, the
uncertainties and contradictions both within and between parts of the
NCB may result in major conflict and incoherence.

Second, the dissemination of information on a 'need-to-know' basis
may be related to attempts to maintain morale in declining activities.
Pessimistic information on markets and finances which is formally
related to specific pits might hinder attempts to exploit profitably
reserves prior to shutdown, or unnecessarily provoke fears of closures.
Further, given the uneven history of the NCB, any classification of a
particular colliery as 'uneconomic' may be unstable. Changes in energy
demand, currency fluctuations, availability of imported coal or
investment in pits may dramatically upset such classifications. The
idea of 'the need-to-know' also reflected a concern with the disclosure
of sensitive information which might upset the centrally determined
planning parameters.

Third, the decoupling permits an ambiguity about autonomy and
accountability which helps contain internal conflict whilst satisfying
external bodies that rationality and bureaucratic accountability

prevails (Meyer and Rowan 1977). The separation has the benefit of isolating the technical core of the NCB (which is concerned with long-term planning or coal getting) from environmental change (which requires sensitivity to marketing and financial problems). The decoupling permits the internal conflict created by such discontinuities to be minimised. For example, Finance can maintain its position by accepting the data and analysis provided by Mining. Conflict can be minimised by Finance accepting a rationalising and clerical role. And the virtue of accounting documents is that whilst they legitimate a concern for profits and the market, they are sufficiently ambiguous to allow for multiple interpretations. Fluctuations in markets or financing need not be, and in the past have not necessarily been, reflected in the assessments of colliery viability. Similarly, at local levels, the extensive accountability procedures give a façade of concern for financial accountability, but on closer inspection they appear to be ritualistic in many respects (Capps et al. 1984).

Last, and importantly, there remains the position of management, most notably the power of the mining engineering profession in the management of the NCB. This management segment attempts to emphasise the importance of production and dismiss the significance of 'markets' as providing relevant signals for planning. The dominant line core is staffed almost exclusively by mining engineers whose socialisation and training is conducted predominantly within the pit. Mining engineering is seen as essential for general management. Moreover, the methods of mining engineers cannot be divorced from the cultures of mining communities from which they are often drawn and with which they continue to interact. Nor can they be divorced from cultural norms reproduced underground (Mouritsen 1984).

A consequence of this dominant operational culture appears to have been the protection of the productive core of the NCB from the environment (especially finance and marketing 'signals') and a belief that environmental fluctuations and 'fashion' have to be significantly dampened before reaching Area and Colliery.

However, the professional dominance of mining engineers is not unchallenged. Returning to the attempts at standard costing mentioned in the second section, it was suggested to us several times that the 'Mining Mafia' (the nickname given to the mining engineers in the then Production (now Mining) Department by non-mining engineers) had not wanted standard costing to succeed. This corresponds with Armstrong's analysis (1985) of the mediation of control by professionals and the contest between accountants and engineers regarding the introduction of scientific management. The failure of standard costing at a time when physical standards remain intact would seem partly to be explained by inter-professional competition to dominate control strategies.

If the management contains similar antagonistic relations as is contained in the process of production then one might expect some expression of such antagonism within management. Managerial conflicts have been discussed in the literature of financial controls and information systems (e.g. Hopwood 1973; Argyris 1971; Mintzberg 1975). It has been increasingly recognised that the mechanistic conceptions of information and financial controls depicted in textbooks and espoused by management often do not operate in the manner described. Often financial information is not used and instead some other criteria form the basis of management decision-making. Indeed the relationship between information and decision-making may be quite problematic. Treating the organisation as an anarchy (March and Olsen 1976; Cooper et al. 1981) or stressing the symbolic legitimising and rationalising dimensions of information (Pettigrew 1979, Burchell et al 1980; March and Feldman 1981) casts doubt on the ability of any single group in an organisation to determine policies. The autonomy of individual managers and groups to create an organisational space for themselves may indeed be related to their use of information. Meyer and Rowan (1977) talk of the 'celebration of rationality' whereby managers can produce an image of rationality and legitimacy by displaying information systems as an allegedly well-used decision support system. Information systems may be 'used' not so much as a basis for decision-making, but as a means of demonstrating the competence of decision-makers. As the previously reported research in this paper evidences, such behaviour abounded in the NCB.

Information may also be withheld or manipulated to create organisational space. We have discussed this in a previous section with regard to the transmission of information down the NCB hierarchy and the pervasiveness of the 'need-to-know' attitude. With regard to upward communication, studies by Cyert and March (1963), Lowe and Shaw (1968) and Berry and Otley (1975) investigated the causes and nature of both deliberate and non-deliberate biasing of estimates in organisations. The latter two studies in particular indicate that in both private and public sector organisations, superiors were unable to counter-bias adequately the estimates of their subordinates. Whilst these studies focus on budgetary information, our own study suggested that 'actual' as well as budget information is manipulated. The NCB has recognised the concept of 'slack' in budget information by instituting 'relaxation factors' in its budgeting procedures

(Monopolies and Mergers Commission 1983) but it has not been able to create an equivalent system to counter the manipulation of actual data (except to recognise the unreliability of all information, whether produced by computerised systems or not). The unreliability of 'actual' information, which has also been recognised in other contexts (e.g. Wilensky, 1967; Hopwood 1973; Otley 1978) renders problematic the informational basis for decision-making.

The image of information as a source of confusion rather than enlightenment is clearly contrary to most popular and commonsense conceptions of information and rational decision-making. And we suspect that, at least in the NCB, some strategies to reduce confusion may, in fact, enhance it. Wilensky's observations on military intelligence (Wilensky 1967) suggest the significance of hierarchy, specialisation, centralisation and mistrust as sources of distortion. 'Hierarchy is conducive to concealment and mis-representation... lines of organisations become lines of loyalty and secrecy; each department restricts information that might advance the competing interests of the others ... An emphasis on secret information ... can demoralise an organisation' (Wilensky 1967: 120–6).

Within the NCB the possibility that information can be a source of confusion is implicitly recognised by the use of multiple channels of communication. No one source of information is relied upon, or indeed trusted. Yet the use of multiple channels increases defensive and evasive behaviour by managers as does the management of information as a strategy to enhance managerial freedom of action. Thus a cycle of confusion and misrepresentation becomes part of the labour process in administration.

Financial information and discourse in organisation

We have sought in the above discussion to emphasise the conflicts that may occur within management and in particular the role of information in creating confusion as well as illumination. We emphasise this dimension of management partly to compensate for the overly rational and deterministic approach found in most discussions of management strategies (Edwards 1979). Yet in doing so, we do not wish to deny the argument that financial control can actively mould the language and taken-for-granted view of the world of all those involved in the labour process. Further, this language and view is heavily loaded in favour of capital (Tinker 1980; Tinker et al. 1982; Cooper and Sherer 1984). All managers we talked to in the NCB believed that the 'bottom line' of the industry was profit; not safety, contribution to society, employment, satisfying work or any other measure of performance. As one manager saw it: 'I don't want to work in a bloody charity'. Although miners and most mining engineers and general managers in the NCB tended to avoid using financial information, they had internalised the logic that profit and loss were the absolute measures of performance, the bottom line. Further, and most significantly, whilst they actively 'managed' or manipulated information in their day-to-day activities, when they were provided with financial information they normally accepted it as unproblematic. They tended not to actively recognise that 'profit' can be calculated in a vast manner of different ways (Hird 1983). Financial controls generally tend to be taken as part of the objective formal structures of control within organisations. Although financial information may not be believed or ostensibly may even be ignored, such information may fundamentally influence almost everyone's view of the world. Together with personnel policies and the development of corporate 'cultures', they may be particularly significant techniques used by senior management to control unobtrusively through influencing decision-makers' premises and values rather than the decisions themselves.

Ouchi (1979) emphasises the structural and motivational mechanisms to create 'clan' cultures and Burawoy (1979) emphasises the subjective factors that help to manufacture consent. Further, as critics of Burawoy have pointed out, organisations may also look to the state to help create a compliant and uncritical workforce. Such considerations illustrate the need to recognise the inter-related roles of corporations and the state in social co-ordination, an issue we develop below. With regard to accounting and finance, it is clear that they provide a 'vocabulary of motive' (Batstone 1979) that facilitates the diffusion of managerialist definitions of situations; they identify what is to be measured, and how, who is to report to whom and what is regarded as valuable (Cooper et al. 1981). Financial information makes possible the identification of the success of segments of an organisation (e.g. a pit) and the success itself becomes defined in terms of the particular regime of measurement.

Implications for the managerial labour process
We have emphasised the contradictory position of management and the significance and variety of uses and consequences of financial information in managing the labour process. Our discussion, based on our observations of managerial practices in the NCB, indicates that not only are control systems mediated through resistance on the part of production workers, but they are similarly shaped by managerial desires for autonomy. Managerial agency and compliance cannot be assumed. Second, fractions of the managerial class are themselves

involved in competition for controls. Interprofessional rivalries may frequently produce unanticipated consequences. Third, systems of realisation are inevitably closely related to systems of control of management. Braverman (1974), for example, states: 'management has become administration, which is itself conducted for the purpose of control within the corporation.' Managers may frequently resist management controls through building in slack, manipulation, over-adherence to rules etc.

Fourth, management is, as has been noted by others (Wright 1976, Crompton 1976) in an ambivalent position within class structures. Whilst not wanting to suggest that mining engineers act as champions for the miners, some overlap of interest occurs. Fifth, managers have to live with some of the contradictions within capitalism. Thus uncertainties not captured in financial data or areas of space to contain conflict not granted, must be accommodated, frequently by amelioration of the measurement and control system itself. Perhaps intuitively, management often acknowledges that to rely exclusively on crude capitalist methods of appropriation would render organisations unmanageable (Friedman 1977). Given its contradictory relationship, management may substantially resist and modify controls according to values and ends that appear to be alternative to those of capital. Finally, we have drawn attention to the hegemonic characteristics of financial information, which means that the very language of management is inherently imbued with assumptions that support capital.

The State, Finance and Control
One significant element of our argument thus far has been that a focus on control at the point of production, as is typical in much of the literature on the labour process (e.g. Edwards 1979; Braverman 1974, Knights et al. 1985), may lead to misleading conclusions about the control of the labour process. In the case of the NCB, formal administrative controls may be largely ineffective and management may display internal conflicts, yet managerial control may still be effected through the discourse of the organisation (profit is the 'bottom line') and through managerial practices such as decoupling. Further, control of the labour process is not a static phenomenon but is constantly changing, partly because of the dynamic nature of capitalism itself.

Thus, a problem with an emphasis on control at the point of production is that links between such controls and developments in capitalism may not be appreciated. Of course it could be argued that the two spheres are themselves largely autonomous, but our observations at the NCB suggest that the autonomy of management and practices within the enterprise can be significantly affected by developments in capitalism more generally. In this section we illustrate how the state has acted to encourage changes in the NCB and how these changes reflect developments in British capitalism. Our focus is undoubtedly partial in that we do not provide a coherent theory of the state and its relationship to capital (Jessop 1982). Nor do we attempt to explore explicity the role of the state in industrial relations (as was evidenced during the coal strike of the 1984-5), in the provision of welfare services and demand management, although these roles may all affect the NCB and nationalised industries more generally. The state can play a significant part in sustaining or undermining specific capitalist enterprises, adjudicating in conflicts between specific capitals or in facilitating (or not) the private accumulation of capital. Whilst there have been important analyses of these roles of the state (e.g. Offe 1984), these have typically not been well connected with discussions about the labour process and the organisation and control of enterprises.

This section attempts to connect analyses of the state with those of the labour process, largely by focusing on the mechanisms by which state policies are translated into the practices of a specific enterprise, namely the NCB. Whilst there have been a few recent attempts to link developments in capitalism and the state with the labour process (Gordon et al. 1982), less attention has been paid to the mechanisms or micro-technologies (Foucault 1977) that link the state to specific enterprises. One illustration of this linking of the state with enterprise policies is Krieger's study (1983) of the introduction of a national wage payment system in the NCB. This section offers a further illustration which focuses on the use of financial controls as a mechanism for linking state policies to enterprise practices. Whilst the illustration is written in the context of our study of the NCB in the early 1980s, similar processes seem to have been occurring elsewhere in British society, notably in the health sector (DHSS 1983) and local government.

In particular, reflections upon our investigation in the NCB reinforce recent arguments that have sought to link the labour process and the state. First, we show how the state, by encouraging and enhancing the finance function in the NCB, can produce changes to management approaches to the control of the labour process. We suggest that the language and approaches of financial management are encouraged as mechanisms for controlling the labour process. Second, we show that the state plays an important role in disciplining labour and securing the accumulation of capital by its industrial and energy policy. By emphasising the international division of labour (Wallerstein 1974; Frobel et al. 1980) and supporting the notion of an international coal market, the state arranges the distribution of surplus value around the economy, notably between private and state capitals and between national and international capitals. The remainder of the paper elaborates these two, interlocking, processes of enhancing finance and emphasising international markets.

The state's involvement in management
An overwhelming impression of our research in the NCB was the way in which the language of financial management was consciously being cultivated in the industry and the increasing role and significance of the finance function in influencing managerial practices. Our observations also suggested that these processes were being stimulated by pressures from the state, notably through the increasing significance of the Treasury and the financial constraints imposed on the industry.

The nationalised industries in Britain have always been subject to intervention by their sponsoring ministry which, in the case of the NCB, is the Department of Energy. Indeed, at various times in the past there has been a concern to develop an energy policy and this has been reflected in various tripartite, corporatist, agreements about the coal mining industry. However, since the late 1970s, the Treasury and the Department of Trade and Industry have taken an increasingly active role. The Treasury has made its influence felt through its pursuit of cash limits and the control of the public sector borrowing requirement (PSBR) and the latter, through the use of *ad hoc* investigations and audits by, the Monopolies and Mergers Commission, has emphasised internal 'efficiency', as defined by private sector conceptions of input-output ratios and 'good management practice'.

As illustrated in Hopwood and Tomkins (1984), such influences are increasingly pervasive in government and the public sector. As one White Paper argued: 'An essential element in departments' plan is therefore better information as a basis of action' (Cmnd, 9058, 1983, p.2). Despite initial enthusiasm (e.g. Cmnd 9297, 1984) the ability to increase the role of financial management in central government remains problematic. Kellner and Hunt (1980) argue that civil servants have consistently been successful in resisting the use of specialists in the Civil Service and the adoption of management methods. Yet the current enthusiasm of at least some individuals to apply 'best business practice' (as indicated in the Treasury and Civil Service Committee 1982) seems to be infecting considerable areas of

Central Government administration. Although current developments may be regarded as part of a long line of failed administrative experiments in the Civil Service (e.g. PPBS, MBO, PESC, programme evaluation), there are grounds to believe that financial information systems are being seen increasingly as a major part of the control of public expenditure and, more significantly for the NCB, in the control of public sector organisations. Indeed, we would suggest that Civil Servants might, in resisting such systems to control the activities of their own departments, have a considerable incentive to demonstrate their loyalty, rationality and therefore commitment to the development of information systems by imposing them on other bodies such as nationalised industries.

The NCB is affected by such developments in the Department of Energy. In 1982 the Department introduced a Department of Energy Management Information System (DEMIS) although up to 1984 it has only committed about £200,000 a year to implementing its espoused plans to improve financial management within the department. It would appear to be more interested in encouraging the nationalised industries to be more efficient and effective. For example, each month members of the finance department of the NCB meet with departmental and Treasury officials to discuss the monthly monitoring return. Together with the Nationalised Industries Financial Information System, these returns serve as the basis for the quarterly accountability meetings between the Board and the Department of Energy (with the Treasury also involved). Since these documents emphasise flow of funds, government financing and the progress of capital projects, it is perhaps not surprising that the role of the finance department in the NCB in this process has increased quite extensively in recent years. Without detailed observation of this process we cannot be sure whether that involvement is more apparent than real, but interviews with headquarters personnel in all departments reinforced our view of the significance of finance in the process and the consequent enhanced status of finance in the NCB. This enhanced status has resulted in the development of financial information systems that challenge the traditional supremacy of the mining department in investment decision-making and planning in general. Further, the finance department increasingly sees a role for itself in the management of Area and collieries; it is beginning to carve its way down the management hierarchy, partly at least through the introduction of new information systems and indicators of performance.

Thus the influence of the state is becoming increasingly evident through finance at NCB headquarters and HQ's presence too, is becoming increasingly evident in Area, both in terms of personnel and attitudes. The introduction of cash limits by the Treasury in the late 1970s, and the use of information systems to monitor performance, together with the recession in coal demand and energy in general, increase the significance of finance and marketing. These functions have increased in external legitimacy since, as we show below, they fit in with current notions of economic fitness and market rationality which appear to dominate thinking about the nationalised industries in the 1980s. In short, the concerns of government departments and HQ functions (and personnel) are permeating the activities of the Areas and, to a degree, the collieries.

However, our discussions at HQ emphasised that this involvement is not concerned with managing Area problems *per se*. Rather the purpose seems to be to make issues of cash flow, return on investment and economic efficiency, also the concerns of the Area. There is increasing pressure to invest in new and more pervasive forms of information and accountability in order to cope with external regulators, to demonstrate the rationality and efficiency of the organisation (Meyer and Rowan 1977). The investment in information is not based primarily on internally generated needs. One consequence of such a strategy is an increasing concern by the technical core (engineering professionals) about the influence of externally legitimated groups. Such concern results not only from the feeling that such influence is unnecessary as far as the internal (production) logic is concerned but also because such influence tends to upset their power, career patterns and expectations. The increasing pervasiveness of the spokesman for the environment into the technical core of the oganisation may produce increasing conflict within management in the future.

Thus we witnessed the increasing pressure of the state being exerted, largely through the finance department, throughout the NCB. Although something of a simplification, it seems that Head Office staff (particularly in finance) and increasingly those in Areas who have upward mobility aspirations, tend to have sympathy for the ideology of market 'fitness', clearly espoused by government. Mining engineers within pits, and those in Area and Headquarters who have less strong career aspirations tend to resist this pressure, instead emphasising the importance of stability of production, safety, strategic issues in national energy policy and the dangers of using market prices (particularly international ones) as a guide to long-term policy.

The different models of management control had been able to co-exist in a decoupled organisation structure and with a powerful mining engineering profession. These are currently being undermined as a result of active government policies. After Mr McGregor's appointment as NCB Chairman in 1983 and the publication of the Monopolies and Mergers Commission Report, a consulting firm was appointed and it became apparent (both from our observations, interviews and from leaks in the press) that central planning and co-ordination at Headquarters were likely to be sharply cut back. Whilst the strike of 1984–5 may have delayed some of these changes, it seems probable that many will be introduced soon after. Marketing and Finance may be delegated to newly constituted Areas. Pits and Areas will cease to be measured and evaluated as production centres but rather as investment or business centres. The accent will be on localised, rather than national wage agreements. If these inferences are correct, then it is likely that they will be justified in terms of economic efficiency, especially with regard to making the organisation more market-orientated.

A consequence of such re-organisation would be to strengthen management's control of the labour process as the union becomes more fragmented and less capable of offering resistance to closures and restructuring of the industry as a whole. The state would have thereby introduced a mechanism whereby the coal mining industry was disciplined by the 'market'. This attempt to de-politicise the industry (a process which may, of course, be seen to reorientate the industry to consider only short-run economic considerations) would weaken the unions and tend to make worker control at the point of production something of an irrelevance.

Further, a decentralised coal industry offers the possibility of changing patterns of ownership and shifting 'profitable' parts to the private sector. As we have indicated previously, the present system of accounting does not clearly identify sub-profitable collieries or Areas. In part this may be deliberate, owing to the inherent uncertainties surrounding such measures if used for predictive purposes, due to the unpredictability and variability in mining conditions. To illustrate, the NCB's colliery costs per tonne of coal 'varied from its average cost per tonne by 16 per cent, so there could be variation from one year to another by over 30 per cent up or down' (MMC 1983, p. 30). Despite the variabilities, newer systems focusing on cash flows and returns on investments are being introduced to evaluate pits. These measures are likely to be seen as part of an 'objective' picture painted by accounting and finance and their introduction is justified on the basis of the logics of markets and efficiency.

Similarly the decentralisation, by stressing competition and differential benefits and losses to workpeople throughout the industry, is likely to weaken the powers of trade unions achieved through national negotiation and action, particularly in the context of high unemployment levels and workers' fears for job security. Given the ability to sectionalise the industry through reorganisation, through a number of competitive divisions, one of the 'problems' identified by Edwards in relation to bureaucratic control, namely the creation of a large fixed labour cost, may be alleviated. Management may once again be in the position to treat a proportion of its labour as a variable cost.

Thus, in short, given the trade union's inability to control the superordinate control structure and ethos of the organisation, the benefits accruing from local resistance to management and from control of underground operations is likely to be localised and transitory. And a strategy of the state to discipline and punish labour coincides conveniently with other elements of the ideology of government, notably a hostility to public ownership, a commitment to market forces and a concern for finance capital (Longstreth 1979; Ingham 1984).

'Arranging' surplus value

As well as influencing management strategies of control, the state has been involved in influencing the distribution of surplus value around the economy. This influence has been achieved through its energy policy (which has normally been implicit) and its industrial and financial policy. In relation to energy policy it is important to recognise the interdependence of the UK energy sector. Over 70 per cent of coal sales are to the electricity supply industry, and until the privatisation of Britoil, much of the British demand for electricity was supplied by state-controlled sources of coal, oil and nuclear energy. Since the recession which began in the late 1970s, the deep mined coal industry has borne the brunt of the reduced demand for electricity. And the role of the state is crucial in this squeeze on the NCB. As O'Donnell argues (1985) 'what needs to be explained is why these (demand) constraints have proved so binding given that the institutional mechanisms necessary to coordinate energy provision within Britain have formally existed since nationalisation' (p. 117). Whilst deep mined coal consumption has slumped, other industries which supply the energy for electricity generation, notably privately owned open cast mining and the nuclear industry, have expanded output and profits.

Similar processes have occurred in relation to industrial policy. The decline of British manufacturing industry, which has been part of the international division of labour and which has been facilitated by various measures initiated by the state (e.g. abolition of exchange controls, trade liberalisation), has had the consequence of halving the British steel industry, which has been the second largest customer, after the electricity generation industry, of deep mined coal. Heavy investment by the NCB in the mid 1970s to make its coal suitable for BSC, had added to the interest burden of the NCB without a matching profit from sales.

The decline in British steel and coal production has been exacerbated by a further aspect of the practices of the UK state. The general rhetoric about 'market' prices and discipline has been translated, at least for the NCB, in the use of a so-called international coal market to discipline the NCB. This market is, in reality, rather thin (only 7 per cent of world coal consumption is based on this market) and prices are highly variable. Further, with over-capacity in the world , prices are so low that coal producers are not trading at a profit. Yet the NCB is expected, in its negotiations with BSC and CEGB, to price its coal in line with these prices and investment funds are restricted because of its failure to make a profit.

One consequence of these energy and industrial policies is that surplus value generated by coal extraction is distributed out of the public sector coal industry and into private industry generally. We are suggesting that one mechanism for the state to influence the labour process in the coal industry is through statements of profit and loss. Profits can be recognised anywhere in the energy and industrial sectors if the state can have influence on pricing and investment policies. This is because the raw material costs of the electricity supply industry are the revenues of the coal industry and the energy costs of industry are the revenues of the electricity supply industry. Cheap coal leaves the NCB with large 'losses' and either the CEGB or industry generally with profits larger than they would otherwise be. Of course, managers committed to 'their' industry may be able to resist crude attempts at manipulation, and it is true that the direction and intensity of state policy in relation to the NCB has been variable since nationalisation; but this is merely to say that the use of a mechanism of state power is variable. Nevertheless, in the recent past, by identifying the NCB as 'loss making', the accounting statements provide the Treasury with a rationale to restrict investment in the industry, and provide NCB management with the ability to control the labour process through closures (and threatened closures). This power to distribute surplus around the economy as a result of the 'objective' messages of relative profitability provided by accounting reports, is rarely recognised or contested by the parties themselves.

The obvious question that arises from this analysis is why has the state not favoured the NCB? It can be argued that searching for the motives, interests or objectives of the state is a fruitless and possibly impossible task (Foucault 1977). Whilst we have some sympathy with this epistemological position, conjectures on this question will, we believe, provide important insights into developments of the British state and the ways in which the state is implicated in the labour process.

Following Offe (1984) and Habermas (1976) our starting point is that the state is enmeshed in the contraditions of capitalism. On the one hand it must sustain the process of accumulation and the private appropriation of resources. The stability of the state relies on those who produce resources – for example, tax revenue is important to sustain state activities. The state has an interest in ensuring the success of the capitalist economy. On the other hand, the state must preserve a belief that it is an impartial arbiter in social conflict. The subordinate class has won historic victories which limit the accumulation of capital – for example, the introduction of a welfare system and of periodic democratic processes. The state is vulnerable to democratic processes and even revolution if its power is not legitimised. The behaviour of the state is likely to change as it responds to crises of accumulation and of legitimation:

'it must maintain the accumulation process without undermining *private* accumulation or the belief in the market as a fair distributor of scarce resources. Intervention into the economy is unavoidable and yet the exercise of political control over the economy risks challenging the traditional basis of the legitimacy of the whole social order – the belief that collective goals can be properly realised only by private individuals acting in competitive isolation and pursuing their sectoral aims with minimal state interference' (Held and Krieger 1984, p. 16).

No particular approach of the state is likely to be permanently adequate for solving the state's problems of crisis management in a capitalist society (Offe 1975). Returning to the NCB-state relationship, we would suggest that the state has, in effect, been arbitrating both between different capitals (notably the international oil companies but also more recently the nuclear and construction industry and the coal industry) and between labour and capital. The more interventionist and hostile actions of the state since 1978 reflect changing balances of social forces. Notably, the failure of corporatist type arrangements for the management of crisis in the mid 1970s provided a legitimate reason for attacking the power of labour and the relative strength of the Coal Board *vis-a-vis* other capitalist enterprises. At the same time the state attempted to de-politicise its own actions by re-asserting the significance of 'neutral' markets. The corporatist form of intervention based on direct intervention and social reforms has given way to a 'private' form of intervention with market-orientated economic management and repressive social policies. Since 1978, the NCB has been encouraged to respond to market pressures, to simulate the market in its own organisation and to roll back the gains made by labour in its control of the labour process. However, the varying success of achieving pit closures indicates that the precise forms, strategies and effects of these interventions are problematic.

Implications for locating the state within the labour and valorisation process
Our discussions of the state's involvement in management by enhancing the role of finance and the state's involvement in the realisation of surplus value in the economy are both intended to emphasise that studying the labour process within an enterprise will provide an inadequate analysis of the control of work and the consequences of that control. We suggest that financial management and accounting statements are mechanisms by which the State can unobtrusively manage the activities of enterprises. We recognise, however that the purpose and outcomes of this management may not result in a consistent strategy, except that of managing periodic crises (for which there may be both an ideological and materialist explanation). We would suggest that our investigations in, and observations of, the NCB reinforce several recent arguments in the literature on the labour process, the state and the new middle classes. First, our discussions parallel Burawoy's arguments about the 'securing and obscuring of surplus value' (Burawoy 1978). The state, by its encouragement of the finance department in the NCB, laid the basis of the ideology of 'free and equal' exchange, based on the 'natural' workings of the market, but projected as a neutral accounting technology. Burawoy (1978, p. 281) summarises the position: 'As Habermas puts it, rationality from below (science as the pursuit of efficiency) merges with rationality from above (science as ideology) and in this way both obscures capitalist relations of production and legitimates state intervention as non-political because scientific (Habermas, 1971). Financial assessments of individual collieries and areas of the industry as a whole are predicated on a system of market exchange which is presented as neutral technique. The ideological basis of management control is shifted from direct discipline in the labour process to an impersonal financial logic which obscures the relationship between work and the realisation of surplus value.

Second, our observations serve to emphasise the importance of social structures of accumulation (Gordon et al. 1982). Whilst such structures include the institutions involved in the reproduction of labour, systems of class struggle and exchange and credit arrangements, we have focused on state involvement in investment and pricing. The state, in its role of determining financing limits and imposing objectives on a nationalised industry (e.g. NCB 1983, p. 3) creates the constraints and opportunities for investment and the possibilities for capital accumulation. As we have seen in our discussion of investment patterns in the NCB, 'the state can enhance investment (through subsidies, enforcement of regulations, greater commodity purchases, and so forth) or diminish it (through taxation, regulation, legitimising unions, and so forth)' (Gordon et al. 1982, p. 24). The relationships between the NCB, CEGB, BR and BSC are indeed complex, but there is at least a reasonable suspicion that both the level of profits and investment in the NCB has been held low through state involvement in the regulation of 'energy policy'. However, this has been an uneven process, affecting some Areas considerably more than others and being more intensive in some periods.

A third issue raised by our analysis of the NCB is the role of professions in the global function of capital and the class position of the new middle class. Following Cardechi (1977), it would appear that the state's involvement in furthering the interests of finance (and the accounting profession) at the expense of production and engineering within the NCB illustrates the process by which the labour process is subordinated to the surplus value producing process. Johnson (1977) emphasises the importance of the accounting profession in the realisation of surplus value and that the fragmentation of that profession may itself be analysed in terms of the differing forms of knowledge (especially indetermination) associated with specific aspects of the realisation of surplus value (i.e. the distinction between bookkeepers and information systems designers). The peculiar and historically very recent significance of the accounting profession in the British capitalist system deserves further study. Although the work of Johnson (1977), Armstrong (1985) and Abercrombie and Urry (1983) suggest links between knowledge, power and surplus value, it would require an international study to elucidate the role of professions and especially the accounting profession in the obscuring and securing of surplus value and the role of the State in enhancing the significance of particular professions (Larson 1977).

Conclusion

This paper, based on a study of control in the NCB, emphasises the importance of financial control strategies in the labour process literature. A consideration of financial control offers the opportunity to systematically consider the relationship between the labour process and the surplus value producing process. Whilst we have not developed these issues as fully as we would wish, the paper can be seen as a statement against determinism and reductionism. Focusing on the point of production fails to recognise the role of finance in obscuring and realising surplus value. This may be affected by structures and agents in society more generally. But recognising that there are social structures of accumulation need not lead to a deterministic approach: the actions of the state and of management are mediated by individual agents and professions. To understand adequately processes of control, it would seem necessary to investigate seriously the specific mechanisms of control. In this paper we have focused on financial controls and management as illustrations of such an approach.

Notes

1. Details of the research site, the research methods, and initial findings of the two initial research phases can be found in Berry et al. (1985a) and Capps et al. (1984). Owing to limitations of space such details are omitted from this paper. To a considerable extent this paper represents a retrospective explanation of events observed during an 'interpretive' oriented study. The change to a more 'radical' framework for analysis was in part due to the inability of 'interpretive' frameworks to explicate satisfactorily phenomena observed, not least conflict at local and national levels of analysis.
2. We do not attempt to theorise the significance of such factors nor whether others (e.g. gender) ought to be considered.
3. It must be stressed that industrial relations was a very minor aspect of the study and the researcher's access to trade unions and miners was restricted. In contrast, we had apparently open access to, and co-operation with, management in relation to their own practices and meetings.

References

Abercrombie, N. and Urry, J. (1983), *Capital, Labour and the Middle Classes*, London: Allen and Unwin.

Argyris, C. (1971), 'Management Information Systems: The Challenge to Rationality and Emotionality', *Management Science*, February, 275–92.

Armstrong, P. (1985), 'Competition Between the Organisational Professions and the Evolution of Management Control Strategies', *Accounting Organisations and Society*.

Baran, P. A., and Sweezy, P. M. (1968) *Monopoly Capital*, Harmondsworth: Penguin.

Batstone, E. (1979), Systems of Domination, Accommodation and Industrial Democracy, in T. R. Burns, L. Karlsson and V. Rus, *Work and Power: The Liberation of Work and Control of Political Power*, London: Sage Publications, 249–72.

Berry, A. J., Capps, T., Cooper, D., Ferguson, P., Hopper, T., and Lowe, T., (1985a), 'Management Control in an Area of the National Coal Board', *Accounting, Organisations and Society*.

Berry, A. J., Capps, T., Cooper, D., Hopper, T. and Lowe, T., (1985b), 'NCB Accounts - A Mine of Misinformation?' *Accountancy*, January.

Berry, A. T. and Otley, D. T. (1975), 'The Aggregation of Estimates in Hierarchical Organisations', *Journal of Management Studies*, **12** (2), May 175-93.

Bower, J. (1970), *Managing the Resource Allocation Process*, Homewood, Illinois: Irwin.

Braverman, H. (1974), *Labor and Monopoly Capital*, New York: Monthly Review Press.

Buchanan, D. and Boddy, D. (1982), *Organisations in the Computer Age: Technological Imperatives and Strategic Choice*, Aldershot: Gower.

Burawoy, M. (1978), 'Toward a Marxist Theory of the Labour Process: Braverman and Beyond', *Politics and Society*, **8**, 247-312.

Burawoy, M. (1979), *Manufacturing Consent: Changes in Labour Process under Monopoly Capitalism*, Chicago: Chicago University Press.

Burawoy, M. (1985), *The Politics of Production*, London: Verso Books.

Burchell, S., Clubb, C., Hopwood, A., Hughes, J. and Nahapiet, J. (1980), 'The Role of Accounting in Organisations and Society', *Accounting, Organisations and Society*, **5**, (1) 5-27.

Burns, A., Newby, M., and Winterton J. (1985), 'The restructuring of the British Coal Industry', *Cambridge Journal of Economics*, **9**, 93-110.

Capps, T., Cooper, D., Hopper, T., and Lowe, E.A. (1984), *Accountability and Control within the North Derbyshire Area of the NCB*, Report to the ERSC.

Cardechi, G., (1977), *On the Economic Identification of Social Classes*, London: Routledge and Kegan Paul.

Cmnd 9058 (1983), *Financial Management in Government Departments*, London: HMSO.

Cmnd 9297 (1983), *Progress in Financial Management in Government*, London: HMSO.

Cooper, D. J., Hayes, D. and Wolf, F. (1981) 'Accounting in Organised Anarchies: Understanding and Designing Accounting Systems in Ambiguous Situations', *Accounting, Organisations and Society* **6**, (3), 175-91.

Cooper, D. J. and Sherer, M. J. (1984), 'The Value of Corporate Annual Reports: Arguments for a Political Economy of Accounting', *Accounting, Organisations and Society*, 207-32.

Crompton, R. (1976), 'Approaches to the study of white collar unionism', *Sociology*, **19**, 407-26.

Crompton, R and Jones, G. (1984), *Proletarisation of Work*, London: Macmillan.

Cyert, R. M. and March, J. J. (1963), *A Behavioural Theory of the Firm*, Englewood Cliffs, N. J.: Prentice-Hall.

Dalton, M. (1959), *Men who Manage*, New York: John Wiley.

Dew, R. and Gee K. (1973), *Management Control and Information*, London: Macmillan.

Douglass, D. and Krieger J. (1983), *A Miner's Life*, London: Routledge and Kegan Paul.

Department of Health & Social Security (DHSS) (1983), *Report of the NHS Management Enquiry* London: HMSO.

Edwards, C. (1983), 'Power and Decision Making in the Workplace: A Study in the Coal Mining Industry', *Industrial Relations Journal*, Spring, 50-69.

Edwards, R. (1979), *Contested Terrain: The Transformation of the Workplace in the Twentieth Century*, New York: Basic Books.

Fine, B., O'Donnell K. and Prevezer M. (1983), 'Coal After Nationalisation', Birkbeck College Discussion Paper, no. 138, March.

140   Managing the Labour Process

Foucault, M. (1977), *Discipline and Punish: The Birth of the Prison*, London: Allen Lane.
Friedman, A. (1977), *Industry and Labour: Class Struggle at Work and Monopoly Capitalism* London: Macmillan.
Frobel, F., Heinrichs J. and Kreye O. (1980), *The New International Division of Labour*, Cambridge: Cambridge University Press.
Giddens, A. (1981), *A Contemporary Critique of Historical Materialism: Vol. 1: Power, Property and the State*, London: Macmillan.
Goffee, R. (1981), 'Incorporation and Conflict: A case study in the coal industry', *Sociological Review*, **29** (3), 475–97.
Gordon, D. M., Evans R. and Reich M. (1982), *Segmented Work, Divided Workers: The Historical Transformation of Labour in the United States*, Cambridge: Cambridge University Press.
Gouldner, A. W. (1954), *Patterns of Industrial Bureaucracy*, New York, Free Press.
Habermas, J. (1971), *Toward a Rational Society*, London: Heinemann Educational.
Habermas, J. (1976), *Legitimation Crisis* London: Heinemann.
Hall, T. (1981), *King Coal*, Harmondsworth: Penguin.
Handy, L. J. (1981), *Wages Policy in the British Coalmining Industry*, Cambridge: Cambridge University Press.
Held, D. and Krieger, J. (1984), 'Theories of the State: Some Competing Claims' in S. Bornstein, D. Hold and J. Krieger (eds) *The State in Capitalist Europe*, London: Allen and Unwin.
Hird, C. (1983), *Challenging the Figures: A Guide to Company Finance & Accounts*, London: Pluto Press.
Hopwood, A. G., (1973), *An Accounting System and Managerial Behaviour*, Farnborough: Saxon House.
Hopwood, A. G., Burchell, S. and Clubb C. (1979), 'The Development of Accounting in the International Context: Past Concerns and Emergent Issues' in A. Roberts (ed.) *An Historical and Contemporary Review of the Development of International Accounting*, Georgia: Georgia State University.
Hopwood, A. G. and Tomkins, C. (eds) (1984) *Issues in Public Sector Accounting*, Oxford: Philip Allan.
Ingham, G. (1984), *Capitalism Divided? The City and Industry in British Social Development*, London: Macmillan.
Jessop, B. (1982), *The Capitalist State*, Oxford: Martin Robertson.
Johnson, T. J. (1977), 'The Professions in the Class Structure' in R. Scase (ed.) *Industrial Society: Class, Cleavage and Control*, London: Allen and Unwin, 93–110.
Kellner, P., and Hunt N. C. (1980), *The Civil Service: A New Ruling Class*, London: Macdonald.
Knights, D., Willmott H, and Collinson D., (eds) (1985), *Job Redesign: Critical Perspectives on the Labour Process*, Aldershot: Gower.
Kotter, J. P. (1982), *The General Managers*, New York: Free Press.
Krieger, J. (1984), *Undermining Capitalism*, working paper: Princeton University Press, London: Pluto Press.
Larson, M. S. (1977), *The Rise of Professionalism: A Sociological Analysis*, London: University of California Press.
Longstreth, F. (1979), 'The City, Industry and the State', in C. Crouch (ed.) *State and Economy in Contemporary Capitalism*, London: Croom Helm, 157–90.
Lowe, E. A. and Shaw, R. W. (1968), 'An analysis of Managerial Biasing: Evidence from a Company's Budgeting Process', *Journal of Management Studies*, **5**, (3).
March, J. G. and Feldman, M. S. (1981), 'Information in Organisations as Signal and Symbol', *Administrative Science Quarterly*, **26**, (2), 171–86.
March, J. G. and Olsen, J. P. (1976), *Ambiguity and Choice in Organisations*, Bergen, Norway: Universitetsforlaget.

Meyer, J. W. and Rowan, B. (1977), Institutionalised Organisation: Formal Structure as Myth and Ceremony, *American Journal of Sociology*, **83**.

Mintzberg, H. (1973), *The Nature of Managerial Work*, New York: Harper and Row.

Mintzberg, H. (1975), *Impediments to the Use of Management Information*, New York: National Association of Accountants.

Monopolies and Mergers Commission (1983), *National Coal Board: Volumes 1 and 2*, Cmnd 8920, London: HMSO.

Mouritsen, J. (1984), *The Role of Financing Collieries*, unpublished M.A. dissertation University of Shefffield.

National Coal Board (1983), *Annual Report and Accounts 1982*-1983, London: NCB.

O'Donnell, K. (1985), 'Brought to Account: The NCB and the Case for Coal' *Capital and Class* **26** (Summer), 105-24.

Offe, C. (1975), 'The Theory of the Capitalist State and the Problem of Policy Formation' in L. Lindberg, R. Alford, C. Crouch and C. Offe (eds), *Stress and Contradiction in Modern Capitalism*, Lexington, Mass: Lexington Books, 245-59.

Offe, C. (1984), *Contradictions of the Welfare State*, London: Hutchinson.

Otley, D.T. (1978), 'Budget Use and Managerial Performance' *Journal of Accounting Research*, **16**, (1) (Spring) 122-49.

Ouchi, W. (1979), 'A Conceptual Framework for the Design of Organisational Control Mechanisms', *Management Science*, **25**, 833-48.

Pettigrew, A. (1979), 'On Studying Organisational Cultures', *Administrative Science Quarterly*, **24**, (4) 570-81.

Plackett, M. W., Ormerod R. J. and Toft F. J. (1982), The National Coal Board Strategic Model, European Journal of Operational Research, **10**, (4) 351-50.

Pollard, S. (1965), *The Genesis of Modern Management*, London: Edward Arnold.

Solomons, D. (1968), 'The Historical Development of Costing' in D. Solomons (ed.) *Studies in Cost Analysis*, London: Sweet and Maxwell.

Storey, J. (1983), *Managerial Prerogative and the Question of Control*, London: Routledge and Kegan Paul.

Tinker, A. M. (1980), 'A Political Economy of Accounting', *Accounting, Organisations and Society*, **5** (1) 147-60.

Tinker, A. M., Merino B. D. and Niemark M. D. (1982), The Normative Origins of Postive Theories, Ideology and Accounting Thought'. *Accounting Organisations and Society* 7 (2) 167-200.

Trist, E. L., Higgin, G. W., Murray, H. and Pollock, A. B. (1963), *Organisational Choice*, London: Tavistock.

Wallerstein, I., (1974), *The Modern World System*, New York: Academic Books.

Wilensky, H. L. (1967), 'The Failure of Intelligence: Knowledge and Policy in Government and Industry', Proceedings of the 19th Annual Winter Conference, Industrial Relations Research Association.

Williams, K. and Haslam, C. (1985), 'Accounting for Failure in the Nationalised Industries', University of Aberystwyth.

Willmott, H. (1984), 'Images and Ideals of Managerial Work: A Critical Examination of Conceptual and Empirical Accounts, *Journal of Management Studies*, **21**, (3) 349-68.

Wright, E. O. (1976), 'Class Boundaries in Advanced Capitalist Societies, *New Left Review*, July-August, 3-41.

Yarrow, M. (1979) 'The Labor Process in Coal Mining: Struggle for Control' in A Zimbalist (ed.) *Case Studies on the Labor Process*, New York: Monthly Review Press.

7 Managerial Labour Processes in Organised Capitalism; the Power of Corporate Management and the Powerlessness of the manager*

Ad W.M. Teulings

Introduction: Management as a Labour Process

The question of role and powers of management is a theme which recurs frequently in current discussions of contemporary society. Whether these focus on problems of restructuring industry, on the possibilities of government intervention on the private market, on the necessity of technological innovation and automation or on the 'causes' of economic crisis, the issue of the power or powerlessness of management comes up recurrently. Sometimes management is presented as all-powerful; and, at other times, as wholly impotent. The objective of this paper is to illuminate this paradox. In doing so, it is to be argued that, with the rise and increasing complexity of organised capitalism, the power of management as a labour process has grown as the power of the individual manager has diminished.

If management is to be the object of our study, this object should first be defined more clearly. Who or what exactly are we talking about when we talk about management? And how can we tackle the question of the power or powerlessness of management more specifically in structural terms? What kind of activities are performed in management? What is the process of management that distinguishes it from other processes in the organisation?

There are various approaches to and definitions of our subject. The approach chosen in this study is based on organisational structuralism. In this perspective, management is not in the first place regarded as a category of society, as a societal class, or even as a collectivity of professionals, but as a combination of *labour processes within organisations*. Or, as Braverman (1974: 267) puts it, 'Management has become administration, which is a labor process

*I wish to thank David Hickson (University of Bradford), Hugh Willmott (University of Aston, Birmingham), Risto Taino and Keijo Räsänen (Helsinki School of Economics) for their help in preparing this paper.

conducted for the purpose of control within the corporation, and conducted moreover as a labor process exactly analogous to the process of production, although it produces no product other than the operation and co-ordination of the corporation.'

The question addressed in this paper is inspired by this aside in Braverman's *Labor and Monopoly Capital*. This aside is in a way in sharp contrast with the rest of his book. In his book Braverman seems to deal exclusively with manual and clerical workers, and analyses the changes in the substance of their work from the labour process perspective. Managerial work operates in opposition to this labour process: it is the other pole of a control structure and dominance relationship, and management and the workers are struggling along the frontiers of control dividing them. The research and theory development that followed Braverman's analysis reflects this perspective. When Braverman's book was welcomed as a theorectical basis for plant activism within the labour movement, the aside on management was passed over quickly.

Braverman suggests that management itself is to be analysed as a labour process. This implies two things. First, of course, that managerial work is also part of the collective labour process at the corporate level in industrial capitalism. Second, that there is a labour process *perspective*, open for further development, and that managerial work is to be analysed with the same conceptual apparatus used by Braverman in his treatment of the development of manual and clerical work. Braverman's *Labor and Monopoly Capital* is only a first part of a research programme. This paper then is an attempt to begin with the execution of this programme. Its focus is on the historical development of managerial work as an object for the labour process approach. The outcome of this analysis is again two-fold. It is described how managerial work is increasingly differentiated into (four) separate labour processes with distinctive, and often contradictory logics of action. And it is suggested that there are – in a way – various 'frontiers of control' within management itself. In much of the post-Braverman debate, however, management is treated as a unitary concept, and the singular 'frontier of control between management and the workers' is located at the operational level. The post-Braverman debate thus serves to avoid the most interesting and nagging theoretical issues involved in the labour process approach, such as the study of the conditions for communality of control interests between (part of the) operational workers and (part of) the management; the precise nature of structural (non-interactive) controls of various levels of management over operational work; and, perhaps of the most immediate relevance for the 'activism oriented' school of the labour process approach, the question how to cope with the increasing number – in some industries the majority -- of employees that are part and parcel of the labour process of management.

The concept of a differentiated management with separate rationalities does not only create a more complex and differentiated programme for workers' control, for those who seek to combine theory and praxis. It also brings the issue of political control right into the factory and corporation. Workers tend, in precisely the same way as described in this paper for managers, to note and confront operational decisions first, and will continue to apply operational rationalities, as long as they have some effectiveness. Only when all evidence turns against using this logic of action, solutions at higher levels of rationality are searched for. One could call these the levels of political bargaining (Teulings 1984; Boreham et; al. in this volume). It is not accidental that these issues turn up more easily within the tradition of German and Dutch Codetermination. Worker representatives in Works Councils, both in Germany and the Netherlands, could not avoid learning how to deal with the various labour processes of management, when participating in managerial decision-making.

It will be suggested that, in larger corporate organisations, the increasing differentiation of the management function produces not just one, but several parallel labour processes. That is why it has become more difficult to define 'the' general management function; there are several discrete objects of investigation. In this paper, we will distinguish four organisationally differentiated management functions: institutional management, strategic management, structuring management and operational management (see Figure 1). The differentiation of these task structures into separate levels of corporate management enables us to compare their relative power and powerlessness. However, when we speak of interdependent arrangements, this does not imply the existence of hierarchical relations between the levels I and II, etc. in a sense of supervisory relations, or of a 'line' organisation. This is feasible, but it is not essential. Rather our starting point will be that every management function develops its own *rationality*, or, following Karpik (1978: 15–68), its specific logics of action. This differentiation of functions is seen as the outcome of an ongoing process of the capitalist division of labour.

Insight into the process of differentiation amongst management functions is of relevance, if only to help us localise the object of our study more precisely. In its most advanced form, *management is a rather comprehensive and extensive whole, the different elements of which can only be reduced to the same denominator by extreme*

Figure 1
Relations between management and market functions

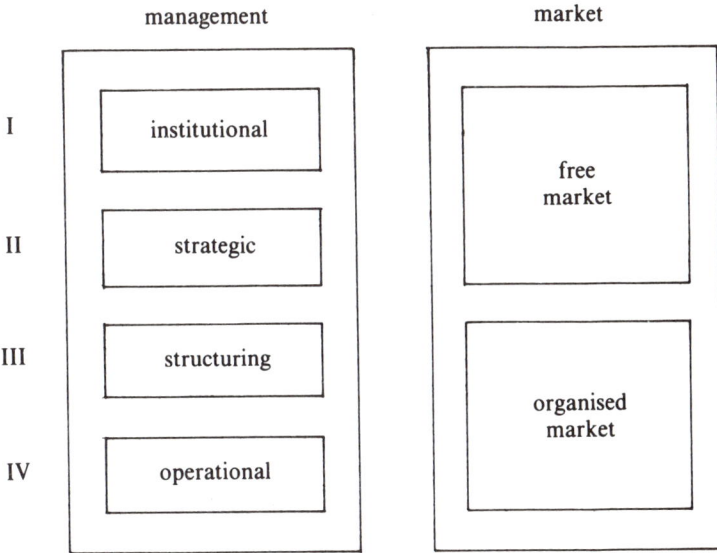

management   market

	management	market
I	institutional	free market
II	strategic	
III	structuring	organised market
IV	operational	

abstraction. The identification of various managerial functions is important in order to get a better view of a relevant part of the quest for control, as it occurs to those who perform specific tasks within management, the managers themselves. As we will see, part of this control problem arises from the relations of the various management functions and managerial structures *with respect to each other.*

The General Function of Management as a Substitute of the Market
On the evidence of his extensive historical investigation into the development of American trade and industry, Chandler (1977: 484ff) arrives at a challenging conclusion: management owes its existence to the possibility of transferring the co-ordinating and allocating function of market mechanisms to administrative/managerial structures. The rise of 'the managers' can, in essence, be considered as the rise of a new economic function: the *administrative* co-ordination and allocation of capital and labour. This conclusion is provocative in its immediate consequences. For what does it imply? That, with the rise of the salaried manager as a new 'sub-species of economic man', as an administrative co-ordinator, the market mechanism as a functional alternative loses importance without actually disappearing. Thus,

Chandler proposes the thesis that the rise of an army of managers is at the same time the decline of the market economy, of the capital market, the product market and the labour market. In short, modern management effects an *'internalisation of transactions'*. Williamson goes one step beyond this proposition, arguing that the survival of market relations, of external transactions, finally becomes an object of managerial discretion in itself. Markets may be kept alive or even 'opened' anew if this appears to be more efficient after all (Williamson 1975: 57–106, 252–4). Large corporations do not comply with the laws of every market, but rather the other way around. For some markets the corporation also determines their survival and their limits. *The functions of management, therefore – in this view – can be considered as former market functions.*

As a result, we may observe, both on the capital market and on the labour market, as well as on the markets of raw materials and finished products, a decompartmentalisation of two kinds of market structures: the classical market, regulated by 'anonymous forces', and the modern market, created and formed by the conscious intervention of management. Decompartmentalisation has also developed within the modern organisation. The internal co-ordination and allocation of capital and labour are not only affected by classical means of administration, within the framework of hierarchical relations between the constituent parts of the organisation, but, quasi-market relations and competitive relations are also created between parts of the organisation partly from the expectation that, with them, the efficacy and efficiency of the organisation as a whole are enhanced.

In sum, at the present stage of organised capitalism, market and management have become ambiguous concepts. The above considerations give rise to a preliminary 'abstract' definition of the management function. Management is defined as a social activity aimed at (or: resulting in) the co-ordination and allocation of the means of production by arranging the relations of subordination (hierarchy) and appropriation (property). Management is thus distinguished from the market by arrangement of the hierarchical relations and the relations of ownership. Whether this arrangement is effected depends on the comparative transaction costs. The cost advantages which can be achieved by transforming market transactions into managerial transactions are sometimes obvious, but ordinarily they are only discovered after much 'trial and error'. For instance:

(a) Opposing interests between sources of supply and demand on the markets of labour, capital, raw material and finished products are accommodated more effectively by managerial structures. The rules of the game are established, a common language of negotiation develops; the expectations of parties with regard to the outcome converge more easily – in short, an institutionalisation of opposing interest becomes possible. If in such an arrangement consultation repeatedly appears to lead to cost advantages, it will become formalised.

(b) The unreliability of free market prices as a means of planning and decision-making (should the volume of production increase or decrease with a change in price?). Many, sometimes fatal, failures in trade and industry can be traced to conclusions drawn too easily from price movements.

(c) The inertia of decision-making via market transactions. The scope of uncertainties confronting a market party often demands a long period of decision-making. The internalisation of market transactions may lead to a reduction of complexity, for with such a rearrangement not all decisions have to be taken at one and the same time. The process of decision-making can be taken apart in a number of steps, and in the course of time, a more flexible adaptation to new insights and data is possible. Management as a process within the division of labour enables a fractioning of decisions in correspondence with the property of limited rationality inherent to processes of decision-making.

(d) The chance of manipulation and opportunism in market transactions. Withholding certain information and knowledge that might be important to the other party belongs to the typical market behaviour of the opposing party on the market. Internalization of these transactions decreases the possibilities of opportunistic presentation, opens up the opportunity for effective supervision and for forcing the opposing party to become involved in one's own interests (Williamson 1975: 20–40).

Management Functions and the Rise of Organised Capitalism

The diagnosis of Chandler and of Williamson is in essence not so new in itself. As early as 1916, the sociologist Werner Sombart coined the term 'organised capitalism' for the tendencies described here (Sombart 1916). According to Sombart, 'organised capitalism' would be the last or 'mature' phase in the development from the free market system of the nineteenth century. This opinion is shown to be partly invalid by Strieder (1916), among others. In the rise of trade and industry, the ideal type of free market system has only been an intermezzo, the climax of which lay in the period 1800–75. Before that time, in early capitalism, monopoly and management structures dominated as the most important forms of industrial organisation and co-ordination. The defractionalisation of industry and the loss of managerial control over the 'environment' of the organisation was, in retrospect, a temporary phenomenon – the result, in particular, of a very fast and turbulent development of mechanisation which enabled and stimulated the formation of small-scale firms, outside the sphere of influence of existing industrial powers (Strieder 1916). Or, in Marx's words: the swift development of the forces of production broke down the existing framework of its social relations. From this historical background, it is understandable that this phase of development is idealised in the classical entrepreneural ideology: the newly gained private ownership of the means of production created opportunities for contemporary personal and social progress, the 'free' market economy meant the liberation from existing monopolies which often controlled an entire industry. But the complexity, the deficiencies and failures of the free market economy are met in the structure of the private enterprise itself. Some of the deficiencies of the labour market are met by the formation of the factory system, the simple supervisory hierarchy. The intermediate product market is partly replaced by forms of vertical integration, and the deficiencies of the capital market are finally met by corporate structuring and conglomeration (see Figure 2). And with each of these transformations, the size and complexity of management in the organisation grows and an increasing differentiation of management functions arises. Or, in Masuch's words, complexity is transformed into contingency – that is to say, into an object suitable for decision-

Figure 2
The substitution of market functions by management

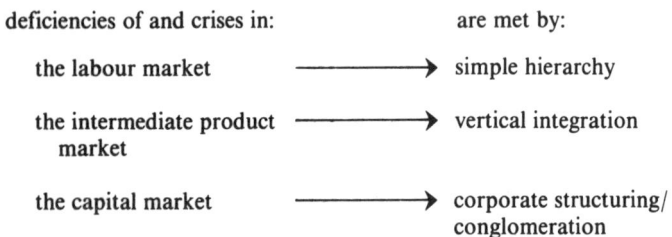

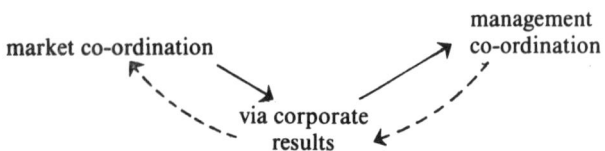

deficiencies of and crises in:		are met by:
the labour market	⟶	simple hierarchy
the intermediate product market	⟶	vertical integration
the capital market	⟶	corporate structuring/ conglomeration

market co-ordination ⟶ via corporate results ⟶ management co-ordination

Figure 3
The life cycles of early capitalism, industrial capitalism, and organised capitalism

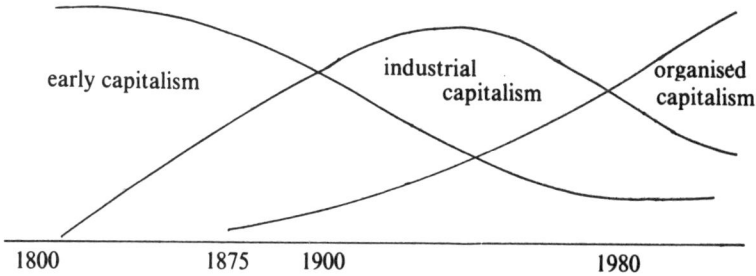

making processes – and this, at the same time, is the material basis for the rise of management (Masuch 1981: 2).

The historian Kocka defines 'simple capitalism' as an economic system which is mainly based on the private ownership and the private control of capital which is applied to the production and trade of goods, for the sake of profit. In this system, the key decisions are made by private entrepreneurs who interact mainly via the mechanism of the private market (Kocka 1980: 21–2; 42–54). 'Industrial capitalism' is characterised particularly by the formation of the factory system, a centralised mode of production on a basis of machines and hired labour. The factory system does not only penetrate the secondary sector to expand at the cost of agriculture, but also the tertiary, service sector. Kocka also sees the industrialisation of the tertiary sector as a last stage in the growth of industrial capitalist production. The dynamics, the motor of this growth, lies in the development of the factory system, opening up (by a rational organisation of machines and men) new opportunities for a rise in productivity. Industrialisation of the service sector is still in progress in our time. The life cycle of industrial capitalism, therefore, has not reached its end, although the system has had its peak. But Kocka suggests the emergence of a new order of organised capitalism long before that, as early as around 1900 (see Figure 3).

Now, what happens with the rise of this organised capitalism?

(a) With regard to the private ownership of capital, a joint development of concentration and combination in branches of industry occurs: on the one hand as a reaction to unequal growth within, and to crises of industrial capitalism; and, on the other hand, as a conscious effort to co-ordinate already existing economic interdependencies.

(b) With regard to the private control of productive capital a division of labour occurs, followed by the separation of relations of ownership and command. Control of capital does not become less private, nor do the goals of the corporation change in any fundamental way, but the separation makes the function of control more accessible to systematic, 'scientific' management, to a further division of labour and the functional specialisation of managerial tasks, in short, to rationalisation of the allocation process and (therefore also) of the co-ordination process in general. In the wake of this development we see the rise of the white collar workers and wage-dependent professions.

(c) With regard to the private markets we see the tendency to substitute individual transactions and contracts for collective agreements – both on the product market, the capital market and the labour market. Again, this does not lessen the private character of these transactions, but its opaque and anonymous element becomes markedly less. Here, again, there is talk of rationalisation, aimed at improved control.

(d) Finally, with regard to the private entrepreneur, a transformation occurs, especially of the position from which strategic decisions are produced. What does this transformation consist of? According to Kocka, it may be described as a tendency to organise and integrate the private sector into the political system (with the result of a continuously expanding public service). Here, it is relevant to note that this tendency is not really opposed to the private economic power, but rather, can be viewed as a more rational form, in terms of the division of labour, of this power. In other words, private economic power is not threatened by its interlocking with the political system, and the latter does not necessarily interfere with the aims of corporate enterprise; on the contrary, it is a precondition for its realisation (Kocka, 1980: 42–3).

Rationalisation of the relations between industrial corporations and the state by means of organisation implies in the first place an increase in the transparency of those relations. It also implies an increase in opportunities for mutual control. Which of the two parties will profit most, the private corporations or the public administration, depends – to put it simply – on the current relations of political bargaining powers.

To summarise this part of the argument. The rise of management and the differentiation of managerial functions is connected with changes, especially in the surface structure of capitalism. The crisis of management, in which the question of its power and powerlessness is asked first and foremost, seems to be connected – in a number of essential points – with problems which are specific to historical phases or episodes of organised capitalism. The processes of rationalisation with regard to the large-scale introduction of machines and men in the factory, which were developed fully in the phase of industrial capitalism (e.g. the factory system, the organised labour market) and which, with regard to the product market and the capital market, were implemented quite pragmatically, seem to stagnate when it comes to the rationalisation of the function of the entrepreneur. Any development in this territory is soon considered as interference with the reputed private character of this function. Paradoxically, this ideological disposition is perhaps a greater threat to the entrepreneurial function than its rational socialisation. Here, too, the preservation or viability of entrepreneurial positions of power is preceded by a necessary process of its division of labour. The separation of the economy and the polity, between corporation and government, no longer exists; instead, we find a great measure of economic interdependence and interlocking relationships. The processes by which this interdependence manifests itself in the field of operation of both parties are mainly unpredictable, opaque and loosely coupled. A more conscious organisation of already existing interdependencies precedes the possibility of an effective implementation of power by whichever 'party'.

The Differentiation of Management Functions
The emergence and growth of management lead to changes not only in external, but also in internal organisation. Management, as a labour process, is differentiated into various (sub)functions. This process also comes about over a rather long period in industrial history. Chandler, for example, describes this 'managerial revolution' in a number of phases (see Figure 4).

If we take the period of expansion of the small factories in the first industrial revolution as a starting point, a first differentiation of management shows up as soon as the production process becomes more complex. This is because components are no longer purchased but incorporated in the production line; because several production lines are brought together on one work-floor, or because parts of the distribution process are incorporated in the industrial corporation. The first separate level of management (A) emerges when entrepreneurs employ 'managers' to take over the co-ordination of these complex physical work flows. In the United States – as opposed to Europe – the definite breakthrough in this development occurs, according to Chandler, first of all in the distribution sector (mass

Figure 4
Differentiation of management functions: Chandler

Differentiation		Emergent differential management functions	Typical emergent institutions
PHASE I	*entrepreneur* workers	————	manufacture, factory, firm
PHASE II	*entrepreneur* *management (A)* workers	'labour process- co-ordination'	subsidiary
PHASE III	*entrepreneur* *management (B)* *management (A)* workers	'allocation of investments'	holding/trust
PHASE IV	*entrepreneur* *management (B)* *management (C)* *management (A)* workers	control of product markets	division

retailers) and only after that in production. Management takes over the co-ordination of what we are now used to calling 'operations' at plant level. Only with a certain volume of economic activity does management co-ordination become more productive and therefore more profitable than market co-ordination. In industry, moreover, a certain level of technological development is needed for only in that case is it possible to bring together different flows of production under one roof (Chandler 1977: 485).

Once this development is successful, managers who are in charge of co-ordinating the workflow, also become responsible for the allocation of resources for future production and distribution. This second level of management (B) does not emerge as an entity separate from the entrepreneurial function, but as a follow-on from the first managerial level (A), although it is going to take up a position in the organisational hierarchy between the entrepreneur and the original level of management. This B-level specialises in – what we would now call – the allocation of financial means and in the development and control of investment plans. The emergence of this level occurs first when mass production and mass distribution are integrated in one large corporation. The typical form in which it occurs is the holding (or – to use a term that has an old-fashioned ring nowadays – the 'trust').

Figure 5
Differentiation of management functions: Touraine

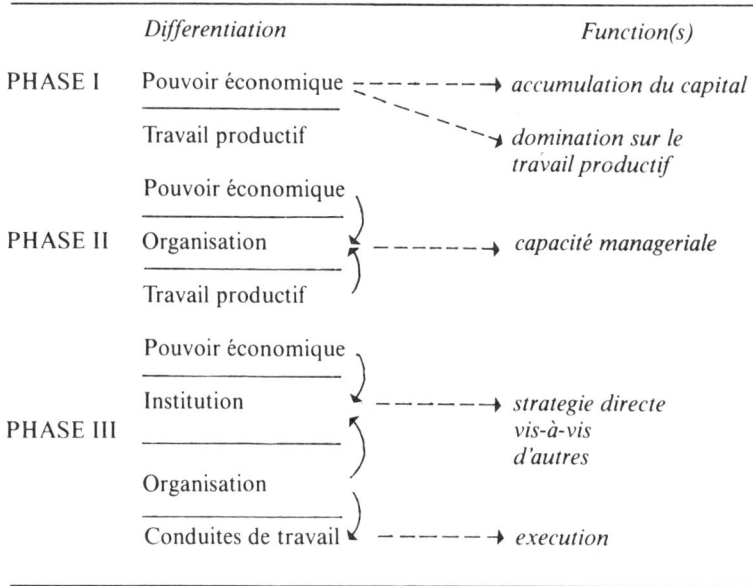

	Differentiation	Function(s)
PHASE I	Pouvoir économique Travail productif	accumulation du capital domination sur le travail productif
PHASE II	Pouvoir économique Organisation Travail productif	capacité manageriale
PHASE III	Pouvoir économique Institution Organisation Conduites de travail	strategie directe vis-à-vis d'autres execution

The succeeding phase in the development of management can be initiated by one of two different strategies, by a defensive or by an offensive strategy. The situation on the product markets (the number of competitors) and the economic situation/climate (growth or contraction) are decisive for this selection of strategy. The defensive strategy is aimed at preventing the possible blockage of supply channels and market outlets or at obstructing potentially new competitors from access to the market. The offensive strategy, with expansion as its goal, is aimed at an optimal use of more competitive means of administrative co-ordination by way of adding new units of production. The quality of the management structure has improved to such an extent that the take-over of firms and distribution networks leads to a further decline in the costs per unit of production. The economies achieved by the system of management co-ordination between various production and/or distribution units appear to be much larger than the economies of scale of the separate units themselves. The new level of management thus emerging is separated from the B-level, and gets its place between (B) and (A) levels of management. In modern jargon we would indicate its function as product market control, and its typical form is the divisional structure (C).

In slightly different words, and with slightly different accents, we find this reconstruction of the process of differentiation of management, in various historical sociological analyses. Touraine, for example (see Figure 5), describes the functions of the management at the phase of 'simple capitalism' – in which the positions of management and entrepreneur are not yet separated – as capital-accumulation, and control and co-ordination of the labour process (*le travail productif*). Both by separating elements of the function of the entrepreneur and by separating elements of the control function, an independent level of management is constituted – an organisational 'apparatus' (Touraine 1969: 202–3). Obviously Chandler describes this phase much more precisely, dividing it into two phases. In Touraine's scheme, finally, an institutional level develops out of the organisational apparatus, as well as out of the entrepreneurial level (the 'level of economic power'), which has as its function the development of a direct strategy (opposed to the lawlessness of the market) towards the competitors. Here, Touraine does actually note the emergence of a separate function of product market control, like Chandler, but, again, its relation to other levels is indicated only roughly. Management on the plant level finally is eroded further into operational management ('execution') (Touraine 1969: 189–260).

Figure 6
Institutionalisation of distinctive management functions at separate levels of management

	functions:	levels:
I	the ownership function — accumulation of capital	institutional management — creation and preservation of legitimations
II	the administrative function — allocation of investments	strategic management — development of objectives
III	the innovative function — product market development	structuring management — new combinations of production factors
IV	the production function — control of the direct labour process	operational management — direction and co-ordination of direct labour

Before we can proceed to determine how the analysis of management differentiation as presented here can throw some light on a number of current problems of management power, it is advisable to bring these historical sociological approaches under one common denominator and connect them with the language of 'management science'. For, in modern 'management science' we also encounter similar distinctions – without explicitly going into the history of its development. These distinctions are not described particularly as functions, but as different levels within management, and connected with 'prescriptions' of what management at a certain level should take as its objectives and which tasks should be fulfilled to that end (Ansoff 1969; Snellen 1981, Van der Schroef 1975).

Levels of Corporate Management

A recapitulation of the result of the process of differentiation of management has been presented in Figure 6 (in the left-hand column). In modern large-scale corporations (and in other kinds of organisation to a lesser extent) these four functions of management can be identified as separate labour processes. We will call them in sequence:

the ownership function
the administrative function
the innovative function, and
the production function.

The ownership function of management is brought about by producing an accumulation of capital, that is to say, by a range of activities that leads to its concentration, preservation and valuation in a transferable form (viz. as property). The administrative function is brought about by the process of determination of the allocation of investments, that is to say, by a range of activities that leads to the allotment of capital and labour to specific productive uses based on rational criteria (including, for instance, the ratio of returns on investment). The innovative function is brought about by a range of activities that leads to the development of new product markets, or to the improvement of existing product market shares, by creating new combinations of production factors. The production function is brought about by a range of activities that allows for an increasing control of the direct labour process, especially of the relations between tasks and machines, between machine operations and between the tasks of employees among themselves.

These distinctions have been deduced from the historical sociological analyses of Kocka, Chandler, Touraine and others. In the literature on management science we may also encounter those four functions as parts of a role-set of the manager – an approach that, both formally and empirically, is no longer adequate. For we are not concerned with a characterisation of individuals or positions, but with separate labour processes of management.

Were we to personify these functions we would indeed get the roles of 'the owner', 'the financier', 'the businessman', and of 'the plant supervisor'. However, in the modern corporate organisation we seldom encounter these figures and most certainly not as the characteristic of one person. *What we do encounter are separate management structures and those who are part of them. These structures guide the complex labour processes and forms of organisation in which the functions of ownership, of the financier, etc. are more or less objectivated.* The participants are subjected to elaborate divisions of labour and processes of rationalisation. Some of them are called 'managers', some are not. But 'management' has to be defined in terms of the processes and divisions of labour that have been developed to fulfill one of the four functions mentioned above. The 'managers' and other employees set to work to accomplish these processes and reinforce these task structures. The division of labour which comes about within these task structures also extends over positions of a strictly manual nature: Being 'part of management' no longer means being spared manual and routinised labour. The formation of 'management apparatuses' even results in a routinisation of most of the managers' activities (Mintzberg 1973).

Snellen (1981) has described the level at which the function of production is localised as *operational* management. It includes a series of tasks that brings about a co-ordination of workers at the shop floor to reach previously determined goals (Snellen 1981: 23). At the next level we encounter *structuring* management. This level is concerned with 'all those tasks which are related to the allocation and organisation of production factors and their combination', the 'weighing and adaptation of alternative combinations of production factors' and 'the structuring of more or less permanent forms of co-operation between various production units' (ibid. 24). The creation of new combinations of production factors (according to Schumpeter), or the new development of (new) product markets, forms the hard core, and the most distinctive feature of this level of management activities. It is an institutionalisation of the innovative function.

At the level of *strategic* management activities are defined which have to lead to the creation and development of new objectives. Snellen rightly notes that 'given' objectives are often taken for granted in traditional definitions of organisations. In a highly changing environment, however, this becomes less self-evident. The formulation of new objectives and the timely adaptation of existing objectives becomes an extensive and specialised work process. The tangible form in which this occurs is the anticipative adoption of changes in the portfolio of investments, on a basis of a systematic comparison of alternative investment possibilites. The administrative management function is institutionalised in this process.

Finally, Snellen discusses the level of *institutional* management. This is described as a range of activities aimed at the creation and preservation of legitimations both externally – towards the public and clients – and internally – towards the employees. The need for these activities is prompted by the fact that an uncontrolled growth of capital and, particularly the uncontrolled transfer of capital – which is possible with private ownership – can hardly find acceptance in our society, let alone appreciation, in view of the extensive consequences this can have both for the employees and for the public. New legitimations must be found continuously; each decision has to find its own functional legitimation; the ownership title alone provides insufficient justification. The increase of activities at the level of institutional management reflects a crisis in the function of ownership.

From the Processes of Management to its Problems
What is the use of a definition of management functions or of levels of management as has briefly been presented? One of the advantages of the conceptual explanation offered is that it helps to visualise a number of current problems of corporate management, and to rephrase them in such a way as to help a better understanding of the nature of these problems. Some current issues that will be specified are:
1. the internal limits of corporate effectiveness
2. the internal limits of social integration and conflict resolution
3. goal-succession by means of goal-displacement
4. the unequal distribution of constraints and control.

1. Permanent Imbalances
In large corporations, the differentiation of management functions not only takes the form of a vertical division between levels of management, but also *produces a relative autonomy of rationalities or logics of action at each level.* Management activities can no longer be brought under one common denominator; they have neither a common 'input' nor a common work flow and 'output' or one coherent objective or outcome. This breaking-down of management functions leads to structurally determined contradictions, to

Figure 7   From process to problems

	processes	problems of management	managers
A	substitution of market functions by management functions	internationalisation vs. externalisation	inflexibility
B	differentiation between management functions	conflicting action logics politicisation	lawlessness (anomia trained incapacity
C	division of labour within management functions	rationalisation	alienation
D	growing autonomy of management functions	incrementalism	inversion

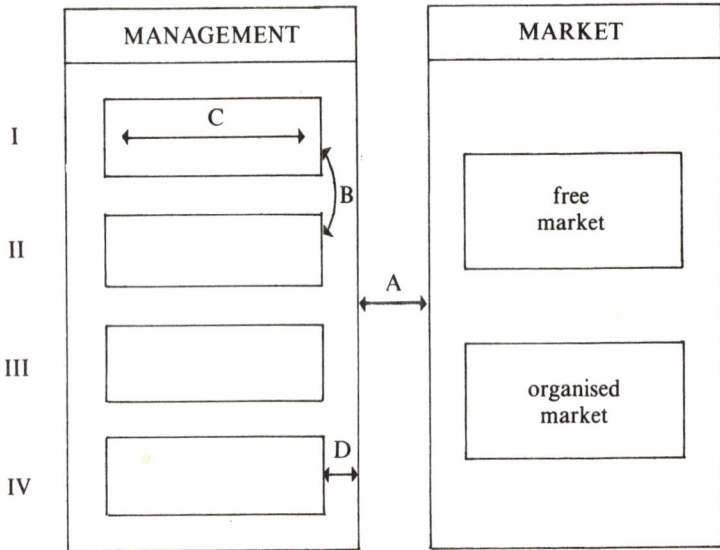

contradictions in the internal functioning of the administrative organisation of the large corporation. That which is logical and necessary to the function of production can be seen to run counter to the function of innovation, etc. Each level of management operates following a rationality or action logic of its own. At the level of production it is rational, for instance, to aim at production units with optimal economies of scale; then capital and labour are used most efficiently. From the perspective of the product market for the innovative management level, however, things may look quite different. There the starting point is, for instance, the life cycle of the product which may intersect at some points with the technical economies of scale. But that point in time is usually far removed from the present. Efficiency at the first level implies inefficiency at the second and vice versa. At the level of strategic management, one may follow yet another logic. The actual range of products may yield reasonable profits, but, if compared with other investment opportunities not yet realised, a move towards new activities or to other producton locations may appear to be more attractive. Finally, at the level of ownership, a change of ownership relations (take-over of firms; government participation) can be considered as desirable, although these changes may seriously endanger the opportunities for growth or profit maximisation of subsidiaries. There is no unique and common reference point for all levels toward which all actions can be orientated. Rationality, effectiveness and efficiency mean different things and have different values at different levels.

The differentiation of management functions and the subsequent formation of various levels of corporate management leads to the juxtaposition of different rationalities and to equally different optimalities. This produces a corporate structure which, as a whole, is always 'out of balance' somewhere. In a period of economic growth this permanent imbalance can be an important source of continuous expansion. Such an imbalance can be accommodated more easily when there is accelerated growth of the organisation. However, in a period of economic recession, the opposite movement occurs: the disparity provides an inexhaustible motive for decline. Moreover, since simultaneous resolution of all disparities is impossible, and because every partial resolution creates new disparities at other levels, a recession can trigger off a downward spiral of disinvestments which – once the fever of reorganisation and efficiency has risen – knows no limits. As soon as one subsidiary has been X-rayed and trimmed, one can be sure of finding new optimal efficiencies at the divisional level, after which one could return again to the subsidiary level for further downward adaptations which – when viewed from the action logic of divisional management – seem to be only natural.

However, a certain degree of inefficiency and inefficacy of the corporate organisation, both of the whole and of its parts, is unavoidable and even desirable. Consequently this limited overall rationality does not in itself form enough cause for either growth or decline. Other 'non-rational' motives and considerations are bound to take up an important place in these decisions. What motives are they? In principle there are two main motives: the opportunities for the preservation or increase of managerial power, and the tendency to defend specific group interests.

Limits of Formal Mechanism for Conflict Resolution
The chances of integrating management functions are limited because they are based on different rationalities. In its institutionalised form this problem emerges as a conflict between levels of management. Adaptation between levels occurs by means of:

(a) **Authoritarian intervention**, that is to say, a unilateral decision which cannot be founded on an irrevocable appeal to requirements of efficiency and efficacy (for such an appeal, depending on the management function from which optimalisation occurs, would turn out differently), but only, in the last resort, on an appeal to the 'naked' power of one of the parties involved.

(b) **Processes of negotiation**, in which an agreement is reached on an outcome that reflects a weighing of the various group interests of the parties involved. The result of such a process is not 'the most effective or efficient solution', but a solution which meets as much as possible the interests of each party in such a manner that open conflicts can be avoided. To arrive at such a solution, it is necessary for both parties to place the problem in a new context, in which concessions and compensations can be talked about. Thus, the sometimes trying process of muddling through, about which so much has been written in organisational literature, takes place primarily in the borderland of the various managerial rationalities, in the intercourse between operational and innovative management; between innovative and strategic management; and finally, between strategic and institutional management.

The managers who get involved in such a boundary conflict often do not know how to proceed. In the first place, if the course of a management process becomes orientated on values and interests, it tends to be considered as 'deviant', as abnormal, sometimes even as something unseemly. It is experienced as incompatible with formal management culture, which is expected to grant priority to efficiency and efficacy. In the second place, it requires specific negotiating behaviour which, as a rule, one is less familiar with, and which has had little attention during the training and education of managers. Consequently, the managers involved are confronted with a considerable amount of role uncertainty when they are forced to take up the authoritarian or negotiator's role. Subsequently, we see quite often that organisations have no formal procedures and decision-making platforms which could give the negotiating process a more controlled course, and a more predictable outcome to both parties.

Finally, it can be noted that authoritarian intervention, which, in the past was still applied rather frequently within corporations, has encountered great resistance since the end of the 1960s. This means that, in most cases, only the model of internal negotiation is available for these situations. The question is how this model is to be institutionalised in the practice of management. We can establish that the organisational model from which the managerial apparatus was originally constructed is hierarchial in nature. The co-ordination and allocation of capital and labour, originally ran along hierarchic lines. The development of forms of participation and co-determination within this structure is, indeed, an adaptation which meets the objections and limitations inherent in the hierarchic model to some extent, but it remains an adaptation within the hierarchical model. Forms of participation and co-determination can be seen as the ultimate confirmation of hierarchy.

The internal differentiation of the management function and the emergence of separate levels of management which function according to different rationalities require, however, the formal establishment of internal procedures and structures of negotiation. The 'informal organisation' of internal negotiating processes must be visualised and integrated into the formal hierarchical structures. The possibility of improving control of the managerial process itself and/or the possibility of integrating the various levels of management seems to depend mainly on social innovations on this point. 'Organisational failures', which can be observed regularly in the assimilation of changes in ownership relations (mergers, conglomerations, government participation in the private sector); of changes in investment and disinvestment programmes; of product market innovations and of new forms of mechanisation and automation, are also caused in many cases by the lack of formal procedures of internal negotiation. The managers who get involved increasingly in this kind of decision, appear to sustain a strong feeling of incapacity in the process of their assimilation. The organisation appears as a 'recalcitrant tool' especially when the hierarchic model of organisation remains the guiding principle of the managers' thought and action.

The paradox of the theory and practice of management
In the theory of management a disproportionately large amount of attention is still paid to rational processes of decision-making. Even when empirical research shows the managers' activities to be largely concerned with everyday, more or less routine actions, it seems hardly

able to correct this theoretical prejudice. Moreover, the experience that it is very difficult to localise the places, moments and positions that are 'decisive' in the whole of these activities, does not lead to a fundamental revision of theoretical starting points either.

A well-known presentation of the process of decision-making is, for instance, the decision tree. General objectives come up for discussion first, then goals and sub-goals, etc. 'Lower' objectives are 'means' within the framework of 'higher' objectives. And again, within every goal-means relation one works with alternatives, evaluations, feed backs and revisions (Abrahamsson 1977: 83–182). As a means to describe the process of management in practice, all this is highly deceptive. In practice, the need for decision-making is felt at the moment that existing procedures and routines do not lead to a solution of the problems. Then, something like a 'crisis' arises which requires special attention. The remarkable thing is that such a crisis is nearly always noted first of all at the level of operational management, in a disturbance of the material 'workflow' (for instance, of purchase – production – sales). Moreover, the answer to the prevailing problem – whatever its nature – is also sought, as a rule, in an adaptation in the operational labour process. The signals that are first caught are, for instance, a drop in sales or a decrease in services, a drop in market shares, a rise of production costs, a decline in productivity, an increase in the labour turnover or absenteeism, of sub-standard delivery times. And the resolutions that are sought, are, for instance, sales promotion, a search for cutting costs, improvement of machine maintenance, a 'programme to fight absenteeism', a more precise monitoring of the times of delivery respectively.

Only when these operational solutions also appear in the long term to be ineffective is the problem lifted to a higher level of management. Only then does one start looking for possible innovations of products, for new markets, for new production processes and for new forms of organising labour. In other words, a second-line adaptation occurs at the level of innovative management. When this proves successful, the processes of management change at a higher level are not set in motion so easily. However, when this adaptation does not appear to lead to the outcomes desired, then a revision of investment pro-grammes will follow, and the time has come for strategic management. An orientation towards new objectives may lead to a cut in some activities, to withdrawal from a traditional market, or to a turning into entirely new roads. Only in the very last resort is a modification of ownership relations undertaken, by repelling subsidiaries, by taking over subcontractors, buyers or competitors, by entering into mergers, or by seeking the participation of banks or of the government

(Chevalier 1977: 37–78). The stubbornness with which this phenomenon – known as the law of retarded reaction (Ansoff 1969), or as the practice of incrementalism (Braybrook and Lindblom 1963) – manifests itself continually, could tempt us to define structures of management as means-directed rather than as goal-directed systems.

Disproportionate pressure on the operational level
The purport of the preceding disquisition was that change and innovation of the organisation are, as a rule, initiated by crises at the operational level on the shop floor, and are in the first instance, also assimilated at that level or at least according to an operational logic of action.

One of its consequences deserves our special attention. For it implies that it is the operational level which is first and foremost under pressure for control and/or change in the organisation. The labour process of direct (manual) labour is more liable to reorganisation than any other labour process, the rank and file is more subject to co-ordination and control than any other category of employees. As indicated by the law of retarded reaction, one can also expect frequent contingency situations, requiring a tightening of controls on the shop floor, for lack of capacity of work control and reorganisation at higher levels of management. The chances of stability of work and labour conditions are not only unequally distributed, but this inequality can also hardly ever find rational legitimation – as it is partly produced by such motives as the preservation of power and the vested interests of higher levels of management. When the adaptation of the organisation to a changing environment regularly affects only the operational level, it is not surprising that is where resistence to change is most developed.

An increase in the autonomy of higher levels of management which can absorb or accomplish environmental changes directly and, to a certain extent, without interfering in the shop floor organisation will lead to a decrease in the pressure on the operational level. But even with the most favourable relationship between levels of management, contradictions between the different managerial rationalities will remain. In so far as the consequences of structuring strategic and institutional management processes also affect the operational management level, integration can only be achieved by forms of negotiation in which the interests of the shop floor employees are weighted against other interests, and in which the distribution of power at each level is also brought into the discussion. It is no coincidence that employees on the shop floor are the first to unionise in defence of their direct interests and the little autonomy that remains in the manual labour process. These conflicts of interests and power appeared unsolvable both within the organisational hierarchy and through ordinary forms of employee participation (c.t. Teulings 1981).

Conclusions: The Manager as Homo Politicus

The manager in large industrial and administrative organisations has become part of an administrative apparatus of the division of labour. He is a participant in a complex labour process of management, fulfils specific tasks in it, sometimes as a specialist, sometimes in a more general capacity. The tasks that are carried out by these managers and the activities they perform, can only be understood in the context of the labour process that, as a whole, is called 'management'.

As organisations grow in size and are confronted with a changing environment, the division of labour in management increases. A differentiation of functions occurs, which, after a lapse of time, can be distinguished as separate 'levels of management'. The separation of these functions into distinct levels implies the presence of different rationalities or logics of action within management. The mutual attunement of the various rationalities cannot be co-ordinated by hierarchical procedures but requires co-ordination through negotiation procedures. Negotiating processes of this kind, in which the parties involved are guided by different rationalities, have a political nature: their object or outcome is the redistribution of power and the revaluation of aquired interests.

With the development of organised capitalism the power of management as a whole (the power of the administrative machinery) has greatly increased. But simultaneously, the power of the individual manager as a participant in the division of labour of the management process has diminished. The powerlessness of the manager is apparent when we consider the relations between and within each level of management that was separately identified. An increasing rationality of the labour process of management is achieved by its differentiation and hierarchical separation of functions. But, at the same time, this makes their inner contradiction more manifest. Rationalisation of management as a labour process results in a politicisation of the relations between levels of management, a development that is widely regarded with feelings of incapacity by the individual manager, who is trained to function in a decomposed and hierarchically structured sub-system. For the rules which lead to success in his own labour process no longer appear to apply, and in any case, no longer appear to work in the process of accommodation with other logics of action. The power of the individual manager (and, in particular, his sense of power) thus lags behind the power of management. The manager

frms part of an extensive machinery of power, without being able to derive from it any real sense of sharing that power.

References

Abrahamsson, B. (1977) *Bureaucracy or Participation, The Logic of Organization*, London/Beverley Hills: Sage.
Ansoff, H. I. (1969), 'Towards a strategic theory of the firm' in H. I. Ansoff, (ed.), *Business Strategy*, Harmondsworth: Penguin.
Braverman, H. (1974), *Labor and Monopoly Capital*, New York: Monthly Review Press.
Braybrook, D. and Lindblom, C. E. (1963), *A Strategy of Decision*, New York: Free Press.
Chandler, A. D. (1977), *The Visible Hand*, Cambridge Mass. and London: Harvard University Press.
Chevalier, J. M. (1977), *L'économie industrièlle en question*, Paris: Calmann-Levy.
Karpik, L. (1978), 'Organizations, Institutions and History' in L. Karpik, *Organizations and Environment*, London and Beverley Hills: Sage.
Kocka, J. (1980), *White Collar Workers in America, 1890-1940*, London and Beverley Hills: Sage.
Masuch, M. (1981), *Kritik der Planung*, Amsterdam: University of Amsterdam (doctoral dissertation).
Mintzberg, H. (1973), *The Nature of Managerial Work*, New York: Harper and Row.
Schroeff, H. J. van der (1975), *Organisatie en bedrijfsleiding*, Amsterdam: Kosmos.
Snellen, I. Th. M. (1981), *Gezondheidszorg en management*, Alphen aan den Rijn: Samsom.
Sombart, W. (1916), *Der moderne Kapitalismus*, München: Duncker and Humblot.
Strieder, J. (1925), *Studien zur Geschichte Kapitalistischer Organisationsformen*, München: Dunker Humblot.
Teulings, A. W. M. (1978), *Herstructurering van de industrie*, Alphen aan den Rijn: Samsom.
Teulings, A. W. M. (1981), *Ondernemingsraadpolitiek in Nederland*, Amsterdam: van Gennep.
Touraine, A. (1969), *La Société Post-Industrielle*, Paris: Editions Denoël.
Williamson, O. E. (1975), *Markets and Hierarchies: Analysis and Antitrust Implications*, New York and London: The Free Press.

8 Technocratic Management: Social and Political Implications

Beverly H. Burris

If justice is beyond us, we would like at least to claim knowledge. (James Burnham 1941, p. 76)

Introduction

Technological and social change has rapidly and dramatically transformed the organisational structure of advanced industrial societies in recent years. Implications for workplace politics have been particularly significant, and yet existing attempts to analyse these transformations have fallen short of a comprehensive understanding. What is needed is an analysis of the organisational control structure which is increasingly characteristic of industrial societies: technocracy.

Technocracy can best be understood as the most recent stage in a dialectical evolution of different organisational control structures: craft/guild control, simple control, bureaucratic control, professional control, technical control, technocratic control. This evolutionary pattern does follow a general chronological sequence, although uneven development and overlapping systems of control are common. Thus, this sequence does not represent a linear process of rationalisation, but rather a *dialectical* process of rationalisation (see Heydebrand 1979): contradictions develop within each control structure which are resolved (partially and temporarily) by the next. Technocratic control both transcends and integrates certain features of these earlier forms of control, particularly bureaucratic, professional, and technical forms: certain aspects of bureaucracy, professionalism, and advanced technology are combined into a radically new type of control structure, with significant social and political implications both within workplaces and in the society at large.

Part I of this paper presents and discusses existing theoretical approaches which are relevant to technocracy. Part II analyses the dialectical process of rationalisation so as to reveal how technocracy emerged out of previous types of control structures. Part III discusses some of the most salient features of contemporary technocracy. Part IV explores some of the political and social implications of technocratic organisation, including existing contradictions which point toward future developments.

I. Theoretical Perspectives on Technocracy

One striking feature of the neo-Marxist 'labour process literature' has been its virtual neglect of managerial, scientific, and technical workers.[1] Braverman's (1974) major contribution to the field extended and updated Marx's work by analysing the implications of recent technological and social developments on the labour process. However, Braverman (ibid.: 3), intent on refuting the view that 'modern work, as a result of the scientific-technical revolution and "automation", requires ever higher levels of education, training, the greater exercise of intelligence and mental effort in general,' has taken an equally partial approach: that the working class, updated and expanded so as to include clerical workers, has been deskilled and dehumanised by advanced workplace technology and corollary management techniques, as exemplified by Taylor's scientific management. Although this perspective is important as a corrective to the paeans of technological progress, as an analysis of the impact of advanced technology on the contemporary capitalist labour process it is not sufficient.[2] In order to reach a more comprehensive vision, one which would consider both deskilling and reskilling (Edwards 1978), it is necessary to cultivate a more systemic perspective.

Given his Marxist emphasis on the degradation of the proletariat, Braverman deals with managers, scientists, and engineers only in passing. The implication is that Taylor represents an ideal type of capitalist managers: 'Modern management came into being on the basis of Taylorist principles'. (Braverman 1974: 120). To the extent that managerial and scientific employees are dealt with, Braverman (as well as later labour process theorists) stresses the fact that they, too, are often deskilled and controlled; that many administrators are largely clerical workers.[3]

Although Braverman made a major contribution, with the dramatic and rapid developments in computerised technology over the past decade, we are now in the position of needing to update Braverman, just as he updated Marx's analysis in volume 1 of *Capital*. Particularly problematic in this regard is his emphasis on Taylorism, a phenomenon characteristic of the early years of this century, which had questionable significance in terms of its long-term impact on work organisations. As Edwards (1978) and Herman (1982) point out, Braverman attributes inordinate importance to Taylorist writings

because he assumes that Taylorist theory was necessarily implemented, whereas very few firms actually followed Taylorist principles
rigorously. Although Taylorism may indeed have symbolic importance which transcends its practical implementation, the contemporary relevance of Taylorism can be understood only by
examining what Taylor's scientific management has become:
technocracy.

Technocracy has been addressed primarily by non-Marxist
theorists. Veblen (1921) stressed the universal interests of engineers
and technicians, and the need to reorganise society according to
technocratic principles, rather than leaving financiers, 'who speak for
Vested Interests' (1921 : 133) in control.[4] According to Burnham
(1941), a 'managerial society' has already emerged, one which
transcends capitalist/socialist distinctions and substitutes technical
expertise and managerial power for more traditional capitalist power.
Theories of post-industrialism and the 'end of ideology' (Bell, 1960,
1973, 1976; Galbraith, 1967; Touraine, 1971b) emphasise the
ascendancy of a *knowledge class* of technical and professional
workers, with technical decision-making and meritocracy replacing
ideology and traditional class policies.

When neo-Marxists have analysed educated workers, they have
tended to focus upon the class position of such workers. New
working-class theorists (Gorz 1968, 1972; Mallet 1975a 1975b;
Touraine 1971a, 1971b) contend that the contradiction between
capitalist imperatives and the exigencies of educated work is
sufficiently extreme to radicalise such workers, causing them often to
side with the working class in opposing capitalist interests. Moreover,
according to new working-class theory, educated workers will tend to
oppose the basic logic of capitalism in a more fundamental and
progressive manner than the more traditional working class, owing to
the fact that it is more integral to capitalist technocracy, and hence
uniquely situated to challenge it.

Professional-Managerial Class theory (Ehrenreich and Ehrenreich
1977a, b; Walker 1978) alleges that new working-class theory, by
emphasising only the contradictions and ignoring the continuities
between educated workers and capitalist interests, has not fully
understood the class situation of such workers. Professional and
managerial workers comprise a distinct class (the PMC) which
involves an objectively antagonistic relationship to *both* capitalists
and the working class, rendering alliances with either problematic.
Educated workers are often in 'contradictory class locations' (Wright
1976, 1979) within the capitalist class structure.

Such debate about the 'new class' of educated workers: how to define, disaggregate, and situate it within the class structure, and which sub-groupings tend towards particular political viewpoints (Brint 1980; Bruce-Briggs 1979; Chomsky 1982, Gouldner 1979), needs to be buttressed by a more structural and historical under-standing of technocracy. Among recent theorists, only Heydebrand (1979, 1981, 1983) has attempted such an analysis, with his understanding of organisational rationalisation as a dialectical process (Heydebrand 1977). Based on empirical studies of the judiciary (Heydebrand 1979) and the educational system (Burris and Heydebrand 1984), Heydebrand analyses technocracy as a dialectical synthesis of the contradiction between professional and bureaucratic control structures. The following analysis builds upon his work.[5]

II. Dialectical Rationalisation of Organisational Control

In contrast to previous definitions, then, technocracy can be best understood as the most recent in a dialectical evolution of organisational control structures. Organisational control structures are relevant at different levels of analysis: individual organisations of diverse types, systems of organisations (e.g. the educational system, the judiciary), and the societal level of integration of different sectors (see Heydebrand 1981: 5). In the following discussion of the evolution of organisational control in the United States, a rough chronological sequence can be traced, although uneven development and coexistence of different control structures is the norm.

This mascrosocial organisational analysis of developing control structures is a useful corrective to the usual analyses of managerial control, which have tended to assume the vantage point of either managers themselves, or of the working class. A more systemic analysis, one which focuses upon the unfolding of contradictions within control structures, how these are dealt with, and how subsequent contradictions develop, is necessary, particularly because technocracy is characterised by its systemic nature. Only by examining the historical process of organisational rationalisation can contemporary technocracy be understood.

Precapitalist control
Precapitalist control structures relied on either family-based produc-tion (subsistence and 'putting out'), or on craft/guild organisation, both of which served as frameworks for apprenticeship. Patriarchal religion provided an overall societal context of authoritarian theocracy which offset the decentralised family and guild organisational structure and provided considerable societal cohesion. However, the extent of decen-tralisation was nonetheless substantial.[6]

Family-based production was subject to patriarchal control, and apprenticeships were essentially structured in a hierarchical and authoritarian manner. However, the hierarchical relationship between master, journeymen, and apprentices differed from later work hierarchies in that the master did a good deal of the actual work in most cases (see Braverman 1974; Reckman 1979). The system of guild organisation and family-based production may not have been particularly democratic, but these pre-capitalist forms of work organisation did include dimensions of collegiality, meritocracy, and decentralisation. In fact, home-based production eventually became seen as overly decentralised and unsupervised: neither the labour process nor the products could be sufficiently controlled to allow for efficient capitalist appropriation and accumulation.

Simple control
With the emergence of capitalism, then, organisational control structures changed dramatically, as the perceived need for control and supervision increased. The implicit authority of expertise (buttressed by religion) gave way to the more coercive authority of capitalist ownership. Early factories (including pre-industrial factories) embraced time discipline (Thompson 1967) and simple control (Edwards 1979; Marglin 1974): entrepreneurial owners of emergent capitalist enterprises relied on direct supervision and coercion to ensure worker output. As Edwards (1979: 25) puts it:

> In the entrepreneurial firm, although the need for control was great, the mechanisms for achieving it were very unsophisticated, and the system of control tended to be informal and unstructured. The personal power and authority of the capitalist constituted the primary mechanism for control. In Stephen Hymer's words, the entrepreneur 'saw everything, knew everything, and decided everything.'

Vestiges of guild organisation were restricted to economic élites (boards of trustees), occupational élites (craft workers and early professionals) and political élites (governing committees).

Bureaucracy
By the late nineteenth century, the scale of capitalist enterprises had increased sufficiently to make simple control increasingly impossible, leading to a 'crisis of control' (Edwards 1979) in both particular organisations and in society in general. Although they are analytically distinct control structures, bureaucracy and professional status groups emerged together during this period, posing alternatives to simple control. Both promised to reduce arbitrary authority, re-establish control, promote efficiency, and 'raise standards'.

Bureaucracy relied upon a series of organisational innovations: differentiation of structure, specialisation of function, specification of job tasks, and formalised rules allowed for efficiency in the context of greater complexity and size. Authority was to be delegated, with a pyramidal hierarchy of control replacing the simple control of entrepreneurial capitalism. Finally, the alleged reliance on objective, standardised criteria for recruitment and promotion was designed to ensure meritocratic allocation with the bureaucracy, a reduction in arbitrary authority and favouritism, and the smooth functioning of the organisation (Weber 1968).

Professionalisation
Professionalisation represented another approach to standardisation and rationalisation. Professional status groups are analogous to craft guild organisation, with the difference being that professional status is dependent on formalised education or training, and credential certification (see Collins 1979). The emergence of universities, with differentiated professional training of diverse types, allowed for such credentialism. Given the alleged esoteric knowledge of the professions, self-regulation and evaluation by the professional status groups (based on 'codes of ethics') emerged as an alternative to bureaucratic control (Edwards 1979; Freidson 1973).

Professionals were presumed to be above politics and self interest, lifted to their exalted, objective position by the universality of science and expertise. Around the turn of the century, progressives saw professionalism as the key to reforming institutions and ridding them of corruption and favouritism. The perception was that 'Professional men...have no personal ends to serve and no special cause to plead' (Tyack 1974: 140). Both professional status groups and bureaucracies were thought to be politically neutral control structures, controlling in the interest of efficiency and rationality, rather than to augment power. Democracy came to be seen as inevitably inefficient and chaotic; one nineteenth-century school administrator said that he would 'as soon think of talking about the democratization of the treatment of appendicitis as to speak of the democratization of schools' (Tyack 1974: 77). In actuality, the politics of the emerging professional status groups undermined these hopes of professional political neutrality (see Collins 1979; Larson 1977).

Professional bureaucratic conflict
Moreover, the parallel emergence and uneasy coexistence of bureaucratic and professional organisational control structures led to 'professional/bureaucratic conflicts', particularly in organisational

contexts where professionals were working within a bureaucracy, as in the educational system and the judiciary. How to reconcile these divergent approaches to control, and how to balance professionals' claims to autonomy with bureaucratic rules were the central questions.

In fact, the 'conflict' between professionalism and bureaucracy is actually a developmental contradiction (Benson 1973; Heydebrand 1981), derived from an inherent incompatibility between the two types of control. Attempts to mediate this contradiction have culminated in the eventual development of technocratic control, which resolves the contradiction through the use of advanced technology.

One way in which such professional/bureaucratic conflicts were initially dealt with was through the attempt to professionalise management and administration so as to streamline the early mechanistic bureaucracies. Taylorism and its search for the scientific basis of management was an early attempt to increase managerial control and organisational efficiency by expanding management's technical understanding of the labour process (see Braverman 1974). Although Taylorism relied on only the most rudimentary science and technical understanding, time and motion studies combined with cost accounting, the attempt to rationalise and legitimate bureaucratic administration by giving it a surer basis in scientific and technical expertise was an important precursor of technocratic control.

Taylor emphasised the capability of engineering science to discover the 'one best way' to solve administrative problems. The bureaucratic apparatus needed to be rationalised by turning it over to professional engineers, who would ensure progress in the form of material development, greater efficiency, and technological advance. The former president of the Society of Civil Engineers termed engineers 'the priests of material development', (Akin 1977: 7). However, although Taylorists brought religious fervour to their reform efforts, the scientific basis of scientific management was too weak to provide sufficient legitimation, and the long-term impact of Taylorism was diluted, especially among professionals (Burris and Heydebrand 1984).

Technical control

The final type of control which emerged antecedent to technocracy was technical control. Edwards (1979: 112) defines technical control as 'designing machinery and planning the flow of work to minimize the problem of transforming labor power into labor as well as to maximize the purely physically based possibilities for achieving efficiencies'.

Although technical control has a history which is as old as the use of machines in a context of occupational subordination (and machine design to further such subordination), it only began to be systematised and perfected in the early twentieth century, heralded by Henry Ford's assembly line. As Edwards (1970: 113) points out, technical control only truly replaces simple control 'when the entire production process of the plant or large segments of it are based on a technology that paces and directs the labor process'.

Technical control is the blue collar/production counterpart of bureaucratic control; both are forms of structural control which serve to veil and legitimate control by embedding it in the structure of either the machine technology or the organisational structure (see Edwards 1979). Such hidden control is less likely to be questioned due to its enhanced probability of being reified by workers. In addition, technical control assumes the powerful legitimating force of scientific and technological progress; technological design is less likely to be scrutinised because it is often viewed as the material manifestation of the benign teleology of science (see Habermas 1968). Finally, technical control relies on the isolation of workers, which becomes more pronounced as workers are increasingly interacting with machines rather than with co-workers or supervisors; job dissatisfaction is thereby rendered more diffuse, and opportunities for worker solidarity are reduced.

By the 1920s, then, the various types of control which would eventually combine to form technocratic control had become manifest: bureaucracy, professional status groups, and technical control. Both Taylor's scientific management and James Burnham's vision of managerial society represented early and premature attempts to conceptualise the emerging technocracy.

In the post-war period, technocracy has become more and more salient. With the increasing size of the state sector, the development of computerised information technology, and the increased need to manage the economic system and perfect long-range planning, technocratic control structures have become increasingly hegemonic. Professionalism, bureaucracy, and technical control have become intergrated into a sophisticated technocracy which transcends each of these previous forms of control, even while it incorporates certain features of each.

III. Aspects of Contemporary Technocracy

Transformation of bureaucracy
Technocracy is not merely a 'technobureaucracy' (Larson, 1972/73) or

Table 1 Bureaucracy contrasted with technocracy

Bureaucracy	Technocracy
Hierarchical division of labour	*Flattening of hierarchy; Polarisation into experts and non-experts*
Organisational complexity	*Technological complexity*
Rank authority emphasised	*Expertise as basis of authority*
Internal labour markets; Seniority as basis of promotion	*Credentialling from without; Mobility barriers based on credentials*
Task specifications at all levels	*Flexible, task-force orientation at technical levels; routinisation at lower levels*
Centralised structure	*Centralisation of control through technological design; functional decentralisation to promote efficiency*

a technical bureaucracy (Gouldner 1976), but a genuine departure from bureaucratic organisation in several respects. Table 1 summarises some of the most salient contrasts between bureaucracy and technocracy.

First, in technocracy, the hierarchical division of labour characteristic of bureaucracy tends to be simplified and broken down, with a certain *polarisation* into experts and non-experts, and a corresponding flattening of the hierarchy occurring within work organisations. This transformation of the division of labour is due to the systematic reorganisation around technological systems, which substitute internal, technical complexity for the organisational complexity characteristic of bureaucracy. Although in some work organisations there is an attempt to retain the bureaucratic division of labour by imposing a proliferation of job titles and hierarchical categories on workers, the underlying tendency of technocratic organisations is towards simplification and polarisation.

Empirical substantiation of this tendency can be found in Kraft's (1979: 86) study of computer programmers. He found that:

> Technical and scientific occupations are not inherently amenable to military-like separation of substantive job tasks or to authority distinctions based on them. An engineer may be more or less experienced, more or less senior, or even more or less competent, but he or she is either an engineer or something else which is not an engineer.

Feldberg and Glenn (1980a,b) also found that polarisation of job categories tended to accompany computerisation of the insurance companies they studied. Peters and Waterman (1982) discuss the flattening of the hierarchical division of labour in the best-managed corporations which they studied.

A corollary of this tendency is that expertise tends to become coterminous with rank authority. Kraft (1979), for instance, found that while some computer analysts emphasised expertise and others emphasised managerial authority, that analysts without sufficient expertise tended to have trouble maintaining their authority, and that there was a trend towards assigning technical and managerial functions to the same person. It appears then, that existing contradictions between technical expertise and traditional managerial authority are pointing towards a convergence of the two. As technocracy becomes more fully consolidated, managers will increasingly need to rely on technical expertise in order to maintain legitimacy within the technocratic system.

Another way in which the bureaucracy is transformed is the decreasing emphasis on internal labour markets and seniority, and the increasing reliance on credentialling by the educational system (Noyelle 1983; Collins 1979). In terms of organisational structure, this implies stringent mobility barriers between the levels of the flattened hierarchy, with a proliferation of job titles within each level, giving the possibility of horizontal rather than vertical mobility.

Finally, some of the rigidity characteristic of bureaucratic rules and task specifications tends to be lost, particularly at higher, technical levels. Tasks tend to become organised around projects and to involve more flexible and collegial forms of work. Peters and Waterman (1982), following Bennis and Slater (1968) discuss the concept of 'adhocracy' and the utility of task forces as necessary alternatives to bureaucracy in modern corporations. Kraft (1979: 65) found that:

> Software work, like other mind-work, does not readily lend itself to this sort of narrow definition of work and tidy division of people into discrete 'job descriptions'. Even today, categories as broad and poorly defined as coder, programmer, and analyst are largely arbitrary and routinely crossed in the practice of writing a program. They are social divisions, as between manager and managed, more than technical divisions of labor, and yield when the realities of the production process demand cooperative effort.

At the non-expert level, however, the tendency is for tasks to become more routinised and regimented (Braverman 1974), although this tendency may be offset through various forms of 'work humanisation'. Peters and Waterman (1982) do discuss autonomy for low-level workers, but in the context of the need to keep it circumscribed. There is an entire spectrum of workplace reform (see Zwerdling 1976) from manipulative pseudo-participation to actual workplace democracy. Managers will increasingly be forced to deal with issues of workplace democracy and the demands of non-expert workers for the sort of self-determination at work which expert-level workers often enjoy.

Centralisation/decentralisation
As a technocracy is organised around a given system of advanced technology, it tends to combine centralisation with decentralisation, in contrast to bureaucracy, which tends to be centralised.

The technological system assumes the form of visible decentralisation (e.g. computer terminals in every office) but with an underlying centralisation of control, which is programmed into the design of the system. Power can therefore be variably distributed according to how the system of technology is designed and implemented. In practice, power tends to be kept highly centralised, with functional structure more decentralised so as to promote efficiency and to give the illusion of decentralised power. As Ellul (1980) points out, this centralisation of administrative power which is associated with computerised systems is largely due to the fact that technology is designed so as to fit into an ongoing political system which is centralised and essentially undemocratic.

Peters and Waterman (1982: 318) discuss the 'coexistence of firm central direction and maximum individual autonomy' at some length. They recommend centralisation around 'core values' and 'maintaining very substantial control where it counts' (ibid.213), while giving managers and workers some autonomy and socialising them into believing that they have a great deal.

That computerisation has tended to augment centralised control and systematisation on a world-wide scale is clear; what is less clear is the extent to which the functional decentralisation provides opportunities for the decentralisation of power. Organisational politics in the coming years will reveal the answer.

Transformation of professionalism
The nature of professional work is also changed fundamentally as professionalism is fused with bureaucratic and technical control. As Heydebrand (1981: 37–8) puts it:

> The growing integration of professionals into organizational routines tends to threaten their exclusive jurisdiction and monopoly over knowledge and skills, their functional and legal autonomy (even though it may enhance their economic autonomy), their discretion and control over those aspects of the content of work

that is affected by the terms and conditions of their employment, and their commitment to a service ideal.

Although some have viewed this process as deprofessionalisation (Haug 1973, 1975) or as proletarianisation of professionals (Larson, 1977), these conceptualisations tend to obscure the fact that professionals working in a technocracy lose some prerogatives while gaining others.

With the convergence of professional and administrative functions, and with the nature of professional expertise becoming increasingly technical in nature, professional power is transformed rather than reduced. As professionals become experts, i.e. technocrats, their autonomy may be somewhat restricted, as the loose regulation of professional status groups gives way to the need to co-ordinate with the exigencies of the technocratic system.

One recent indication of this convergence of function was the 1978 Supreme Court decision concerning Yeshiva University which declared that professors were in effect 'managers' of the university, and hence ineligible to form a union or engage in collective bargaining with the administration (see Burris and Heydebrand 1984). In this decision, the Supreme Court legitimitated an actual trend, the technocratic convergence of professional and managerial work, while circum-scribing any democratic tendencies, since students and non-professional staff are to be managed rather than integrally included in the educational system.

How much autonomy is retained will vary according to profession and setting. At one extreme, professionals may become mere functionaries, or paraprofessionals, implementing a technology which is centrally devised and controlled. At the other extreme, they may become expert administrators of an increasingly powerful technical apparatus, which both simplifies certain tasks and augments their power. As more and more professionals become integrated into technocratic organisations, this contradictory transformation of professionalism will become more pronounced, with parapro-fessionals and technicians often used to mediate the tension.

Finally, it is the *systemic* quality of technocracy which is its most distinctive feature: technocratic systems of work organisation are now world-wide in scope, and carry the cumulative legitimation of bureaucratic authority, professional expertise, and scientific/technical rationality. As Heydebrand (1979: 38) puts it:

If bureaucratic conservatism, according to Karl Mannheim, tends to 'turn problems of politics into problems of administration,' and if 'professionals tend to turn every problem of decisionmaking into a question of expertise' ... then the technocratic strategy can be said to turn problems of politics, expertise, and administration into problems of cybernetic systems control, the ultimate form of the 'administration of things.'

IV. The Implications of Technocracy

Relation to capitalism

Some theorists (e.g. Veblen 1921; Larson 1972/3; new working class theorists) have conceptualised technocracy as fundamentally challenging the basic logic of capitalism, in that it would substitute rational production centred around use value for the irrational capitalist market economy, and authority based on expertise for authority based on ownership. However, contemporary technocracy appears to be compatible with capitalism, and indeed seems to have resulted in an increasingly hegemonic world capitalist system.[8]

Technocracy has been perfected in response to capitalist crises, and in particular economic crises (O'Connor 1973; Heydebrand 1979, 1981), but has resulted in the perpetuation and transformation of capitalism, rather than its supercession. Heydebrand (1981, 1983) uses the term 'technocratic corporatism' to convey the nature of this transformation of capitalism, with its increased emphasis on state intervention, planning, and technical decision-making. Technocratic forces of production have been developed so as to harmonise with existing capitalist relations of production (Gorz 1972; Ellul 1980) in particular through the design of technological systems and the structuring of systems of higher education.

However, technocratic rationality is also antagonistic to capitalism. The exaltation of knowledge and expertise as alternative sources of power and authority, leading to the creation of a 'cultural bourgeoisie' (Gouldner 1979), may result in contradictions with market rationality and displaced crisis tendencies in advanced capitalism (Block and Hirschorn 1979; Larson 1972/73). Capitalist interests may be threatened by certain aspects of technocratic rationality. In particular, the competitive, small business sector will be at a disadvantage as large-scale technocratic systems augment monopolisation and diminish market rationality. Moreover, the transformation of bureaucratic hierarchies into expert/non-expert polarities and the increased role of expertise in decision-making may undermine the traditional prerogatives of capitalists and managers.

Critically important in evaluating the relationship between technocracy and capitalism is the education/work nexus and the political economy of *knowledge capital* (Gouldner 1979). Theorists who assume that technocracy implies meritocracy (Bell 1973; Touraine 1971b) ignore the facts of 'cartelisation' of knowledge capital

(Gouldner 1979), 'feudalisation of power' (Martins 1972/73) and monopolies of 'cultural capital' (Bourdieu 1979), all of which serve to undermine any meritocratic tendencies within technocratic rationality and to make technocratic experts unlikely to become a 'new working class'.

And yet, technocratic élitism coexists with some tendencies towards meritocracy and universality, with the latter potentially coming into contradiction with capitalist imperatives, much as new working-class theorists have predicted. For instance, when educated workers are unable to use their education on the job because of the exigencies of capitalist technocracy (Berg 1970; Burris 1983), then the contradiction between the meritocratic potential of technocracy and the reality of power imperatives may become pronounced. Technocracy's emphasis on planning may instill expectations of a rational social order which will be thwarted as deindustrialisation and recurrent crises indicate the limitations of technocratic rationality (Habermas 1975; Bluestone and Harrison 1982). Technocracy represents a 'flawed universalism' (Gouldner 1979), and hence is inherently contradictory.

Technocracy and social stratification
One large class of workers which technocracy has helped to create is the unemployed. In the contemporary US, the reality of de-industrialisation continues to thwart the post-industrialist dream of a leisure society.

Among the employed labour force, if the division of labour within work organisations is broken down, the greater visibility of occupational groups may tend to promote political solidarity and heightened political consciousness, although the proliferation of job titles, the intermediate group of technicians, and the isolating tendencies of technical control will tend to counteract and obscure the structural polarisation. At the societal level, the different types of knowledge and expertise will result in division among the working class which may be difficult to overcome.[9] Moreover, the world-wide division of labour involves a geographical dispersion of the working class which is an even more difficult obstacle to organising.

In general, technocracy seeks to undermine traditional class groupings by substituting overall system imperatives for the labour/management polarity. The synthesis of bureaucratic, professional, and technical control also implies a synthetic and powerful legitimating ideology. To the extent that the expert/non-expert polarity is accepted as rational and meritocratic, traditional labour/management conflict may be reduced. Alternatively, work-place conflicts may be transformed from conflicts centering around authority and control to those ostensibly centering around differences in expertise. Cultural capital and 'conspicuous expertise' will become increasingly salient currencies in workplace politics, tending to obscure and mystify workplace conflicts (Bourdieu and Passeron 1977; Burris 1983, Collins 1979).

Less obscured, however, is the impact of technocracy on gender and minority relations. The polarisation of the occupational sector into skilled and non-skilled jobs is paralleling and reinforcing a sexist and racist division of labour, so that women and racial minorities are disproportionately found in the non-expert, deskilled jobs and white men are in the majority among expert, skilled workers (Kraft 1979; Feldberg and Glenn 1980a, b; Zimmerman 1983). This tendency is most marked in the international division of labour, where young women comprise 85–90 per cent of workers in the Third World's Export Processing Zones of US based multinationals (Fernandez-Kelly 1983). As a technocracy reinforces sex and race segmentation, it will also reinforce sexist and racist conceptions about the inability of women and minorities to work with skill and judgement, and perpetuate divisions among the working class.

Finally, it appears that technological systems are now being designed so that women can operate computer terminals in their homes, so that they can more readily combine family and work roles (Zimmerman 1983). This return to home-based production, albeit in a technologically advanced form, raises serious questions about the shape of gender relations in the future. The resulting isolation of women workers, and the re-emphasis on the traditional female role of homemaker and mother would have far-reaching effects on both gender politics and on labour politics in general. Women workers, minorities, and the male working class, must become more integrally involved in the design and implementation of technological systems if they are to have any control over their future working lives.[10]

Conclusion
Technocracy, as an emergent form of control, is becoming increasingly apparent in diverse work settings. Analysts of the labour process should add technocratic control to their lexicon of types of control: simple control, technical control, bureaucratic control, professional control, and technocratic control (Edwards 1979; Freidson 1973; Heydebrand 1977, 1979, 1981), and should use the concept of technocracy in future studies of the workplace.

In a technocracy, there is an attempt to reduce political questions to technical considerations: that there is 'one best way', that this way can only be understood and found by the experts, and that the parameters of choice are dictated by technical imperatives, rather than political ones (Straussman 1978). Like the 'end of ideology' theory, technocracy rests on an 'ideology of non-ideology' (Heydebrand 1981): the view that political conflict is a non-rational vestige which will wither away as technocratic rationality continues to expand.[11]

Straussman (1978) has documented the expansion of technocratic expertise at the federal level since the Second World War. He concludes from his analysis that the experts have served various functions, including guidance, legitimation, diffusion of political conflict, and catalysis of the centralisation of power. Straussman's analysis refutes the technocratic ideology of non-ideology by revealing how 'technopolitics' are veiled but not eliminated: reports get 'sanitised' according to political motives, and the assumptions of technocratic planners involve political decisions which go unexamined, often leading to self-fulfilling prophecies (see also Cole 1973). To make the values and assumptions of technocratic experts explicit is to risk conflict, and is resisted on the grounds of technocratic rationality.

Within work organisations, similar sorts of 'technopolitics' are becoming apparent. Expertise, or the semblance of it, is increasingly used to buttress and legitimate managerial authority. Extra-work cultures, such as those based on class, race, sex and education, are becoming increasingly salient precursors of the cultural capital which is an important component of expertise (Bourdieu and Passeron 1977; Burris 1983; Collins 1979). Politicking has been transformed, but not eliminated.

If the 'flawed universalism' of technocracy is to be made less flawed, the 'one best way' ideology must be challenged by a re-politicised and educated public, both within work organisations and in society at large. The emphasis on functional rationality must be offset by substantive rationality and democratisation. Ongoing economic and political crises will create the potential for a questioning of the legitimacy of technocratic rationality (Habermas 1975); whether this potential will be realised remains to be seen.

One important component of this democratisation of technocracy is the de-reification of technology. As Noble (1983) points out: 'Technological determinism – the domination of the present by the past – and technological progress – the domination of the present by the future – have combined in our minds to annihilate the technological present' (p. 10). If we are to avoid 'technological hubris' (Peters and Waterman 1982: 135), the technological present must be reclaimed as a realm of democratic decision-making.

Technocracy, with its reduction of some of the rigidity and hierarchy of bureaucracy, with the power of advanced technology, and with its emphasis on knowledge as a possible source of more legitimate authority, does involve the potential for human liberation. However, there is also 'decadence' within technocracy (Gouldner 1976) and the potential for a technically-based authoritarianism. Technocratic experts will not automatically serve the public interest, and technical decisions are not free of political considerations. Only through democratic debate and old-fashioned politics can the universalistic potential of technocracy begin to be realised.

Notes

1. For instance, *Case Studies on the Labor Process*, edited by Zimbalist (1979) contains only one article concerning technical or managerial work: Kraft's piece on computer programmers (see also Kraft 1977). Edwards (1978, 1979) also departs from the usual trend of viewing workplace control from the vantage point of the proletariat, as his is a more systemic perspective.

2. The usual criticism of Braverman concerns his inattention to worker resistance against Taylorism and subsequent managerial control (Edwards 1978; Stark 1981). While this is true, it is an epiphenomenon of another limitation: his lack of a systemic perspective which focuses upon contradictions (including contradictions between workers and managers) as dynamic tendencies. Inattention to this essential feature of the Marxist dialectical method is a more telling deficiency in Braverman.

3. See, for instance, p. 246, where an analysis of recent changes in management is reduced to a discussion of the 'mass of clerical workers' now involved in administration.

4. Veblen (1921) became the manifesto of the Technocracy Movement of the 1920s and 1930s. See Akin (1977), Elsner (1967) for histories of this prescient movement, its internal conflicts, and its long-term impact on American society.

5. My approach differs from Heydebrand in that it focuses more on historical developments which led up to technocracy, it considers technocracy as a tripartite synthesis of professional, bureaucratic, *and technical* control structures (as compared with Heydebrand's synthesis of professional and bureaucratic forms of control), and it deals with the question of the implications of technocracy somewhat differently.

6. Clark (1978) makes this decentralisation clear in describing educational guilds: 'Faculty (and sometimes students) banded together in guilds, attempted to govern themselves through collegial principles, and manoeuvred as best they could against the somewhat removed officials of state and church' (p. 104).

7. Peters and Waterman (1982), for instance, do discuss the possibility of giving low-level workers more autonomy, but this concern is clearly secondary to the need for autonomy at higher levels.

8. It should be noted that although the present analysis is limited to advanced capitalist countries, technocracy is not only characteristic of capitalist societies, but of state socialist societies as well. Socialist technocracy is somewhat different from capitalist technocracy, although certain common features are apparent. See Mallet 1970; Bahro 1979.

9. This argument is similar to that of Gordon, Edwards and Reich (1982), although they fail to distinguish between organisational and societal levels of analysis.

10. Some trade unions in the US are beginning to make this a concern. See the International Machinists' 'Technology Bill of Rights' (1983).

11. These claims are similar to those which were made for bureaucracy in the nineteenth century: that bureaucratic reforms would 'take the schools out of politics' for instance.

References

Akin, W.E. (1977), *Technocracy and the American Dream*, Berkeley: University of California Press.
Bahro, R. (1979), *The Alternative in Eastern Europe*, New York: Schocken Books.
Bell, D. (1960), *The End of Ideology*, Glencoe, Ill.: The Free Press.
Bell, D. (1973), *The Coming of Post-Industrial Society*, New York: Basic Books.
Bell, D. (1976), *Introduction to The Coming of Post-Industrial Society*, New York: Basic Books.
Dennis, W. G. and Slater, P. (1968), *The Temporary Society*, New York: Harper.
Benson, J. (1973), 'The analysis of bureaucratic-professional conflict: functional vs. dialectical approaches', *Sociological Quarterly*, **14**: 376–94.
Berg, I. (1970), *Education and Jobs: The Great Training Robbery*, New York: Praeger.
Block, F. and Hirschhorn L. (1979), 'New productive forces and the contradictions of contemporary capitalism', *Theory and Society*, **7** (3): 363–95.
Bluestone, B. and Harrison, B. (1982), *The Deindustrialization of America*, New York: Basic Books.
Bourdieu, P. and Passeron J. (1977), *Reproduction in Education, Society, and Culture*, Beverly Hills, Calif.: Sage Publications.
Bourdieu, P. and Passeron, J. (1979), *The Inheritors*, Chicago: University of Chicago Press.
Braverman, H. (1974), *Labor and Monopoly Capital*, New York: Monthly Review Press.
Brint, S. (1980), ' "New Class" or new scapegoat?', *Contemporary Sociology*, **9**: (5), 651–53.
Bruce-Briggs, B. (ed.), (1979), *The New Class?*, New Brunswick, N.J.: Transaction Books.
Burnham, J. (1941), *The Managerial Revolution*, New York: John Day.
Burris, B. (1983), *No Room at the Top: Underemployment and Alienation in the Corporation*, New York: Praeger.
Burris, B. and Heydebrand W. (1984), 'Technocratic administration and educational control' in Fischer and Sirianni (eds) *Critical Studies in Organization and Bureaucracy*, Philadelphia, Pa.: Temple University Press.
Carter, M. A. (1976), 'Contradiction and correspondence: an analysis of the relation of schooling to work' in Carnoy and Levin (eds), *The Limits of Educational Reform*, New York: David McKay.
Chomsky, N. (1982), *Towards a New Cold War*, New York: Harper and Row.
Clark, B.R. (1962), *Educating the Expert Society*, San Francisco: Chandler.
Clark, B.R. (1978) 'United States' in Van de Graaf et al. (eds), *Academic Power: Patterns of Authority in Seven National Systems of Higher Education*, New York: Praeger.
Cockburn, C. (1983), *Brothers: Male Dominance and Technological Change*, London: Pluto Books.
Cole, H. S. D. et al. (1973), *Models of Doom: A Critique of the Limits to Growth*, New York: Universe Books.
Collins, R. (1979), *The Credential Society*, New York: Academic Press.
Dickson, D. (1981), 'Limiting democracy: technocrats and the liberal state', *Democracy* **1** (1), 61–79.
Edwards, R. (1978), 'The Social Relations of Productions and the Point of Production', *Insurgent Sociologist* **8** (2/3), 109–25.
Edwards, R. (1979), *Contested Terrain*, New York: Basic Books.
Ehrenreich, B. and J. (1977a), 'The professional-managerial class', *Radical America,* **11** (2) .
Ehrenreich B. and J. (1977b) 'The new left and the professional-managerial class', *Radical America*, **11** (3).
Ellul, J. (1980), *The Technological System*, New York: Continuum.

Elsner, H. (1967), *The Technocrats: Prophets of Automation*, Syracuse: Syracuse University Press.
Feldberg, R. and Glenn E. (1980a), 'Effects of technological change on clerical work: review and reassessment', Paper presented at the 1980 ASA Meeting, New York.
Feldberg, R. and Glenn E. (1980b) 'Technology and work degradation: re-examining the impacts of office automation', unpublished paper, Boston University.
Fernandez-Kelly, M. P. (1983), 'Gender and industry on Mexico's new frontier' in Zimmerman (ed.), *The Technological Woman*, New York: Praeger.
Freidson, E. (ed.) (1973), *The Professions and Their Prospects*, Beverly Hills: Sage.
Galbraith, J. K. (1967), *The New Industrial State*, Boston: Houghton Mifflin.
Gordon, D., Edwards, R.; Reich, M. (1982), *Segmented Work, Divided Workers*, New York: Cambridge.
Gorz, A. (1968), *Strategy for Labor*, Boston: Beacon Press.
Gorz, A. (1972), 'Technical intelligence and the capitalist division of labor'. *Telos*, **1** 27–41.
Gouldner, A. W. (1975/6), 'Prologue to a theory of revolutionary intellectuals', *Telos* **26**, 3–36.
Gouldner, A. W. (1976), *The Dialectic of Ideology and Technology*, New York: Oxford.
Gouldern, A. W. (1979), *The Future of Intellectuals and the Rise of the New Class*, New York: Seabury Press.
Habermas, J. (1968), *Toward a Rational Society*, Boston: Beacon Press.
Habermas, J. (1975), *Legitimation Crisis*. Boston: Beacon Press.
Haug, M. (1973), 'Deprofessionalization: An alternate hypothesis for the future' *Sociological Review* Monograph no. 20: 195–211.
Haug, M. (1975), 'The deprofessionalization of everyone?', *Sociological Focus* **8**, 197–213.
Herman, A. (1982), 'Conceptualizing control: domination and hegemony in the capitalist labor process', *Insurgent Sociologist* **9** (3): 7–22.
Heydebrand, W. (1977), 'Organizational contradictions in public bureaucracies', *Sociological Quarterly* **18**, 83–107.
Heydebrand, W. (1979), 'The technocratic administration of justice', *Research in Law and Society* **2**, 29–64.
Heydebrand, W. (1981), 'Technocratic corporatism: toward a theory of organizational change', Unpublished paper, New York University.
Heyderbrand, W. (1983), 'Technocratic corporatism: Towards a theory of occupational and organizational transformation', in *Organizational Theory and Public Policy*, R. Ball and R. Quinn (eds), Beverly Hills, Calif.: Sage.
International Association of Machinists (1983), 'Workers' technology bill of rights' *Democracy* **3** (2), 25–27.
Kraft, P. (1977), *Programmers and Managers*, New York: Springer-Verlag.
Kraft, P. (1979), 'The industrialization of computer programming' in Zimbalist (ed.), *Case Studies on the Labor Process*, New York: Monthly Review Press.
Larson, M. S., (1972/73), 'Notes on technocracy: Some problems of theory, ideology and power', *Berkeley Journal of Sociology* **17**, 1–34.
Larson, M. S. (1977), *The Rise of Professionalism*, Berkeley: University of California Press.
Loeb, H. (1933), *Life in a Technocracy*, New York: Viking Press.
Mallet, S. (1970), 'Bureaucracy and technocracy in the socialist countries', *Socialist Revolution* **1** (3), 44–75.
Mallet, S. (1975a), *Essays on the New Working Class*, edited and translated by D. Howard and D. Savage, St Louis: Telos Press.
Mallet, S. (1975b), *The New Working Class*, Bristol: Spokesman Books.
Marglin, S. A. (1974), 'What do bosses do? The origins and functions of hierarchy in capitalist production', *Review of Radical Political Economics* **6**, 33–60.

Martins, C. E. (1972/73), 'Technocratic rule or technological counsel?' *Berkeley Journal of Sociology* **17**, 35-56.

Meynaud, J. (1964), *Technocracy*, New York: Free Press.

Noble, D. (1983), 'Present tense technology', *Democracy* **3** (2), 8-24.

Noyelle, T. J. (1983), 'Employment and career opportunities for women and minorities in a changing economy', Unpublished paper, Columbia University: Institute for the Conservation of Human Resources.

O'Connor, J. (1973), *The Fiscal Crisis of the State*, New York: St Martins' Press.

Peters, T. J. and Waterman R. (1982), *In Search of Excellence*, New York: Warner Books.

Reckman, B. (1979), 'Carpentry: the craft and trade', in Zimbalist (ed.), *Case Studies on the Labor Process*, New York: Monthly Review Press.

Stark, D. (1981), 'Consciousness in command', *Socialist Review*, **57**.

Straussman, J. D. (1978), *The Limits of Technocratic Politics*. New Brunswick, N. J.: Transaction Books.

Thompson, E. P. (1967), 'Time, work-discipline, and industrial capitalism', *Past and Present*, **38**.

Touraine, A. (1971a), *The May Movement*, New York; Random House.

Touraine, A. (1971b), *The Post-Industrial Society*, New York: Random House.

Tyack, D. B., *The One Best System*, Cambridge, Mass.: Harvard University Press.

Veblen, T. (1921), *The Engineers and the Price System*, New York: Viking.

Walke, P. (ed.), (1978), *Between Labor and Capital: The Professional-Managerial Class*, Boston: South End Press.

Weber, M. (1968), *Economy and Society*, vol.2, Roth and Wittich (eds), New York: Bedminster Press.

Wright, E. O. (1976), 'Class boundaries in advanced capitalist societies', *New Left Review*, **98**.

Wright, E. O. (1979), *Class, Crisis and the State*, London: Verso Editions.

Zimmerman, J. (1983), *The Technological Woman*, New York: Praeger.

Zwerdling, D. (1976), *Workplace Democracy*, New York: Harper and Row.

9　The Institutional Management of Class Politics: Beyond the Labour Process and Corporatist Debates

Paul Boreham, Stewart Clegg, Geoff Dow

Introduction: The Politics of Production

Braverman's notable contribution to the study of the labour process[1] initiated a major reformulation of theories of control in the study of organisations. Braverman, following Marx, set forth a detailed exposition of the realisation of capitalist control over the labour process, which argued that scientific management provided the vehicle for effecting the progressive investment of decision-making powers in the hands of capitalists and the removal of control from workers. The management techniques elaborated in the systems of Taylor, Ford and others consitute the extension of capitalist relations to all levels of work organisations. These techniques involved elaborate systems of stratification which created strictly demarcated hierarchies, the formulation of specific methods of wage payment, particularly, piece-work rates and incentive payments, and the extended fragmentation and deskilling of the workforce through an elaborate division of labour and the creation of intermediate management functions.

Within the 'labour process' perspective, class is re-instituted as one of the more traditional concerns of industrial/organisational sociology. For instance, it is argued that once skill or knowledge is removed from the control of workers and placed in the hands of 'management' whose task it is to plan and control the work process, there are significant advantages which may accrue to capital. Labour will be cheapened and made more easily transferable as aspects of planning and design of work themselves become infused with managerial control and removed from labour. According to Braverman, skills formerly exercised by workers are absorbed not only by management but also by modern technological systems and the work arrangements upon which they are predicated. The significance of locating technology in this context is that it provides a clear mechanism for the extension of direct control strategies under the guise of rationalisation and technological progress.[2] Braverman's thesis is that the logic of capitalist intervention into the labour process has focused on the differentiation of once unified functions of conception and execution. This now constitutes the major locus of differentiation in contemporary industry.[3] Finally, it is argued that the nature of these developments has been determined by conscious strategies of the contending classes:

> The bureaucratic reorganization of the labour process developed, then, not through some technological imperative but through a historically specific process of class struggle which was understood and articulated as such by the contending parties.[4]

A measure of the impact of *Labor and Monopoly Capital* is the critical debate which has surrounded its findings.[5] Three major elements of this debate are important to our argument. The first point is that the labour process is but one of a number of avenues through which influence and control are brought to bear on workers. Such control often appears redundant. Educational institutions, the family and the media of communication and socialisation are scarcely likely to utilise a vocabulary of motives which could provide unskilled workers with a legitimate and plausible rationale for that resistance to managerial prerogatives which, in its rituals and rules, provides much of the sense of locale which is work.[6] What is political is not experienced *as* political, but as, simply, the games people play to make work bearable. It is more than likely that labourers enter the workplace individually prepared to co-operate and contribute to a degree conventionally regarded as appropriate. Clearly, such conventions do not impact passively on working-class groups but are negotiated and modified in the light of objective conditions and experiences. Nevertheless, it seems likely that the forms of control of the labour process do connect with non-work experiences which reflect the valuations imposed by the distribution of economic and political power in the wider society. Thus, to emphasise control in the labour process is to obfuscate other structural forces whose impact may be overriding.

The second concern surrounding Braverman's analysis derives from the relative lack of emphasis on the consequences of working-class consciousness and resistance. This has led to the recognition that the development of a clear-cut relationship between capitalist production methods and the skill structure of the workforce is significantly constrained by worker resistance. While there may have been a general trend toward deskilling, the difficulty which Braverman's unidirectional thesis encounters is that when the fact of worker resistance is admitted, the theorisation of class relations is thrown into disarray. The design of work involves a critical interaction of

structures of management control, employee resistance and
subsequent adjustments and counter pressures which management
attempts to employ.[7] There are two issues which flow from this
contention. One is that Braverman's analysis proposes a mechanistic
notion of a capitalist class whose degree of intersubjectivity is such as
to determine a unitary capital logic.[8] The second point is that the
actual levels of skill or technical knowledge employed by the worker
in any particular location may be less relevant to employers' needs to
control the labour process and to enhance the conditions for
accumulation than the extent to which workers have or have not 'been
accepted as skilled within the politics of the workplace.'[9] Clearly, the
specific conditions circumscribing the actions of both labour and
capital within the workplace affect the degree of intervention
possible.[10] This highlights the essential variability of the outcomes of
worker resistance. 'Some changes are resisted more than others, some
groups resist more than others, some groups achieve a 'negotiated
order', whilst some groups become a privileged élite.'[11] In this process
both jobs and workers acquire certain social statuses to which accrue
expectations and regulations concerning rates of pay and conditions.[12]
These differentials are not only intraorganisational,[13] but also become
interorganisational and regionally specific in the world-wide division
of labour, and hence, not specific to the politics of a particular labour
process.

The third issue which has been raised with respect to Braverman's
work concerns the complexity and variety of influences on the
structure of employment. The development of mechanisms at the level
of the workplace constitutes only one of a complex and interacting set
of factors shaping the workforce. Included among these factors are
changes in levels of national and international economic activity
reflected in levels of employment. Interregional changes in the
distribution of economic growth or the availability of political
subsidies, development of new markets, changes in tax structures and
the growth of new industries and products.[14] Equally important to
employers are alternative income sources external to the production
process. Factors such as commodity and currency speculation, money
market transactions and credit manipulation have important
consequences for the development of economic activity. Thus,
accumulation may have more important origins in mechanisms in the
sphere of circulation than in the labour process.[15] Indeed, where
workplace relations have assumed a 'negotiated order' and where the
expression of industrial conflict has been routinised through
structural and procedural mechanisms, employers will be placed in a
situation allowing them to devote a considerable proportion of their

energies to concerns other than production.

In the light of these reflections on orientations initiated by Braverman, sociological attention has focused on resistance within the labour process to managerial control. It may, however, be argued that the usual register of collective resistance to organisation and control – industrial militancy – is an imperfect guide to the strength and effectiveness of labour movement strategies. Comparative analysis of national statistics concerning worker resistance indicates that further, complementary dimensions of extra-enterprise struggles and of existing and emerging parliamentary and extra-parliamentary institutions warrant attention. These dimensions embrace questions of political mobilisation and political strategy concerning macro-economic conditions and the institutional sites of their formulation. If these broader considerations are implicated in structuring the forms and outcomes of labour process-centred resistance then the development of political institutions wherein labour's perspective on decisions affecting capital accumulation needs to become the focus of class-based strategies and of class analysis.

One argument which engages with this line of reasoning suggests that cyclical factors surrounding crises in accumulation in the 1930s and again in the 1970s created the circumstances in which large numbers of workers were effectively deskilled.[16] In this analysis it is the articulation of technological innovation and accumulation, and particularly the cycle of fixed capital renewal, that must provide the focus of analysis of contemporary changes in the mode of production. These changes may, once in motion, generate dislocation and crises which activate the search for alternative strategies for valorisation and accumulation. The orientation and 'success' of capitalist strategies to redress the outcomes of such crises must be viewed as contingent upon the response of working-class organisation and its political practice.[17] However, as Rutigliano[18] has pointed out, such opposition is frequently less an 'offensive' and more a 'defensive' manoeuvre against some of the grosser exploitative features of the reorganisation of work. This may be done because the modes of political action which seem to be available or appropriate are structured not only by historical and immediate material conditions and by the formal nature of trade union organisation and action, but also by the historical and contemporary bonds between workers' organisations and labour parties. The structural limitations of a trade unionism which is confined to the role of permanent opposition do permit the bargaining for conditions and rewards within work organisations but they also restrict the occasions for any direct promotion of macro-level social and economic change.

Braverman's conceptions of organisational and economic actors are highly unitaristic. Managers are unambiguously part of 'capital', workers are clearly 'labour' and problems of assigning positions to categories are underplayed. Consequently, both Braverman's account and many of those influenced by him tend to assume, in the allegories of a dichotomous class model, much that cannot be assumed. (In this respect they are not unlike those prescriptive and descriptive texts on management, which assume the goal-orientedness of managerial action to 'capital's' requirements as an overarching principal.) Contrary to this view are those qualifications advised by writers such as Loveridge.[19] Under certain circumstances of capital concentration, there need be no more a necessary unity of interest between particular local managements and a central capital-raising entity, than a necessary opposition of interests between a local management and the labour force it employs. Loveridge demonstrates how increasingly state intervention into federally fragmented organisation structures can increase both workforce-management conflict locally and local management-strategic management conflict overall. The outcome of these state interventions, he intimates, is a tighter capital discipline over both management and the workers, often achieved through liquidating undisciplined centres or divisions.

The contribution by Loveridge, albeit that it is addressed primarily to the managerial labour process, displays an accord with recent literature on the labour process in general. Perhaps no single point has been reiterated more emphatically in recent debates than the importance of studying resistance to organisational controls. Resistance can take many forms from rule-breaking, slowdowns and working to rule, to more explicit forms of sabotage and collective action. It can include the limitations to 'strategic choice'[20] which Loveridge identifies at the level of operational management's discretion, as well as more classic forms of labour resistance, such as the strike.

Arenas of Conflict and Political Power

In what follows we wish to argue on two interrelated fronts. First, taking up the 'resistance of labour' issue, we will argue beyond the simple zero-sum game assumptions of the labour/capital allegories. Second, developing the 'limitations to strategic choice' issue we will identify a set of constraints located in a particular type of institutional conjuncture, that of radical, politically bargained corporatism. These constraints, we will argue, derive from outside the conceptions of the simple zero-sum game, yet have important effects on the strength of the actors conceptualised. Paradoxically, however, in terms of the 'resistance' issue, these effects are not registerable within the terms of the dichotomous model. Consequently, the institutional management of what the labour process perspective has regarded as class politics, can not be seen to enter into these politics. The result of this is to produce an overly 'productivist' view of politics.

The most explicit collective action is the strike, defined as a temporary stoppage of work by a group of employees who withdraw their labour in order to express a grievance or enforce a demand.[21] From a labour process perspective strikes as a collective form of action and resistance would have to be regarded as a sign of working-class power. However, a contrary position could be put: that shop-floor power is less potent than other strategies that may be open to a labour movement, when viewed in an internationally comparative perspective. In the light of these data, we would suggest that in the aggregate, a high level of strikes is not a necessary or sufficient index of shopfloor power.

An elucidation of this statement lies in an appreciation of the linkages between the political and industrial arenas, political parties and collective action. These linkages can be constituted through a 'power-difference' model of conflict as Korpi[22] terms it. The less unequal the parties are in a social relationship the less it will be marked by social conflict. The more unequal the parties are in a social relationship the less it will be marked by social conflict. The reasons for this are clear. Manifest conflict typified by the exercise of power (getting others to do something they would not otherwise have done, even against their resistance) occurs only where the weaker party is at least strong enough to formulate and act on an alternative course of action. In other words 'a great disadvantage in power resources makes successful action by the weaker party unlikely.'[23] Where there is a smaller, or over time, decreasing, power-difference one would anticipate that there would be an increase in conflict 'since the weaker party will attempt to change the unequal terms of exchange and the stronger party to maintain them.'[24] Moreover, where there is more than just one arena of conflict, it is advantageous to the weaker party to move the power process and its conflict manifestations to the arena in which they have least disadvantage.

In liberal democracy there is ample evidence to suggest that the working class is at a greater disadvantage in the arena of private property and its relations of production than in the political arena. Not least relevant is the fact that in the latter, equal and universal suffrage allows for the sacking of the political masters by the mass: no such power resides in the normal organisation of relations of production. Hence, given the achievement of universal suffrage, then to the extent that the working class through its organisations for collective action is able to achieve strong and stable control over the executive, the conflicts of interest between labour and capital will increasingly be fought out in the political arena and industrial conflict will decline.[25]

High levels of strikes do not necessarily signal a strong and highly resistant labour movement. This may appear to be the case as a result of an exclusive focus on the point of production and resistance to it within a specific national framework. We would, however, propose a different relationship between class, politics and strikes. High levels of strike action may in fact be interpreted as a sign of blockage of the working class at the more effective level of class action and mobilisation: the political level. Moreover, it signals that the institutional arrangements arrived at in the political arena are themselves partly an effect of the balance of class forces at any particular conjuncture. Certain institutional aspects of past victories or defeats will be inscribed within this arena in a sedimented form, shaping further struggles of class forces.

Within this arena the central focus of struggle will be, as Lindblom suggests 'the degree to which market replaces government or government replaces market'.[26] Perhaps the most significant issue over which this struggle will occur will be that of economic policy, because of its impact upon property rights, relations of production, the control of the labour process and the labour market. These are the central structural features of the industrial arena. To the extent that labour movements attempt to affect these, they may do so through a number of strategies. Two polar ideal types were identified by Beatrice and Sydney Webb: these are 'the method of legal enactment' and 'the method of collective bargaining'.[27] The former method is one whose primary locus is the political arena of the state, while the latter focuses on specific industries and firms as its more appropriate site. Hence, the former may be termed a political strategy, oriented towards the subsumption of market to government, while the latter is a market strategy oriented towards 'free' (i.e. without state interference and regulation) collective bargaining.

As ideal types, such strategies will never be found in reality in their pure form, but always as somewhat mixed and contradictory. The balance of class forces and the development of a labour movement strategy are never voluntaristically 'chosen' of course. Nor are they subject to endogenous determination alone. No state is a political island. All states are part of an international network of alliances and oppositions which necessarily have effects on the balance of domestic forces.

Strikes have been a central issue of concern in society at large, ever since their efficacy began to be registered in legislative attempts to neutralise or outlaw them, at the end of the eighteenth century in Britain. A leitmotif of much of the writing done by industrial relations specialists in the 1950s and early 1960s on the social structure of the advanced societies, was the 'withering away of class' as Westergaard has extensively documented.[28] Linking class and struggle was the finding that strikes, as the dramatic focus of their expressive unity, were at the centre of this 'withering'.[29] It became conventional wisdom to point to the decline in strikes, internationally, as a post-war trend. Trends, however, have often been constructed out of what, with hindsight, proves to have been an extrapolation from a cycle rather than a linear tendency. Such appears to have been the case in the interpretation of comparative data on industrial conflict.

With all due caution,[30] it may be observed that the level of strike activity in the world's advanced industrial capitalist economies increased quite notably in the period from 1969, such that some commentators have spoken of the outbreak of a world strike wave.[31] After 1968-9 through to 1976, in the OECD states, the total number of working days lost in disputes, on the average, more than doubled

Figure 1
Labour mobilisation and political strategy in 18 OECD countries,
1945-1976

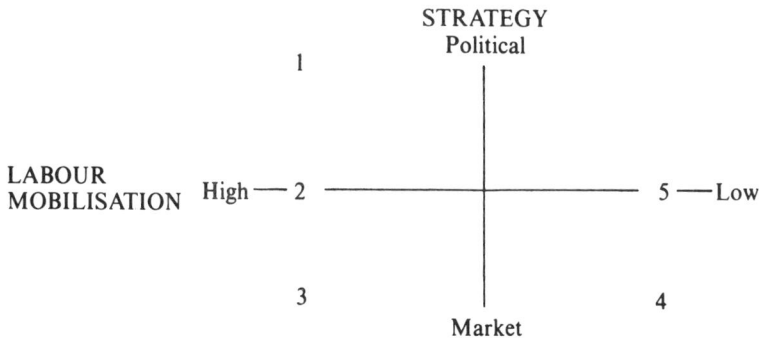

1. High labour mobilisation: stable left political control: Sweden, Austria Norway.
2. High labour mobilisation; occasional left control of politics: Denmark, New Zealand, United Kingdom, Belgium.
3. Medium-high labour mobilisation: little left-political control: Australia, Finland, France, Italy, Japan.
4. Low labour mobilisation: exclusion of left influence in politics: Canada, United States, Ireland.
5. Low labour mobilisation: partial left-political participation in politics: Germany, The Netherlands, Switzerland.

compared with the 1951–67 period. The incidence of this strike wave has been put in an historical context by the work of Korpi and Shalev for 18 industrial capitalist societies from 1900 to 1976.[32] The focus of this analysis is the extent of non-agricultural workforce involvement in strike activity.

The post-1968–9 strike wave is not the first this century. The period from the turn of the century until 1920 saw an upward trend in strike activity (except in the United States and Canada), with the years around 1920 providing the benchmark for an international strike wave, which was followed by a decrease in the 1920s. During the latter part of the 1930s in about half of the major OECD countries, there was an increase in strike activity (the exceptions were countries in which fascism was dominant or in which a labour party had gained office). Immediately after the Second World War there was another international strike wave of short duration, giving way to quite divergent post-war patterns (see Figure 1), which have continued to the present.

The correlations between the different patterns of industrial mobilisation and political involvement are significant, particularly in the three 'social democrat' examples of a political strategy of high mobilisation and stable control, the level of involvement and volume of strikes are very low. What makes these findings more significant is that in the period before the social democrats became the normal party of government in both Sweden and Norway (which, unlike Austria, did not have a fascist pre-war government), the strike volume and involvement were very high. This declined sharply with the accession to government of the social democrats (1932 in Sweden, 1945 in Norway).

Sweden is the strongest illustrative case of the general argument for a political strategy, for it is only after the beginning of social democratic rule from 1932 onwards that its high and prolonged levels of strike action receded. Their decrease was due to the emergence of a set of economic and social policies which partially transformed the reproduction of capitalist relations of production. To propose this account of the changing pattern of strike action in Sweden is to distance ourselves from some alternative accounts. Conventionally, the reasons that are often advanced for the lessening of strike action under democratic socialist governments stress the ability of 'parliamentary socialism' to incorporate the working-class leadership, which is then prevailed upon to extend this incorporation to the rank and file, in order to manage capitalism more efficiently.[33] The question of specific policies as more or less reproductive/transformative of particular class-structured inequalities will be taken up next.

The Production of Politics

Walter Korpi[34] has used the phrase 'democratic class struggle' to refer to conflicts of interest that are manifested in the political arena but which derive from the class structure of OECD-type countries. Conflict over the economic organisation of production when collectively represented in class-based unions, can produce a shift in power to wage-earners and undermine capitalist social relations even without resistance organised through industrial militancy. Similarly, as Higgins argues, there is a 'political trade-unionism' which, provided it has assumed a combative and bargaining role in relations with the state, has frequently won battles to encroach on bourgeois prerogatives.[35]

Increasingly since 1945 the primary arena of class conflict has become the institutions which decide and conduct macro-economic policy. The issues which constitute this conflict are familiar ones: political versus market control of the national economy. This contestation has been apparent ever since debates over intervention into the economy intensified in the 1930s. Since then, a number of new institutions have emerged as arenas of political struggle – over the extent to which market mechanisms have purged economic decisions of any overtly political content. The current economic crisis, along with the more significant political responses to it, therefore provides an opportunity for further evaluation of those decision-making arenas that have been termed corporatist.

In so far as new political institutions involving some functional input from and representation of labour, capital and the state are being created in some countries in the 1980s, some intellectual and political defences of them can be examined. The case must be presented in general terms, but an obvious Australian example of what we have in mind is provided by the now extant permanent successors to the spectacular 1983 National Economic Summit Conference, the Economic Policy Advisory Council (EPAC) and associated industry councils. As many countries are further down the corporatist road than Australia the evaluations we can offer will draw on international, especially OECD, experience.

Both programmatic and analytical aspects of our argument are presented in the context of the recession which began in 1974 and invoke the explanation of this current crisis that derives from post-Keynesian political economy, especially in the writings of Michal Kalecki and Joan Robinson. This body of analysis incorporates a politically sophisticated understanding of both unemployment and inflation.

In this view, the apparently anomalous experience of simultaneous unemployment and inflation is less surprising and less perplexing than has been commonly supposed. In the 1930s and 1940s, both Keynes and Kalecki argued the case for sustained and substantial government intervention on the grounds that because normally functioning private enterprise economies do not necessarily produce full employment, a self-regulating equilibrium or social harmony, a 'somewhat comprehensive socialization of investment will prove the only means of securing an approximation to full employment.'[36] The Keynesian critique of liberalism emerged from the patent observation that economic activity which was privately profitable was not necessarily socially desirable.[37] Consequently the basis for subsequent post-war argument over the extent of political control (as opposed to market determination) of investment was laid. Keynes and Kalecki argued not merely for an increase in public sector spending to stimulate economic activity but for socialised control over the direction of the macro-economy.

In 1943, Kalecki, understanding both the affinity with Marx's expectations of sectoral imbalance and the political objections that bourgeois interests would mount against any fully-fledged interventionism, pointed out that Keynes's scenario would be unlikely to eventuate. Instead of political institutions to expand the economy and guarantee full employment, there would be a political trade cycle, an era of 'stop-go'. Conservatives 'would probably find more than one economist to declare that the situation was manifestly unsound', predicted Kalecki.[38] Intervention and expansion would be introduced for opportunistic and electoral reasons from time to time, but, with intellectual support, neither governments nor business would opt for permanent full employment or for maximum levels of economic growth or capital accumulation. The reasons for this caution are opaque to many contemporary writers on corporatism but depend mainly on the increased class power and bargaining strength which accrues to organised labour in times of full employment and economic upswing. This institutional strength typically derives not only from the ability to demand and receive high wages, but also from the ability thereby created to influence, either through the state or directly, the economic prerogatives of management and investment calculus more generally. The common legacy of the classical, Marxian and Keynesian traditions of economic analysis shows that the key to the dynamics of a capitalist economy is the behaviour of investment. Private control of investment decisions is what causes crises in capitalist development; hence, a more democratic control of investment is essential for full employment – and for consistently higher levels of economic activity, incomes, living standards and so on. Nonetheless, such democratisation of the economy will be opposed by anti-labour forces simply because, at moments of crisis, continued control of private prerogatives is preferred to profitability. Capitalists will oppose capital accumulation and full employment conditions when their political power is threatened.

It is for these reasons that political opposition to reflationary strategies persists and that the radical implications of Keynesian prescriptions were bastardised. Instead of the socialisation of investment, the post-war era produced 'fine-tuning' (fiscal and monetary policies) and the long boom ensued under bourgeois auspices. The welfare state's subsequent development was under bourgeois instead of labour movement hegemony in most OECD countries.[39]

With the onset, again, of recession in the 1970s there was no reversion to or acceptance of interventionist policies. The reasons are, first, that the anti-market arguments were never conceded by conservatives or market-liberals. Von Hayek has insisted throughout the post-war decades that Keynes was wrong to emphasise macro-economic aspects of market behaviour and that the proper function of economic analysis and advice was to preserve freedom by keeping governments away from concern with the level or content of production. None of this type of economic writing has ever acknowledged Keynes's conclusions that free market mechanisms do *not* normally lead to optimal resource allocation.

The second, associated, reason for the post-1974 refusal to explore extra-market possibilities concerns the generalised fear of an expanded role for government. This manufactured paranoia derives from Treasuries, Reserve Banks, financial institutions and some international agencies. Except in so far as state institutions are direct facilitators of business activity, encroachment of any innovative nature has been resisted, especially in the UK, USA and Australia.

The third reason for this hostility, however, is probably the most important: the alleged problem of inflation. This concern is well-known and is exemplified in this utterance from a speech by the (then) British Prime Minister, James Callaghan, in 1976:

> We used to think that you could just spend your way out of a recession and increase employment by cutting taxes and boosting government spending. I tell you, in all candour, that that option no longer exists, and in so far as it ever did exist, it worked only by injecting bigger doses of inflation into the economy followed by higher levels of unemployment as the next step. That is the history of the past twenty years.[40]

Similar conceptions could readily be retrieved from Labour

Treasurers Bill Hayden and Paul Keating in Australia. The belief that demand stimulation, public sector deficits, economic expansion and anti-recessionary policy necessarily embody the danger of inflation is as pervasive as it is inaccurate. Labour leaders are consequently proud to broadcast their economic conservatism as standard-bearers of economic responsibility.

While Keynes and Kalecki did not directly address the problem of inflation, neither was unaware that inflation was a likely consequence of labour movements buttressed by full employment. If labour does secure wage rises and if these cost increases are responded to by capital in the form of price increases, then the result is inflation. This type of inflation is possible only when labour is institutionally strong. In the 1930s neither capital nor labour had the institutional strength to set this train of consequences in motion. In the depression of the 1930s businesses failed and wages were reduced. In the 1970s and 1980s, however, more concentrated industry and monopoly pricing policies allowed business to increase prices despite declining turnovers. Strengthened labour movements were able to continue successful wage bargaining in the industrial arena despite increasing unemployment. Inflation in a recession became a major economic fact of life. Wage rises can cause inflation even when the real value of those wages is falling, even when price rises far exceed wage gains.

Hence, the post-Keynesians view inflation as a consequence of recession-induced conflict over the distribution of income. When the total size of the cake is not increasing and when total income is insufficient to absorb competing demands from both labour and capital, the result is inflation. Inflation in a recession is a symptom of class struggle, that is, conflict between wages and profits. In this fundamental distributional arena, the contemporary impact of class structure on other aspects of civil society is amply affirmed.

The monetarist view, on the other hand, sees inflation as a sign of institutionalised profilgacy and government-induced increases in the money supply. The irony is that for the left, wage rises *do* cause inflation: for the right, the cause is not wages (or unions), but government. For the left, the centrality of class conflict (over distribution of income) is established: for the right, neo-liberal hostility to collectivism is entrenched.

The policy concomitants of this analysis have far-reaching consequences for political strategies and arenas. To control unemployment, we need political control of the economy – and this means new arenas and agencies of economic decision-making, imposing some limitations to managerial 'strategic choice'. To control inflation, we need political control of income distribution – and this means social contracts, price and incomes policies, government-business-union 'accords' in the industrial arena, thus eroding some 'resistance of labour' as it has been conceived in traditional labour process terms. Overriding this need for new political institutions to reflect the increased power of democratic anti-liberal forces, however, is the primacy of a politically astute anti-recessionary strategy. Unions must be cautious in their support for what is proposed as anti-inflationary policy. No 'accord' should be endorsed by labour unless it is primarily an anti-recessionary strategy, that is, a set of serious proposals for industry restructure, political control of the economy, expansion of the social wage and maintenance (at the least) of real incomes. It must be recognised by labour governments that costs do *not* cause generalised recession – in fact high wages, because of their effect on industry efficiency and aggregate demand, help prevent the onslaught of economic decline. In addition, government spending does *not* cause inflation (in times of full utilisation of labour and resources, any spending can be inflationary, public sector dollars are no more or less culpable than any others); and inflation does *not* cause recession.

The two functions of new political institutions, therefore, are (a) to control investment and (b) to control the distribution of income. (It should be remembered, too, that the distribution between wages and profits in a capitalist society is not fixed – it varies according to stages of the business cycle, with the profits share typically increasing in the upswing and the wages share increasing in the downswing. The wages *share* can increase relative to profits even when real wages are falling.)

The upshot of this analysis is not only the call for new institutions to develop arenas not previously embraced by the institutions of liberal democracy. It is also to show that permanent full employment and capitalism are fundamentally incompatible unless the proposed arenas can be called into existence to adjudicate the content and distribution of the economy's output. When labour is made *institutionally* powerful, recession cannot be used to weaken labour and rationalise industry in an anti-social, pro-market manner. Unregulated capitalism cannot guarantee full employment, economic growth or social stability. Moreover, the terms on which levels of employment, growth and stability eventuate are mediated by political struggles through the state. Where the principal actors in these struggles are trade unions and employers, employing divergent and contradictory analyses, it seems reasonable to talk of class struggle. This is the underlying conception of capitalism which we are using to evaluate contemporary corporatist developments.

Corporatism as Class Politics

Because a robust, healthy capitalist economy with high growth rates and high standards of living is incompatible with capitalist social relations (wage labour, private profitability as the criterion for investment, resource-allocation according to market mechanisms as well as managerial prerogatives in the labour process) the displacement of decision-making to tripartite bodies involving the state, capital and labour must be seen as potentially progressive. Our argument, along with that of Korpi[41] and Higgins and Apple[42] is that class-representation of labour and capital is necessary both for economic recovery and the transition to post-capitalist social relations. However much incomes policies pursued by labour governments in the past have had the effect of reducing wages or demobilising unions' support, this fact remains: institutions where *conflict* over economic decisions *is* expressed are necessary. The ones currently being established in Australia therefore should be embraced. They legitimate union involvement in economic decision-making by taking corporate investment decisions out of the board room and into a more public arena: they make income distribution overtly political by publicly guaranteeing to maintain real wages – something which in the normal course of recession would not occur. In addition, they help to expose the inability of liberal institutions to acknowledge the conflicts implied by economic growth. No community of common interest exists. Corporatism then, to the extent that it means the involvement of business and unions in the making of economic policy, represents an expansion, not a diminution, of democratic control of the economy. It represents an affirmation of the central significance of class politics in contemporary circumstances. The myriad of cleavages in civil society – cleavages which may affect political allegiances and personal experience much more immediately than struggles over wages and expansionary economic policy – do not dissipate this fundamental aspect of societies in which the capitalist mode of production prevails: democratic class struggle over full employment and wages can simultaneously assist in the development of the forces of production and contribute to the erosion of exploitative relations of production.

The literature on corporatism is, of course, insistent on the risks and hidden agendas of such arrangements. Leo Panitch's impressive survey[43] of post-war experience with incomes policies in Britain shows undeniably that union memberships have usually suffered as a result of social contracts and incomes policies negotiated and forced upon them by their leaderships. Bargaining constraints thus imposed are not *necessarily* detrimental to labour, but the evidence sounds *caveats* that need to be taken very seriously. It is clear to us, however, that Panitch's conclusions are in some respects incorrect. Corporatism in liberal democracies need not become a means of reinforcing bourgeois dominance, wage restraint does not necessarily mean reductions in real wages, tripartism need not rule out redistributive policy, expansion of profits and capital accumulation does not necessarily imply wages squeeze (or vice versa), and corporatist structures need not lead to instability and state coercion.[44] The lesson for labour movements is that they should opt out of the contracts, arrangements, arenas and decisions either if real wages commence to fall or if governments abrogate commitments to expansionary policy, industrial restructuring and economic democracy.

A second, more convoluted objection to these developments comes from Claus Offe[45] who focuses more on the interest representation aspects of corporatism than the tripartite structures allow. In an argument almost identical to the 'overloaded government' thesis of Daniel Bell, Richard Rose and others, Offe suggests, from a left perspective, that the state's dependence on 'competitive party democracy' is subjected to conflicting interest group demands which it cannot meet. The underlying tendency has been referred to by Bell as a 'revolution of rising expectations':[46] it is taken by new right commentators as an indication that liberal democracy has become too flaccid, too subservient to the unreasonable desires of its constituencies, too unwilling to say no. In his application, Offe equates Keynesianism, the welfare state and the 'new demands' placed upon the state – especially those of environmental, women's and other special interest groups. Consequently, the resulting *ad hoc* unrepresentative arenas established under state auspices (Enquiries, Task Forces, Special Committees of Review) are inherently contradictory. They perform the same role with the same effects as the anti-pluralist, singular, compulsory, dependent mediating agencies that are defined as corporatist in Schmitter's well-known definition.[47] This objection is alleviated, according to Offe, only to the extent that parties are 'articulatory' rather than 'aggregative' – that is, to the extent that political parties assume or are forced to accept an obligation to the whole (working) class rather than merely voice the host of usually incompatible and disparate interest representations that emerge in more pluralist conditions.

A final general criticism of corporatist structures centres on the extent to which memberships of working-class organisations may feel unrepresented by the conditions accepted at 'peak' negotiations. Marino Regini and Gösta Esping-Anderson[48] have argued that conflicting demands are likely to arise between a union organisation's membership and the broader constituency union leaders are invited to consider. It is argued that particular memberships might be unwilling to make sacrifices in the interest of some distantly defined 'common economic good'. As before, the unstable potential of this situation is dissipated to the extent that the unions involved in corporatist arrangements are explicitly class-oriented unions, rather than 'associational' unions.

In Australia, objections to corporatism have been based in the main on the disquiet felt about the newly elected Labour government's National Economic Summit Conference (NESC) in April 1983 and its accompanying rhetoric of consensus. At the time this seemed to suggest the existence of a labour government intent upon pursuing policies as if no fundamental conflicts existed in society, as if negotiation alone could establish a coalescence of interests and as if only élite groups needed to be involved in such machinations. From what we have argued so far, it is clear that it is possible to accept the desirability of new institutions and arenas without the specific rhetoric of pluralism and consensus. In the final section we argue that the posturings of party leaders are virtually irrelevant to whether the NESC and its permanent institutional successor, the Economic Policy Advisory Council (EPAC) succeed or not. It is important not to take rhetoric at face value. Tripartite corporatism (as opposed to any less radical, pluralist corporatism which we are not defending) does not imply a quest for consensus, but a quest for decisions. Institutions which produce economic policies or which become arenas for decisions concerning capital formation are necessarily sites of conflict. Disputation over the content, location and pace of capital accumulation is the most important form of class conflict. Bourgeois interests are best served not by maintaining economic growth or by sponsoring rapid accumulation but by ensuring that their own prerogatives are preserved. In liberal democracy, parliaments, by separating the economy from democratic interventions, are an ideal way of doing this. In a post-bourgeois polity, economic decisions will need to be opened up to general scrutiny and involvement. This would complement rather than displace parliament; the latter would still serve the democratic representative role it currently has. The long-standing Marxist critique of parliamentary democracy has been that crucial decisions have never come within its arena, not that it is useless.[49] The current Australian debates reproduce misunderstandings that have accompanied corporatist developments elsewhere.

David Kemp, an advisor to the former Conservative government, has produced a broad-ranging critique of tendencies implied by the summit conference and also takes the rhetoric seriously by assuming both that the new institutions are faced with a need to resolve 'unresolvable tensions' and that there must be an erosion of 'popular control' when attempts have been made to deal with them.[50] His argument however misses the basic argument that the function of EPAC and the associated advisory councils for manufacturing industry is not to provide information but to *make decisions* on industrial structure which have never before been subjected to extra-market deliberation. It is wholly acceptable that in these decisions conflict will be manifest and one side will win. Even if short-term compromises are effected between the union movement and industrialists – flowing from their common commitment to manufacturing industry and expansionary policy, say – the fundamental antipathy between labour's interest in maximum economic performance and capitalists' control of the economy remains. The disunity in ruling class organisations, splits in the Confederation of Australian Industry, the non-comprehensive coverage of the new, hastily formed, Business Council of Australia and a continuing difference of perspective between manufacturing and resource/finance-based corporations in Australia attest to this. The tensions are not between authoritative and non-authoritative organisational solutions to burgeoning problems but between the need to establish a more broadly-based input to investment decisions and business's presumption of the illegitimacy of that process.

Some of the same misconceptions could be found in left critiques of the summit conference (*qua* corporatism),[51] which have sharply criticised NESC'S and EPAC'S failure fully to represent welfare groups, the non-waged, the majority of women, etc. It seems to us that these charges are misdirected. EPAC and the other 'tripartite' institutions have an enormous potential to allow the involvement of groups previously denied access to the control of income distribution and investment; they establish new arenas of decision-making never permitted by parliamentary processes: and they create new sites of struggle. People excluded from the capital/labour relationship are benefited by anti-recessionary policies whether they know it or not. To compile lists of token representatives for peak negotiations without grass roots mobilisation is to invite discord in a forum where it can be ill afforded. If labour movements have been historically sexist and have performed other exclusivist practices in the past, then the appropriate reforms within their own institutions are as urgent as the quite distinct need for new political institutions.

Macro-economic Consequences of Corporatism

The objections outlined above become even less pertinent, we wish to

Figure 2
Political and economic conditions in 18 OECD countires, 1974–1978

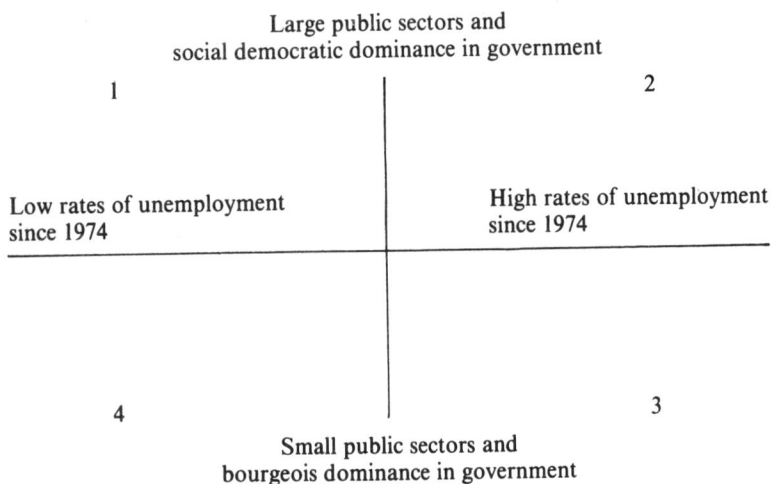

Large public sectors and
social democratic dominance in government

1	2
Low rates of unemployment since 1974	High rates of unemployment since 1974
4	3

Small public sectors and
bourgeois dominance in government

1. Active 'welfare capitalism' with tendencies towards corporatist modes of regulation: Sweden, Luxembourg, Norway, Austria.
2. Passive 'welfare capitalism' with tendencies towards liberal modes of regulation: UK, Denmark, Germany, Netherlands, Finland, Belgium.
3. Passive market economies with tendencies towards authoritarian/competitive modes of regulation, weak welfare state: Australia, Canada, US, France, Italy.
4. Active market economies with tendencies towards corporatist and paternalist modes of regulation: Japan, New Zealand, Switzerland.
   Source: Schmidt (1982, pp. 158-59) adapted.

argue, once the determinants of macro-economic outcomes, the political determinants of effective state policies, are identified. In empirical, as well as in theoretical terms, it can be shown that extra-parliamentary arenas (especially those which influence investment and income distribution) are essential for the political control of the economy, for the achievement of low rates of both unemployment and inflation and for the forging of some measure of national autonomy. All of these have been achieved where the balance in public policy-making has shifted from market to political mechanisms and from parliamentary to more explicitly class-based forms of representation.

In the Australian case, as in Britain, therefore, it is important not to attribute too much effectivity to the presence of particular individuals and particular personalities, or the vicissitudes of policy manifestos or even to the parties themselves. To the extent that labour leaders and labour parties fail to honour constituencies, pledges and platforms, the fault lies as much with the weaknesses and non-assertiveness of the broader labour movement itself as it does with the more identifiable targets. It is not intentions which determine whether what transpires is desirable – but a well-known complex of structural and historical circumstances.

Although no nation state exercises complete control over its own macro-economic destiny, Manfred Schmidt's [52] empirical study of the impact of political processes on anti-recessionary policies in most OECD countries has shown the conditions which need to be attained for a regeneration of anti-capitalist politics in a politically pragmatic, significant and non-rhetorical mode. This study extends work begun by Andrew Martin[53] which used the Swedish experience of long-lived parties of labour in office to comment on the likelihood of democratic advance in the US by ranking different national economies according to both their ability to control unemployment and inflation during recession (1974–8) and the degree of labour movement hegemony. Figure 2 shows Schmidt's results.

Control over the economy is best achieved when *laissez-faire* liberalism is subject to the following encroachments:

(i) When an extra-parliamentary distribution of power (measured by strength of the left-wing vote and levels of trade union membership) indicates a 'left milieu':
(ii) When labour or social democratic parties are in office for long periods:
(iii) When public sectors are large and there is a commensurately active welfare state (suggested by universal non-means-tested state services):
(iv) When high levels of public sector spending are accompanied by high taxes (especially income and wealth taxes) and therefore relatively low levels of discretionary incomes:
(v) When industry is protected and isolated from dramatic changes in the international division of labour and production:
(vi) when there are very low levels of labour market segmentation, few if any distinct job categories where exclusion rules apply, and no racially, ethnically, regionally, sexually or socially distinct groups able to be regulated into an industrial reserve army:
(vii) When labour 'markets' themselves are usurped by the erosion of managerial prerogatives over hiring and firing and where labour hoarding and retraining schemes are the preferred enterpreneurial way of dealing with workers who would otherwise be sacked:
(viii) When the bourgeois parties are weak (electorally, or with respect to industry policy):

(ix) When there is fairly little exercise of bourgeois 'rights', for example, over the direction of investment, the location of economic activity, employment policy, wage policy, labour process, organisation and new capital formation – ownership need not imply control:

(x) When the extent of state intervention by way of the full range of social and economic policy is well developed:

(xi) When a large and increasing proportion of production is de-commodified (that is, not sold on the market, but produced directly for use, either collectively or otherwise): and

(xii) When there exist established forms of collective, capital formation (for example, via pension funds or wage earner funds) which portend a lack of control over their deployment by capital.

These conditions amount to corporatist modes of regulation which strengthen labour and weaken the bourgeoisie: *laissez-faire* is always deflationary and always anti-labour. The OECD experience which reveals these conditions does not, of course, suggest that corporatism is always democratic or that the institutions thus proposed cannot be used against labour. What we are pointing out is that labour cannot possibly hope to control the pace and content of capital accumulation without these new political institutions. An anti-market, anti-competitive milieu is essential. In the words of C. B. Macpherson,[54] we need a 'post-liberal democracy', a resurgence of class politics to replace the atomised competitive, interest-group politics to which we've grown accustomed. Furthermore, the 12 conditions enumerated above tend to be interactive rather than merely additive;[55] hence, to the extent that some of them are not attained, the effect of the others is undermined and the postulated macro-economic outcomes jeopardised. This explains why no national instance has perfect control of its domestic economy – no state has complete autonomy.

Significantly, then, the countries which rank highly with respect to political versus market determinants of economic activity – where non-market criteria for resource allocation and non-financial criteria for investment are well entrenched – are the countries with less serious recessions, a more equal distribution of income, higher material living standards and more chance of achieving collective control over the formation and accumulation of capital. Kalecki would not have been surprised.

Corporatism matters. There can be no economic recovery without a strong labour movement. Macro-economic outcomes, whether expansionary or not, depend not just on parties, policies, parliaments and politicians but on the ability or otherwise of a broader anti-market strategy to develop a longer-term institutional counter to the hegemony of private enterprise in the political arena and the industrial arena. This is so whether it is 'private' enterprise in wage bargaining by unions or 'private enterprise' in the normal sense. There needs to be a perpetual struggle against the limitations of liberalism.

High growth economies demand non-market patterns of production: they demand sustained high rates of investment and capital accumulation. But ultimately, high rates of capital accumulation, as Marx's reproduction models show, are incompatible with capitalist social relations.

Conclusion

Interest in the labour process debate has to some extent encouraged a normative commitment and advocacy of the importance of 'resistance'. The arguments set out in this chapter are proposed as an alternative to such views. The enthusiasm for a 'resistance' perspective, we have argued, is embedded within an overly simple model analogous to a two-player zero-sum game. Employing assumptions of this model, cross-national strike statistics were proposed to stand as a partial index of 'resistance' on a comparative basis. Inspection of these data yielded some interesting implications, when placed in the context of political strategy. It was argued that 'corporatism', in particular forms, might advance the strength of labour, but not in ways which are visible in terms of the labour process concern with 'resistance'. From the latter perspective, corporatism appears to weaken labour. We argued that this interpretation should be revised in certain conjunctures when the institutional management of politics in terms of its limitation of enterprises' 'strategic choice' is considered. Looked at this way, declining 'resistance' may not mean weakening power, but increasing power registered through politics by other (and as we have proposed elsewhere,[56] more effective) means and arenas. As a corollary, increasing resistance, might, under conditions of liberal democracy, imply diminishing power because of a restriction of arenas within which to constitute it.

Managing the labour process is not simply an issue of intra-organisational specificity. Consideration of this question must entail analysis of the political conjuncture within which this management takes place. Contrary to recent popular political analysis by both the right and the left, we do not propose either a practical or theoretical restriction of concern to the enterprise. In this respect the 'labour process perspective' has introduced only a limited politics into the analysis of organisations. Our proposal is simply to extend those limits.

Notes

1. Braverman, H. (1974), *Labor and Monopoly Capital*, New York: Monthly Review Press.
2. Cummings, L. and Greenbaum, J. (1978), 'The Struggle over Productivity: Workers, Management and Technology' in *Union for Radical Political Economics* (eds). *U.S. Capitalism in Crisis*, New York: URPE Publications, 55–62.
3. Salaman, G. (1981), *Class and the Corporation*, London: Fontana.
4. Clawson, D., (1980), *Bureaucracy and the Labor Process*, New York: Monthly Review Press.
5. See for example, Wood. S. (ed.) (1982), *The Degradation of Work? Skill, Deskilling and the Labour Process*, London: Hutchinson.
6. Burawoy, M. (1979), *Manufacturing Consent*, Chicago: University of Chicago Press.
7. See Littler, C. R. (1980), 'International Contract and the Transition to Modern Work Systems: Britain and Japan' in D. Dunkerley and G. Salaman (eds), *The International Yearbook of Organization Studies 1979*, London: Routledge and Kegan Paul, 157–85; Littler, C. R. 'Deskilling and Changing Structures of Control' in Wood op. cit. pp. 122–45 and Friedman, A. L. (1977), *Industry and Labour*, London: Macmillan.
8. Zimbalist, A. (1979), Case Studies on the Labor Process, New York: Monthly Review Press, and Aronowitz, S. (1978), 'Marx, Braverman and the Logic of Capital', *The Insurgent Sociologist*, **8** pp. 126–46.
9. Lee, D. J. (1981), 'Skill, Craft and Class: A Theoretical Critique and a Critical Case', *Sociology*, **15**, 58.
10. Elgar, A. (1979), 'Valorization and Deskilling - a Critique of Braverman', *Capital and Class*, **7**, 58–100.
11. Littler, C. R. and Salaman, G. (1982), 'Bravermania and Beyond: Recent Theories of the Labour Process', *Sociology*, **16**, 256.
12. Lee, op. cit., pp. 56–78.
13. Clegg, S. (1981), 'Organization and Control', *Administrative Science Quarterly*, **26** (4) 545–62.
14. Lee, op. cit., 59.
15. Littler and Salaman, op. cit., 251–69.
16. Boreham, P. and Dow, G. (1980), 'The Labour Process and Capitalist Crisis' in P. Boreham and G. Dow (eds), *Work and Inequality, Vol. 1*, Melbourne: Macmillan, 1–27 and Lee, op. cit.
17. Boreham, P. (1980), 'The Dialectic of Theory and Control' in D. Dunkerley and G. Salaman (eds), *The International Yearbook of Organization Studies 1980*, London: Routledge and Kegan Paul, 16–35.
18. Rutigliano, E. (1977), 'The Ideology of Labor and Capitalist Rationality in Gramsci', *Telos*, **31**, 91–9.
19. Loveridge, R. (1982), 'Business Strategy and Community Culture: Policy as a Structural Accommodation of Conflict' in D. Dunkerley and G. Salaman (eds). *The International Yearbook of Organization Studies*, London: Routledge and Kegan Paul, 26–58.
20. Child, J. (1972), 'Organization Structure, environment and performance: the role of strategic choice', *Sociology*, **6**, 1–22.
21. Griffin, J. (1939), *Strikes: a Study in Quantative Economics*, New York: Columbia University Press.
22. Korpi, W. (1974), 'Conflict, Power and Relative Deprivation', *American Political Science Review*, **LXVIII** (4) 1569–78.
23. Korpi, W. and Shalev, M. (1980), 'Strikes, Power and Politics in the Western Nations, 1900–1976', in M. Zeitlin (ed.), *Political Power and Social Theory*, vol. 1, Greenwich: JAI Press, 307.

24. Ibid, p.308.
25. Ibid.
26. Lindblom, C. E. (1977), *Politics and Markets*, New York: Basic Books, 14.
27. Webb, S. and B. (1924), *The History of Trade Unionism*, London: Longmans.
28. Westergaard, J. H. (1965), 'The Withering away of Class: a Contemporary Myth', in P. Anderson and R. Blackburn (eds), *Towards Socialism*, London: Fontana, 77–113 and Westergaard, J. H. (1972), 'Sociology: the Myth of Classlessness' in R. Blackburn (ed.), *Ideology in Social Science: Readings in Critical Social Theory*, London: Fontana, 119–63.
29. Ross, A. M. and Hartman, P. T. (1960), *Patterns of Industrial Conflict*, New York: Wiley.
30. Shalev, M. (1983), 'Strikes and the Crisis: Industrial Conflict and Unemployment in the Western Nations', *Economic and Industrial Democracy*, 4 (4) 417–60.
31. Sweet, T. G. and Jackson, D. (1977), 'The World Strike Wave: 1969 to 197?', University of Aston Management Centre, Working Paper Series, no. 63; and Sweet, T. G. and Jackson, D. (1978), 'The Classification and Interpretation of Strike Statistics: An International Comparative Analysis', University of Aston Management Centre, Working Paper Series, no. 97.
32. Korpi and Shalev, op. cit. 301–39.
33. Miliband, R. (1965), 'Marx and the State' in R. Miliband and J. Saville (eds). *The Socialist Register*, London: Merlin, and Panitch. L. (1979) 'The Development of Corporatism in Liberal Democracies' in P.C. Schmitter and G. Lehmbruch (eds), *Trends Towards Corporatist Intermediation*, London: Sage.
34. Korpi, W. (1983), *The Democratic Class Struggle*, London: Routledge and Kegan Paul.
35. Higgins, W., (1984), 'Socialist Strategy in the Hawke Era', unpublished manuscript, forthcoming.
36. Keynes. J. M. (1936), *The General Theory of Employment, Interest and Money*, London: Macmillan, 378.
37. Ibid, p. 157.
38. Kalecki, M. (1943), 'Political Aspects of Full Employment' *Politcal Quarterly*, 14 (4).
39. Apple, N. (1983), 'The Historical Transformation of Class Struggle in Late Capitalist Liberal Democracies' in S. Clegg, G. Dow, and P. Boreham (eds), *The State, Class and the Recession,* London: Croom Helm 72–128.
40. Callaghan, J., Speech to Labour Party Conference: 28 September 1976, extracted in A. G. Frank (1980), *Crisis in the World Economy*, London: Heinemann.
41. Korpi, op cit.
42. Higgins, W. and Apple, N. (1983) 'How Limited is Reformism? A Critique of Przeworski and Panitch', *Theory and Society*, 12 (5).
43. Panitch, L. (1976), *Social Democracy and Industrial Militancy: The Labour Party, the Trade Unions and Incomes Policy, 1945-1974*, Cambridge: Cambridge: University Press.
44. Panitch, 1979. op. cit.
45. Offe, C. (1983), 'Competitive Party Democracy and the Keynesian Welfare State: Some Reflections on their Historical Limits' in Clegg, Dow and Boreham, op. cit. 51–71.
46. Bell, D. (1976), *The Cultural Contradiction of Capitalism*, New York: Basic Books, 1976. See also Rose, R. (ed.) (1980), *Challenge to Governance*, London: Sage.
47. Schmitter, P. C. (1979), 'Still the century of Corporatism' in Schmitter and Lehmbruch, op. cit., 7–52.
48. Regini, M. and Esping-Anderson, G. (1980), 'Trade Union Strategies and Social Policy in Italy and Sweden', *West European Politics*, 3 (1) 107–23; and Regini, M. (1983), 'The Crisis of Representation in Class-Oriented Unions: Some Reflections

on the Italian Case' in Clegg, Dow and Boreham, op. cit. 239–56.
49. Tomlinson, J. (1981), 'Corporatism: A Further Sociologisation of Marxism', *Politics and Power, Four*, London, Routledge and Kegan Paul.
50. Kemp, D., (1983), 'The National Economic Summit: Authority, Persuasion and Exchange', *The Economic Record*, **166** (59).
51. Belharz, P., (1983) 'The View from the Summit', *Arena*, **64**; Stilwell, F. (1983) 'The Economic Summit and Beyond', *Arena*, **63**; and Cox, E. (1983), 'The Summit: Nothing from the Underside', *Australian Financial Review*, 27 April.
52. Schmidt, M. G. (1982), 'The Role of Parties in Shaping Macroeconomic Policy' in F. Castles (ed.), *The Impact of Parties*, London: Sage, 97–176.
53. Martin, A. (1975), 'Is Democratic Control of Capitalist Economies Possible?' in L. Lindberg et al. (eds), *Stress and Contradiction In Modern Capitalism: Public Policy and the Theory of the State*, Lexington: D.C. Heath.
54. Macpherson, C. B., (1973), 'Post-Liberal Democracy' in *Democratic Theory: Essays in Retrieval*, Oxford: Clarendon Press, 170–84.
55. Stephens, J. D. (1979), *The Transition from Capitalism to Socialism*, London: Macmillan.
56. Clegg, S., Boreham, P. and Dow, G., (1986), *Class, Politics and the Economy*, London: Routledge and Kegan Paul.

Index

Ehrenreich, B. and J., 168
electricity supply industry, 133, 134
Elger, T., 4, 21
élites, 170, 179, 188
    professional, 27–8, 32, 38–40, 90, 93–5
Ellul, J., 176, 178
Emery, F.E., 55
employers' associations, 34
    Donovan Report (1968), 36, 37
employment
    full, 35, 36–7, 196–8, 199, 200
    relations, 7, 98–9
    state, 85–6, 93–5, 97–9, 101, 103
    structure, 188–9
    see also labour; unemployment;
        workers
Energy, Department of, 129, 130
energy policy, 12, 129, 131, 133–4, 137
engineers, 31–2
    mining, 115, 118, 119, 121, 123, 126,
        127, 131–2, 137
    scientific management and, 9, 22–7
    technocracy and, 167, 168, 172
entrepreneurs, 26, 29, 152, 154, 170
    private, 149, 150, 151
Esland, G., 33
Esping-Anderson, G., 201
Evans, C., 44
Evans, J., 69
expertise
    authority and, 13, 170, 174, 178, 182
    technocratic, 168, 170, 174–81 *passim*
Export Processing Zones, 180

factory system, 148, 149, 151, 170
Fairbrother, P., 99
family-based production, 24, 31, 169–70
Fayol, H., 1
Feldberg, R.L., 48, 175, 180
Feldman, M.S., 124
Fernandez-Kelly, M.P., 180
Fielding, A., 29
financial control (NCB)
    decoupling and, 119–21, 124
    information and, 12, 125–6, 129–31
    labour process control and, 12, 109,
        111, 117–27, 136, 138
    State (role), 12, 109–10, 112, 127–38
Fine, B., 112
Flanders, A., 36
Ford, Henry, 34, 173
Fores, M., 36
Foucault, M., 128, 135

Fox, A., 2, 36
Francis, A., 77
Frankel, B., 89–90, 99
Freidson, E., 171, 180
Friedman, A.L., 4, 21, 22, 69, 87, 127
Frobel, F., 129
Frost, P., 28
Fryer, B., 85
functionalism, 6, 9, 21, 22, 39

Galbraith, J.K., 168
Gee, K., 111
General Motors, 30–31
Germany, 31–2, 144
Giddens, A., 5, 6, 46, 76, 114
Glenn, E., 48, 175, 180
Glover, I., 36
goal-means relation, 157, 162–3
Goffee, R., 114
Golding, D., 2, 8
Goldman, P., 4
Gordon, D.M., 21, 22, 34, 109, 128,
    137
Gorz, A., 168, 178
Gospel, H.F., 87
Gough, I., 88, 99, 103
Gouldner, A.W., 2, 112, 169, 174, 178–9,
    182
government policy, *see* State (role)
Griffiths Report, 105 (*note* 16)
Gubbay, J., 87
guilds, 166, 169, 170, 171

Habakkuk, H.J., 31
Habermas, J., 85, 89–90, 91, 96–7, 101,
    135, 136, 173, 179, 181
Hackman, J.R., 55
Hall, T., 112
Ham, C., 86, 87
Handy, L.J., 112
Harrison, B., 179
Haslam, C., 121
Haug, M., 177
Hawkins, K.H., 36
Hayden, Bill, 198
Haywood, S., 86, 96
health care, *see* National Health
    Service
Herman, A., 167
Heydebrand, W., 166, 169, 172, 176–7,
    178, 180–81
hierarchical model, 92, 161, 164